Reviewing Basic Grammar

Reviewing Basic Grammar

Fourth Edition

Mary Laine Yarber

Robert E. Yarber

Emeritus, San Diego Mesa College

LONGMAN

An imprint of Addison Wesley Longman, Inc.

New York • Reading, Massachusetts • Menlo Park, California • Harlow, England
Don Mills, Ontario • Sydney • Mexico City • Madrid • Amsterdam

Acquisitions Editor: ELLEN SCHATZ
Project Coordination and Text Design: YORK PRODUCTION SERVICES
Electronic Production Manager: VALERIE ZABORSKI
Manufacturing Manager: HELENE G. LANDERS
Electronic Page Makeup: YORK PRODUCTION SERVICES
Printer and Binder: R.R. DONNELLEY & SONS COMPANY
Cover Printer: THE LEHIGH PRESS, INC.

Library of Congress Cataloging-in-Publication Data

Yarber, Robert E.
    Reviewing basic grammar/Robert E. Yarber, Mary Laine Yarber.—4th ed.
        p.   cm.
    Includes index.
    ISBN 0-673-99941-6—ISBN 0-673-99942-4
    1. English language—Grammar.   2. English language—Rhetoric.   I. Yarber, Mary Laine.
II. Title.
PE1417.Y33   1996
428.2—dc20   95–51008
                                                                           CIP

Copyright © 1997 by Addison-Wesley Educational Publishers Inc.

ISBN 0-673-99941-6 (Student Edition)
ISBN 0-673-99942-4 (Instructor's Edition)

12345678910—DOC—99989796

Contents

© 1997 Addison-Wesley Educational Publishers Inc.

To the Instructor

This new edition of *Reviewing Basic Grammar* continues to stress the needs of students who are preparing for the demands of freshman composition. At the same time, it incorporates several new features that ensure that it will remain one of the finest textbooks available for grammar review.

Users of previous editions will recognize that the following principles have guided this revision of *Reviewing Basic Grammar:*

- It must emphasize the essentials of sentence structure, grammar, punctuation, and spelling, with a minimum of abstract terminology.
- It must include writing, because grammar and usage cannot be taught in a vacuum. The writing assignments must be meaningful and reflect students' interests and concerns.
- It must be concise, clear, and interesting to both the student and the instructor, with abundant exercises and opportunities for evaluation.
- It must recognize the ethnic and cultural diversity of today's student body.

Like previous editions, each self-contained chapter features clear explanations and examples, as well as exercises in a variety of formats that require the student's active participation. In response to user suggestions, new writing exercises are included at the end of each chapter to complement the sections on paragraph writing and outlining.

Additional exercises and explanations have been added, and the number of review exercises at the end of each chapter has been doubled. The series of chapter tests and final examinations in the Instructor's Manual has been expanded; each is equal in difficulty and identical in format, thus offering the instructor greater variety and flexibility. We continue to be sensitive to the needs and interests of today's students, as reflected in our discussions of sexism in language and in our use of contemporary allusions.

As before, each chapter sequentially presents a complete and concise lesson in one of the common problems in basic usage and writing:

1. Sentence fragments, comma-splices, and fused sentences.
2. Subject-verb agreement.
3. Pronoun-antecedent.
4. Confusion of the subject and object forms of pronouns.
5. Use of adjectives for adverbs and vice versa.
6. Use of indefinite pronouns such as *anyone, anybody, someone, neither,* and *none.*
7. Use of verbs.
8. Punctuation, possessives, numbers, and capitals.
9. Writing of paragraphs that are unified, developed, and coherent.
10. Outlining as an aid in organizing an essay.

We believe that this new edition of *Reviewing Basic Grammar* offers the student and instructor a thorough presentation of the elements of grammar and usage that is pedagogically solid. We are grateful to the many instructors in colleges and universities throughout the country who have expressed their pleasure with the previous editions of *Reviewing Basic Grammar.* Among those who offered helpful suggestions, we would like to acknowledge the contributions of Susan Clair Imbarrato, Caffey College; Carolyn Kershaw, Allegany Community College; Sims C. Poindexter, Central Carolina Community College; and Andrew Hoffman, San Diego Mesa College.

Mary Laine Yarber wishes to express her gratitude to Rosetta Cohen, Ray Ducharme, Michael Gorra, Robert Hosmer, Al Rudnitsky, Margaret Shook, and Susan Van Dyne at Smith College in Northampton, Massachusetts for nourishing her passion for reading, writing and teaching; Mark Berger, Bill Clawson, Diana Garcia, Lorri Horn, Carol Jago, Ron Mills-Coyne, Cindy Milwe, Sylvia Rousseau, and Robert Thais at Santa Monica High School for encouraging and humoring her; April Quaker, Sherry Talsky, Shana Frazin, Kelly Cannon, and Ginny Tal for needed diversions; and Terry Wolverton for teaching her the precise yet colorful use of language. She also thanks her patient and supportive family: Robert E. Yarber, Mary Winzerling Yarber, and Charles Yarborough.

As in the previous edition, Robert E. Yarber gratefully acknowledges the contributions of his daughter and co-author, Mary Laine Yarber. Her energy, knowledge, wit, and uncompromising point of view have given this edition of *Reviewing Basic Grammar* a relevance needed for today's student. He also acknowledges with equal gratitude the enthusiastic participation of his wife, Mary Winzerling Yarber, whose cooperation made it all possible.

Mary Laine Yarber
Robert E. Yarber

© 1997 Addison-Wesley Educational Publishers Inc.

To the Student

By following the suggestions in this book and the advice of your instructor, you will become a better and more confident writer this semester. Fortunately, you already know and unconsciously follow most of the principles of standard written English. The chapters that follow will build on that knowledge and structure.

Almost every class that you will take in college requires writing of some kind. You will be expected to write exams, reports, essays, and term papers that are not only well organized, logical, and convincing, but also free of serious mistakes in grammar, spelling, and punctuation. But the ability to write effectively is not a skill that is helpful only in college. Many jobs include writing as an important tool. In today's work world, reports, proposals, summaries, and letters are typically required.

To be an effective writer—both in the classroom and on the job—you will have to follow certain principles of standard written English, the kind of English that you find in reports, books, papers, and articles, and that you hear spoken by news announcers on television or radio and by your instructors in classrooms. In informal conversations, of course, you can ignore many of the principles of standard written English. Most slang, for example, is perfectly acceptable to many speakers of American English. But if such expressions appeared in writing, they would get in the way of the writer's ideas and distract the reader.

Perhaps an analogy will illustrate this point. The clothes you wear while working on your car or painting your room would not be appropriate for a job interview. Nor would the expressions you use with your friends be appropriate when you speak to a traffic judge whom you are trying to impress. To be a good writer, therefore, you will be expected to follow the principles of standard written English—in other words, to use language that is right for the job. If your writing does not follow those principles—if it is filled with errors in grammar, spelling, and punctuation—it will confuse and mislead your reader. It could even convince him or her that you and your ideas should not be taken seriously.

The chapters that follow will give you a quick review of the parts of speech and then deal with the most serious kinds of errors that writers encounter. You will also review the most important rules of punctuation and spelling. But do not get the idea that the avoidance of errors equals good writing. You also need practice in writing sentences and paragraphs that are interesting, coherent, and correct. To put into action the skills that you will be acquiring, sections on sentence and paragraph writing and outlining follow the chapters and appear at the end of this book.

As this semester progresses, you will notice an improvement in your command of effective English. More important, you will experience success and pride in your writing assignments in future years.

Mary Laine Yarber
Robert E. Yarber

Chapter 1

The Parts of Speech: A Review

Whenever you study a subject, you have to acquire the right vocabulary to discuss it. Whether the subject is baseball, biology, or backpacking, you have to learn the right terms so that you can talk about it intelligently and precisely. So it is with the English language. Although it has over a half-million words and is adding thousands of new ones every year, all of these words—long or short, familiar or strange—can be divided into only eight categories: the eight parts of speech. When you learn to recognize the parts of speech, you will be on your way to understanding how the English language works. Even more important, you will be able to identify the tools that will help you to write clear, interesting, and correct sentences and paragraphs and to become a more confident writer. Our study of grammar and usage begins, therefore, by examining the parts of speech.

The Noun

We will start with the noun because every English sentence either contains one or is about one. *A noun is a word that names something—a person, a place, a thing, or an idea.*

   David Letterman, Texas, skillet, jealousy

   Some nouns refer to a general class of persons, places, or things. They are called *common nouns*, and they are not capitalized unless they are used to begin a sentence.

   inventor, city, automobile

1

Some nouns refer to specific persons, places, or things. They are called *proper nouns*, and they are always capitalized.

George Washington Carver, St. Louis, Ford Mustang

As you will see in later chapters, nouns are important because they can work as several parts of the sentence.

A TIP FOR SPOTTING NOUNS

If you can put a word in the slot in the following sentence, it is a noun: "A (or An) _____ is remarkable."

Example: "An elephant is *remarkable*."
            "A rainbow is *remarkable*."

The Pronoun

We could not get along without nouns. But occasionally, in order to avoid repetition and monotony, we use other words in place of nouns. The words that we substitute for nouns are called *pronouns*.

As Kenisha looked over Kenisha's biology examination, Kenisha realized that the high-est score on the test was Kenisha's.

This sentence is obviously monotonous because of its overuse of *Kenisha*. We can improve it by using pronouns:

As Kenisha looked over *her* biology examination, *she* realized that the highest score on the test was *hers*.

The pronouns in this sentence are *her*, *she*, and *hers*, and their *antecedent* (the word to which they refer) is *Kenisha*. Here is another sentence with pronouns and an antecedent:

The driver waved to his crew as he drove the victory lap around the track, and the crowd cheered him.

What are the pronouns in this sentence? What is their antecedent?

Unlike a noun, a pronoun does not name a specific person, place, thing, or idea. You will learn more about pronouns and their uses in Chapters 4 and 5. Meanwhile, you should try to recognize the most common pronouns, listed on the next page.

I, me, my, mine

you, your, yours

he, him, his

she, her, hers

it, its

who, whose, whom

we, us, our, ours

they, them, their, theirs

anybody, everybody, someone

everyone, no one, somebody

something, some, all, many, any

each, none, one, this, that, these, those, which, what

Exercise 1-1

Underline the nouns and circle the pronouns.

1. Although he died in 1977, Elvis Presley continues to be the subject of books and documentaries, and he has become one of our country's musical legends.
2. Elvis was born in 1935 in Tupelo, Mississippi, but he later moved with his parents to Memphis, Tennessee.
3. His father and mother were uneducated and "dirt poor," according to friends of the family; nevertheless, they encouraged their son's interest in music and bought him a guitar.
4. While working as a truck driver, Elvis began to sing in church basements, at school, in neighbors' backyards, and for anyone who would listen to him.
5. He was fascinated by Southern gospel songs, country-and-western music, and the musical style of black performers who were popular in the South during the 1950s.
6. To develop his own stage personality and to conceal his nervousness, he wore far-out clothes and combed his hair in a grease-laden pompadour.
7. He made a few records at a local studio and began to tour with a show throughout the South.
8. Those records, whose value today continues to increase, caught the attention of Colonel Tom Parker, who was to become his manager.
9. Parker urged Elvis to emphasize the rhythm-and-blues style of black musicians.
10. In 1956 his first big hit, "Heartbreak Hotel," was released, and its success launched his career.
11. For the next sixteen months his recordings were among the top ten national best sellers, and their popularity spread to Europe, where they soon dominated the sales charts.
12. His television appearances and concerts attracted mobs of screaming teenagers, but many regarded his gyrations and music as symbols of decay in our society.
13. After a brief Army career, Elvis starred in several movies in the 1960s; they were ridiculed by the critics but praised by his fans.
14. His sudden death in 1977 shocked his millions of fans throughout the world; a common reaction was that one of our national idols had fallen.

15.   Today his admirers come to pay their respects at his grave in Graceland, his home in Tennessee.

The Verb

Every sentence that you speak or write contains a *verb*. Sometimes the verb is only implied; usually, however, it is stated. When you can recognize and use verbs correctly, you have taken a big step toward being a better speaker and writer.

A *verb* is a word that expresses action or a state of being and thereby tells us what a noun or pronoun does or what it is. If the verb tells us what a noun or pronoun does, it is an *action verb*.

Roberta paints beautiful portraits, which she gives to her friends.

Neil Armstrong landed on the moon in 1969.

Huang attends medical school in California.

If the verb expresses a state of being rather than action, it is a *linking verb*. Linking verbs do not express action; instead, they connect a noun or pronoun with a word or group of words that describe or rename the subject:

The subject of tonight's debate *is* prayers in public school. (*Subject* is linked by the verb *is* to *prayers*, a word that renames it.)

I.Q. tests *are* unreliable predictors of academic success, according to many educators. (*Tests* is linked to *predictors* by the verb *are*.)

My new speakers *sound* much better than my old ones. (*Speakers* is linked to the word that describes it—*better*—by the verb *sound*.)

Computers were very expensive for the average family to purchase in the 1970s. (What words are linked? What word links them?)

Belize is a small nation in Central America. (What word renames Belize? How are the two words linked?)

The most common linking verbs are formed from the verb *to be*: *am, are, is, was,* and *were*. Others often used as linking verbs are *appear, become, grow, remain,* and *seem,* and the "sense" verbs: *feel, look, smell, sound,* and *taste.*

Verbs are the only words that change their spelling to show *tense*. *Tense* is the time when the action of the verb occurs. Notice in the following sentences how the tense or time of the action is changed by the spelling of the verb:

Our mayor *delivers* an annual message to the citizens of our city. (Present tense)

Last week she *delivered* her message on television. (Past tense)

You will learn more about the use of tense in Chapter 6.

To show additional differences in meaning, verbs often use helping words that suggest the time at which the action of the verb takes place and other kinds of meaning. These words are called *helping verbs*, and they always come before the main verb. Verbs that consist of helping verbs and a main verb are called *verb phrases*. Look carefully at the following sentences.

I *will* study.

He *had* practiced.

Juan *did* not *want* lunch.

The sisters *were* united.

The child *was* photographed.

They *might have been* selected.

Each of the verbs in the preceding sentences consists of a helping verb (or "auxiliary") and a main verb. Here are the common helping verbs. You should memorize them.

can, could, may, might, must, ought, shall, should, will, would, have, has, had, do, does, did, am, is, are, was, were, been

Some verbs can be either helping verbs or main verbs. In other words, if they appear alone without a helping verb, they are main verbs. But if they precede a main verb, they are helping verbs. The following verbs can be either helping verbs or main verbs. You should memorize them.

Forms of "to be": *am, is, are, was, were*

Forms of "to do": *do, does, did*

Forms of "to have": *has, have, had*

Look at the following sentences carefully:

Victims of the earthquake *were* unable to drink the water. (*Were* is the main verb in this sentence.)

Victims of the earthquake *were given* food and clothing by the Red Cross. (*Were given* is a verb phrase. The main verb is *given*, and the helping verb is *were*.)

Tanya *has* a new car. (*Has* is the main verb in this sentence.)

She *has* already *driven* it two thousand miles. (*Has driven* is a verb phrase. The main verb is *driven*, and the helping verb is *has*.)

TIPS FOR RECOGNIZING VERBS

An *action verb* is a word that fits in the slot in the following sentence:
"*I* (or *He* or *They*) usually _____."

Examples: *I usually* jog.
He usually sneezes.
They usually help.

A linking verb is a word that fits in the slot in the following sentence:
"*I* (or *He* or *They*) _____ *happy.*"

Examples: *I* am *happy.*
He is *happy.*
They were *happy.*

Exercise 1-2

If the italicized word in each sentence is an action verb, write "1"; if the italicized word is a linking verb, write "2"; if the italicized word is a helping ("auxiliary") verb, write "3." Use the space provided on the left.

_____   1.   The differing conversational styles of men and women *have been* analyzed by several modern psychologists and linguists.

_____   2.   They claim that men and women *talk* in completely different ways.

_____   3.   For women, they *argue*, conversation is a means of promoting intimacy and cooperation.

_____   4.   For men, it *is* a kind of competition, a way to show their independence or authority.

_____   5.   Men, for example, never want to ask for directions because it *involves* admitting ignorance.

_____   6.   Women, on the other hand, value the personal contact involved and *have* no such difficulty.

_____   7.   Many of the ways that women talk *are* merely conversational rituals designed to save face for the other person.

_____   8.   For example, a typical woman boss *might* gently ask her secretary if she would mind typing a letter.

_____   9.   Some men *would* think that she lacked confidence.

_____   10.   In fact, however, she *felt* so confident that she did not think she had to appear authoritative or aloof.

_____   11.   Saying "I'm sorry" frequently *is* another conversational ritual that many women use.

_____   12.   Such an expression *may* make them sound less self-confident than they really are.

© 1997 Addison-Wesley Educational Publishers Inc.

_____ 13. Most workplaces *favor* male-style communication, particularly when it is used by men.

_____ 14. As a result, many men misinterpret remarks by women, and many women *do* not realize the impressions created by those remarks.

_____ 15. The solution, according to one authority on the subject, *is* to observe a person's performance and not judge prematurely.

The Adjective

In your writing you will often want to modify (or describe) a noun or pronoun. The word you will use will be an *adjective*, a word that modifies nouns and pronouns. Adjectives usually answer one of the following questions: *How many? What kind? Which one? What color?*

How many?   *Many* students believe that the Social Security System will be bankrupt before they will be old enough to retire. (*Many* modifies *students*.)

What kind?   *Loud* noises from the back of the auditorium forced the speaker to interrupt his speech. (*Loud* modifies *noises*.)

Which one?   *This* knapsack was found in the cafeteria. (*This* modifies *knapsack*.)

What color? His *purple* socks did not complement his blue suit. (*Purple* modifies *socks*.)

The adjectives in the sentences above came immediately before the nouns they modified. Some adjectives, however, come after linking verbs and describe the subject of the verb. Adjectives in this position are called *predicate adjectives*. Study the following sentences carefully:

We were surprised to learn that old pairs of jeans in Russia are very *expensive*. (*Expensive* is a predicate adjective because it comes after a linking verb—*are*—and modifies the noun *jeans*.)

After waiting in the hot sun for three hours, the refugees became *angry*. (*Angry* is a predicate adjective because it comes after a linking verb—*became*—and modifies the noun *refugees*.)

Possessive pronouns (pronouns that show ownership such as *my, your, her, his, our, their*) are adjectives when they come before nouns. Notice the following examples:

our *condominium*

their *vacation*

my *sister-in-law*

Demonstrative pronouns (pronouns that point out or indicate) are adjectives when they come before nouns. Notice the following examples:

this *building*   these *flowers*
that *statement*   those *books*

A special type of adjective is called the *article*. The English language contains three articles: *a, an* (before words that begin with a vowel sound), and *the*.

After an absence of sixteen years, Jane returned to the city of her birth and a parade in her honor.

TIPS FOR SPOTTING ADJECTIVES

1. You can add *-er* and *-est* or *more* and *most* to adjectives:

    big, bigger, biggest
    beautiful, more *beautiful,* most *beautiful*

2. An adjective will fill the blank in this sentence:

    The (noun) *is* _____

    Example: The tire is *flat.*

3. Adjectives describe nouns and pronouns:

    The heavy *surf pounded the coastline.*
    She is lucky *that she avoided the accident.*

4. Adjectives tell *how many, what kind, which one,* and *what color.*

Exercise 1-3

A. *In the space before each sentence, write the noun or pronoun that is modified by the italicized adjective.*

_____   1.   A classic example of a *false* rumor that swept the country was the alleged death of Paul McCartney, the Beatle.
_____   2.   In 1969 a Detroit disc jockey casually mentioned a *fictional* story about McCartney's death.
_____   3.   Within a *few* days the rumor of his death had spread throughout the world.

_____   4.   According to one version, McCartney had been killed in an automobile accident *several* years previously.

_____   5.   His record company had replaced him with a look-alike and persuaded the *remaining* Beatles to conceal the event.

_____   6.   But the Beatles, according to the rumor, had inserted *various* clues about McCartney's death in their records to let others in on the secret.

_____   7.   In the weeks following, their fans searched the Beatles' albums for these *alleged* clues.

_____   8.   They held up Beatles' album covers to mirrors, hoping to find some message in the *reverse* image.

_____   9.   *Repeated* denials by record-company officials failed to have much impact on the rumor.

_____   10.   Finally, Paul McCartney issued a *public* statement disproving the truth of the rumor, adding, "If I were dead, I'd be the last to know about it."

B. *In the space before each sentence, write the predicate adjective that modifies the italicized noun or pronoun.*

_____   1.   The *sense* of smell is the least understood of the five senses.

_____   2.   The human *nose* is able to distinguish over ten thousand odors.

_____   3.   The *eye*, by contrast, is capable of recognizing only a few thousand colors.

_____   4.   Scientists believe that individual *genes* are active in the nose and nowhere else in the human body.

_____   5.   The *nose* and the *eye* are different in the ways they process information.

_____   6.   Odor *receptors* in the nose are similar to magnets.

_____   7.   Their *function* is critical: to attract and discriminate among the odor molecules that drift into the nasal cavity.

_____   8.   These *receptors* are responsible for sending signals to the region of the brain that identifies fragrances.

_____   9.   The *sense* of smell was very important to primitive animals.

_____   10.   Among humans, *it* remains vital as a source of information about one's environment.

The Adverb

Adverbs are words that describe or modify verbs, adjectives, and other adverbs. Study these sentences carefully:

The tall guard dribbled the basketball slowly. (Slowly *modifies the verb* dribbled.)

The extremely *tall guard dribbled the basketball slowly.* (Extremely *modifies the adjective* tall.)

The tall guard dribbled the basketball very *slowly.* (Very *modifies the adverb* slowly.)

Adverbs usually answer the following questions: *When? Where? How? To what extent?*

When?	*Hector* immediately *realized that he had confused Jo Ann with her sister.* (*The adverb* immediately *modifies the verb* realized.)
Where?	*Please wait* here. (*The adverb* here *modifies the verb* wait.)
How?	*The dolphin struggled* unsuccessfully *to escape the net.* (*The adverb* unsuccessfully *modifies the verb* struggled.)
To what extent?	*The state capitol building was* completely *remodeled after the tornado.* (*The adverb* completely *modifies the verb* was remodeled.)

Adjectives and adverbs are often confused. Remember that *adjectives* describe nouns and pronouns, and that *adverbs* modify verbs, adjectives, and other adverbs. Notice the differences in the following sentences:

Her loud *hiccups distracted the speaker.* (Loud *is an adjective because it modifies the noun* hiccups.)

If you sneeze loudly, *you will distract the speaker.* (Loudly *is an adverb because it modifies the verb* sneeze.)

Many adverbs are formed by adding *-ly* to the adjective (as in *loudly,* in the sentence above). But keep in mind that some adverbs do not end in *-ly* (*above, never, there, very,* and so on). On the other hand, some words that end in *-ly* are not adverbs (words such as *silly, friendly,* and *lovely*).

TIPS FOR RECOGNIZING ADVERBS

1. Adverbs are words that will fit in the following slot:

   "He will do it _____."

   Examples: *He will do it* later. *(when)*
   He will do it here. *(where)*
   He will do it quietly. *(how)*
   He will do it slightly. *(to what extent)*

2. Adverbs tell *when, where, how,* and *to what extent.*

Exercise 1-4

A. In the space before each sentence, write the adjective, verb, or adverb modified by the italicized adverb.

_____ 1.   *Approximately* twenty million Americans attend monster truck spectaculars every year.

_____ 2.   Monster trucks have huge tires that enable them to scoot up a ramp, take off and travel through the air 100 feet, thirty feet off the ground, then crash *dramatically* back to earth without being smashed to pieces.

_____ 3.   A common feat is to land on a car, *preferably* a Japanese import, and crush it.

_____ 4.   Other *very* popular events at truck shows include mud racing and dropping drivers strapped in their cars 170 feet in the air onto several vans.

_____ 5.   The appeal of monster trucks *probably* derives from the roar and the mud.

_____ 6.   It also stems *partly* from the fantasy most of us have experienced as we have been trapped in traffic, wishing we could push aside the cars around us.

_____ 7.   The trucks *inevitably* have colorful names such as Carolina Crusher, Bearfoot, and Grave Digger, among others.

_____ 8.   But the *most* famous is Bigfoot, the product of Bob Chandler, the originator of the monster truck.

_____ 9.   Bigfoot-licensed products and souvenirs sold at truck shows gross over 300 million dollars *annually*.

_____ 10. Over 700 monster truck shows a year are held throughout the world, and the *most* popular drivers enjoy the kind of fame reserved for movie stars.

B. In the space before each sentence, write the adverb that modifies the italicized word or words.

_____ 1.   As is well *known*, Wolfgang Amadeus Mozart was a child prodigy of extraordinary musical talent.

_____ 2.   In Vienna, Munich, Rome, and London he played, improvised, and composed before audiences that *cheered* wildly.

_____ 3.   Despite such a beginning, Mozart's adult life was filled with very *tumultuous* and *disappointing* events.

_____ 4.   He became increasingly *absorbed* in a world of music without friends or companions.

_____ 5.   The Emperor Joseph II finally *hired* him as a court composer.

_____ 6.   Despite his father's protests, he married Constanze Weber, and there is evidence that they were very *fond* of each other.

_____ 7.   In the years that followed, Mozart wrote several great piano concertos and became increasingly *interested* in the mechanical aspects and design of the piano.

_____ 8.   He also *wrote* several successful operas, including *The Marriage of Figaro*.

_____   9.   Despite the success of his operas and concert tours, Mozart became financially *desperate*.

_____   10.   He became seriously *ill* while writing his *Requiem Mass* and died in 1791.

The Preposition

Prepositions are connecting words—they do not have any meaning or content in or of themselves. They exist only to show relationships between other words. For this reason they must simply be learned or remembered. Prepositions are words like *at, by, from,* and *with* that are usually followed by a noun or pronoun (*at home, by herself, from Toledo, with you*). The word following the preposition is called its *object;* the preposition and its object are called a *prepositional phrase.*

Here are some prepositional phrases. The object in each prepositional phrase is italicized. Notice that a preposition can have more than one object, and that some prepositions are made up of more than one word.

according to *authorities*   in addition to *requirements in science*

after *the meeting*   through *the final week*

below *the deck*   together with *the coach and manager*

between *you and me*   within *the hour*

from *one coast to another*   without *a clue*

Here are some of the most common prepositions. As noted above, some prepositions consist of more than one word.

about	below	in
above	beneath	in addition to
according to	besides	in front of
across	between	inside
after	beyond	instead of
against	but (when it means *except*)	into
ahead of	by	like
along	concerning	near
among	despite	next to
around	down	of
at	due to	off
away from	during	on
because of	except	onto
before	for	on account of
behind	from	out

out of	through	until
outside	to	up
over	together with	upon
past	toward	with
regarding	under	within
round	underneath	without
since	unlike	

Prepositional phrases may serve the same function as either adjectives or adverbs in a sentence.

adjective: Rumors *of an impending attack* panicked the village. (The italicized phrase modifies the noun *Rumors*.)

adjective: The ushers *in blue suits* were college football players. (The italicized phrase modifies the noun *ushers*.)

adverb: Tod and Jan left *during the intermission*. (The italicized phrase modifies the verb *left*.)

adverb: The President spoke *with emotion*. (The italicized phrase modifies the verb *spoke*.)

TIPS FOR RECOGNIZING PREPOSITIONS

1. A preposition is a word that will fill the slot in the following sentence:

    "The airplane flew _____ *the clouds."*

2. A preposition is a word that will fit the slot in the following sentence:

    "I saw him _____ *the game."*

Some prepositions, of course, will not fit either sentence, and they must be learned.

Exercise 1-5

Underline the prepositional phrases in each sentence; write "adv" above the phrase if it is used as an adverbial modifier, or "adj" if it is used as an adjectival modifier.

1. The first symptom of Alzheimer's disease in most older people is loss of memory.
2. Most patients are not aware of the problem and don't realize the need for an appointment with a doctor.

3. Alzheimer's disease affects the hippocampus, one of the areas of the brain.
4. The hippocampus is involved in learning something initially, and then that information is stored or processed in other areas of the brain.
5. For that reason, most Alzheimer's patients have problems with learning and remembering new things, but are better at remembering old things.
6. Billions of cells make up the brain like bricks that make up a house.
7. The dendrite is the part of the cell that receives information, and the axon is the part that sends information out.
8. The axons and dendrites are important to memory because they connect one brain cell to another.
9. One of the theories held by scientists is that the axons and dendrites shrink in Alzheimer's patients.
10. As a result, loss of memory is one of the first effects when these connections are disrupted.

The Conjunction

A *conjunction* is a word that joins words or groups of words. In a sense, conjunctions are like prepositions: they do not represent things or qualities. Instead, they merely show different kinds of relationships between other words or groups of words. There are two kinds of conjunctions you will need to recognize: *coordinating* and *subordinating*.

Coordinating conjunctions join words and word groups of equal importance or rank. You should memorize these coordinating conjunctions:

and, but, so, for, nor, or, yet

The following sentences show how coordinating conjunctions join single words and groups of words:

Maria speaks both English *and* Spanish fluently. (*and* links two words)

Nguyen was born in Vietnam, *but* he moved to the United States at the age of four. (*but* links two independent clauses)

Do you prefer fish *or* chicken? (*or* links two words)

You should talk to a counselor, *or* you might take the wrong courses. (*or* links two independent clauses)

In Chapter 7 you will see how coordinating conjunctions are used in compound sentences. Incidentally, it used to be considered ungrammatical to begin a sentence with one of these words, but this "rule" is no longer observed, even by the best writers.

Some coordinating conjunctions combine with other words to form *correlative conjunctions*. The most common correlative conjunctions are *both . . . and; either . . . or; neither . . . nor;* and *not only . . . but also*. Notice the following examples.

Both *Denver* and *Miami are major league expansion teams*.

Ray will either *go to summer school* or *work in his father's store*.

John Kennedy was *not only* the first Roman Catholic President *but also* the first President born in the twentieth century.

Subordinating conjunctions, like coordinating conjunctions, join groups of words. Unlike coordinating conjunctions, however, they join unequal word groups or grammatical units that are "subordinate." You will study subordinating conjunctions in greater detail in Chapters 7 and 8, especially with respect to complex sentences and fragments.

Some conjunctions like *after, before, for, since, but,* and *until* can also function as prepositions:

The popularity of leisure suits declined after *the presidency of Richard Nixon*. (preposition)

Harold sold his leisure suit after *Richard Nixon wore one*. (conjunction)

Jim bought flowers for *his girlfriend*. (preposition)

Jim bought flowers, for *he knew his girlfriend was angry*. (conjunction)

Every member of the General Assembly but *Cuba voted for the motion*. (preposition)

Every member voted, but *Cuba demanded a recount*. (conjunction)

Exercise 1-6

Underline the coordinating conjunctions in the sentences below.

1. The savings and loan disaster cost the government millions of dollars, but the greatest loss was to the lives of investors.
2. The relationship between smoking and cancer has been established, yet many young people continue to smoke.
3. Neither the Israelis nor the Palestinians would comment on the negotiations.
4. Because he had a car alarm and had parked in front of a church, he was surprised and angry to discover that his new Cadillac was either stolen or towed away.
5. Leon bought a fax machine, but he didn't know how to use it.

The Interjection

The *interjection* (or *exclamation*, as it is sometimes called) is a word that expresses emotion and has no grammatical relationship with the rest of the sentence.

Mild interjections are followed by a comma:

No, *it's too early*.

Oh, *I suppose so*.

Yes, *that would be fine*.

Strong interjections require an exclamation mark:

Wow! *I won the lottery!*

Ouch! *That hurts!*

Fire!

A Word of Caution

Many words do double or triple duty; that is, they can be (for instance) a noun in one sentence and a verb in another sentence. The situation is much like a football player who lines up as a tight end on one play and a halfback on another. His function in each play is different; and so it is with words and parts of speech. A word like *light*, for example, can be used as a verb:

We always light *our Christmas tree after the children are asleep.*

It can also be used as an adjective:

Many beer drinkers prefer light *beer.*

Light can also be used as a noun:

All colors depend on light.

What part of speech is *light*, then? It depends on the sentence; no word exists in a vacuum. To determine the part of speech of a particular word, you must determine its function or use in the sentence.

Reviewing the Chapter: Writing Sentences

This review exercise gives you a chance to show that you can recognize the parts of speech. It also lets you show your originality by writing sentences of your own. When writing your sentences, do not hesitate to review the appropriate pages in this chapter as needed.

1. Write two original sentences; in each sentence use a common noun and a proper noun. Circle the nouns.
2. Write two original sentences; in each sentence use at least one pronoun from the list on page 3. Circle the pronouns.
3. Write a sentence containing an action verb. Circle the action verb.
4. Write a sentence containing a linking verb. Circle the linking verb.
5. Write a sentence containing a helping ("auxiliary") verb and a main verb. Circle the helping verb.
6. Write a sentence containing a predicate adjective. Circle the predicate adjective.
7. Write a sentence containing at least one adverb. Circle the adverb.
8. Write a sentence containing at least two prepositional phrases. Circle each prepositional phrase.

1-A

REVIEW EXERCISE

A. *Identify the parts of speech of the italicized words by using the appropriate letter in the space provided.*

a. noun   b. pronoun   c. adjective   d. adverb

_____ 1. Hal painted his old Chevrolet *yesterday*.
_____ 2. Several *states* reported huge deficits in their budgets.
_____ 3. The detectives found a *bloody* shirt in the closet of the bedroom.
_____ 4. *Some* of the amendments to the proposed law were defeated by a narrow vote.
_____ 5. Children without accompanying *adults* will not be allowed to enter the theater.
_____ 6. The report of the Surgeon General listed three main *causes* of lung cancer.
_____ 7. Governors of the Midwestern states sent petitions to *their* Senators.
_____ 8. By taking aspirin *daily*, men can reduce the likelihood of heart attacks, according to my physician.
_____ 9. *Most* of my conversations with Theresa were about her problems with math.
_____ 10. By shopping early we were able to find *several* bargains.

B. *Identify the parts of speech of the italicized words by using the appropriate letter in the space provided.*

a. preposition   b. conjunction   c. interjection

_____ 11. Most of the workers and their supervisors complained *about* the smell coming from the nearby river.
_____ 12. Michael played point guard in high school *but* started as center in college.
_____ 13. *Well*, I'm not surprised by her decision.
_____ 14. Because of my new antenna, my shortwave radio can now pick up signals *throughout* the East coast.
_____ 15. Andrew *and* Cathie are saving money now for their infant son's college education.

C. *Identify the italicized words by using the appropriate letter in the space provided.*

a. action verb   *b. linking verb*   *c. helping verb*

_____ 16. Dr. Garcia warned the class that the final examination *would* include the topics from his lectures.

_____ 17. I *would have gone* to the Rolling Stones concert if tickets had been available.

_____ 18. Some business instructors at my college *will* insist that their students have access to personal computers next semester.

_____ 19. Benjamin Franklin *held* the patent on several inventions.

_____ 20. How many languages *are spoken* by the students in your college?

_____ 21. Customers needing help *were* assisted by the clerks.

_____ 22. The mosaics *were* by an unknown Roman artist.

_____ 23. At first glance, Elaine *seems* shy and even unfriendly.

_____ 24. The opposing teams *eyed* each other warily.

_____ 25. Greg finally *found* a repairman for his old manual typewriter.

1-B

REVIEW EXERCISE

A. *Identify the parts of speech of the italicized words by using the appropriate letter in the space provided.*

a. noun   *b. pronoun*   *c. adjective*   *d. adverb*

_____   1.   The windows were washed with ammonia *yesterday*.
_____   2.   Investigators discovered three *gold* coins in the safe.
_____   3.   Lois likes to watch *wrestling* matches on television.
_____   4.   *One* of the demonstrators revealed plans for disrupting the meeting.
_____   5.   Manuscripts without *postage* will be ignored, according to the publisher.
_____   6.   The reception at the White House attracted *delegates* from over 150 nations.
_____   7.   The owner of the shopping mall sponsored *roller-skating* on the sidewalks.
_____   8.   By using sonar, *they* were able to find the sunken ship.
_____   9.   Professor Alvarez's book is about early Southwestern *architecture*.
_____   10. Scores on the Scholastic Aptitude Test have risen *gradually*.

B. *Identify the parts of speech of the italicized words by using the appropriate letter in the space provided.*

a. preposition   *b. conjunction*   *c. interjection*

_____   11. Several athletes *and* their trainers were disqualified because of the use of steroids.
_____   12. Herb was employed as a guard at the local bank *but* went to school at night.
_____   13. *Yes*, I think we ought to leave before it begins to rain.
_____   14. A sonic boom sent vibrations *throughout* the neighborhood.
_____   15. The audience enjoyed the songs *of* the drummer.

C. *Identify the italicized words by using the appropriate letter in the space provided.*

a. action verb   *b. linking verb*   *c. helping verb*

_____ 16. The Weather Bureau *issued* a tornado alert twenty minutes ago.

_____ 17. Pete Rose *had been* a professional baseball player since he was nineteen years old.

_____ 18. You *will* receive a ticket if you park in the red zone.

_____ 19. Joseph Smith *founded* the Mormon Church.

_____ 20. The piano concerto *was performed* by a young girl from South Korea.

_____ 21. Harvard *was* founded in 1636 by New England clergymen.

_____ 22. The painting *was* by Salvador Dali, the Spanish artist.

_____ 23. The witness *appeared* nervous as he took the stand.

_____ 24. The prosecuting attorney *presented* evidence to the jury.

_____ 25. The governor *warned* the legislature of the impending financial crisis.

Chapter 2

Finding the Subject and Verb in the Sentence

Sentences are the building blocks of writing. To improve your writing you should master the sentence and its two main parts, the *subject* and the *verb*.

The Subject and the Verb

The *subject* of a sentence names a person, place, thing, or idea; it tells us *who* or *what* the sentence is about. The *verb* describes the action or state of being of the subject; it tells us what the subject *does*, what the subject *is*, or what the subject *receives*.

    (subject)   (verb)
Francis Scott Key wrote the words to our national anthem.

   (subject) (verb)
Tallahassee is the capital of Florida.

    (subject)   (verb)
Gertrude Ederle was the first woman to swim the English Channel.

    (subject)   (verb)
Martin Luther King, Jr., received the Nobel Prize for Peace in 1964.

 (subject) (verb)
I rarely *eat* this much supper.

Each of the above sentences contains a subject and a verb, and each makes a complete statement. In other words, they convey a sense of completeness. In conversation, sentences often lack stated subjects and verbs, but their context—the words and sentences that surround them—makes clear the missing subject or verb. For example:

"Studying your sociology?"

"Yes. Big test tomorrow."

"Ready for it?"

"Hope so. Flunked the last one."

If this conversation were written in formal sentences, the missing subjects and verbs would be supplied, and the exchange might look something like this:

"Are you studying your sociology?"

"Yes. I have a big test tomorrow."

"Are you ready for it?"

"I hope so. I flunked the last one."

All sentences, then, have subjects and verbs, either stated or implied. Before proceeding further, therefore, it is important that you be able to locate the subject and the verb in a sentence. Because it is usually the easiest to locate, the verb is the best place to begin.

Finding the Verb

You will remember from Chapter 1 that the verb may be a single word (He *sleeps*) or a verb phrase of two, three, or even four words (He *had slept*, He *had been sleeping*, He *must have been sleeping*). Remember, too, that parts of the verb can be separated by adverbs (He *must* not *have been sleeping*).

Action Verbs

As you saw in Chapter 1, action verbs tell what the subject does.

Carbohydrates provide energy for body function and activity by supplying immediate calories. (What action takes place in this sentence? What do carbohydrates do? They *provide*. Therefore, the verb in this sentence is *provide*.)

Texas leads the nation in energy consumption. (What does Texas do? It *leads*. The verb in this sentence is *leads*.)

The students boarded the plane for Mexico City. (What did the students do? They *boarded*. The verb in this sentence is *boarded*.)

© 1997 Addison-Wesley Educational Publishers Inc.

Oceans cover three quarters of the earth's surface. (What action takes place in this sentence? What do the oceans do? They *cover*. Therefore, the verb in this sentence is *cover*.)

Blood returning from the body tissues enters the right atrium. (What does the blood do? It *enters*. The verb in this sentence is *enters*.)

Visitors to Disneyland buy souvenirs to show their friends at home. (What do visitors do? They *buy* souvenirs. The verb is *buy*.)

Exercise 2-1

Each of the following sentences contains one or more action verbs. Circle them.

1. When the siren of an ambulance wails, sound waves vibrate in all directions.
2. Scientists describe the effect as an acoustical sphere.
3. If the ambulance moves forward, the sound waves in front of it bunch up as new waves pile up behind older waves.
4. Behind the ambulance, the opposite happens, as individual waves stretch out.
5. The frequency of these sound waves changes their pitch.
6. As the ambulance comes toward you, the frequency of the waves increases.
7. This creates a higher pitch.
8. It reaches its pinnacle as the ambulance passes closest to you.
9. After that, the pitch declines as the sound waves stretch out until they no longer reach your ear.
10. Scientists call this phenomenon the Doppler effect.

Linking Verbs

Some verbs do not show action. Instead, they express a condition or state of being. They are called *linking* verbs, and they link the subject to another word that renames or describes the subject. You will recall from Chapter 1 that most linking verbs are formed from the verb "to be" and include *am*, *are*, *is*, *was*, and *were*. Several other verbs often used as linking verbs are *appear*, *become*, *feel*, *grow*, *look*, *remain*, *seem*, *smell*, *sound*, and *taste*.

The verbs in the following sentences are *linking verbs*. They link their subjects to words that rename or describe them.

My parents *seem* happy in their new apartment. (The linking verb *seem* connects the subject *parents* with the word that describes them: *happy*.)

French *is* the language of the province of Quebec in Canada. (The linking verb *is* connects the subject *French* with the word that renames it: *language*.)

The first-graders *remained* calm during the earthquake. (The verb *remained* connects the subject *first-graders* with the word that describes them: *calm*.)

Steve Martin *has become* an actor as well as comedian. (The linking verb *has become* connects the subject *Steve Martin* with the word that renames it: *actor*.)

Lord Kelvin *was* a founder of the science of thermodynamics. (The linking verb *was* connects the subject *Lord Kelvin* with the word that renames it: *founder*.)

Exercise 2-2

Each of the following sentences contains a linking verb; circle it.

1. Senator Edmonds was not very enthusiastic about the law regarding term limits.
2. Her motives became clear after our discussion.
3. Norman felt powerless to correct the situation.
4. The winner of the marathon appeared near collapse after the race.
5. To an American in a foreign country, nothing tastes as good as a hamburger.
6. The survivors were not anxious to talk about their experiences.
7. Yo-Yo Ma is one of the world's greatest cellists.
8. Soccer seems to be more popular today than a decade ago.
9. Are you ready to leave for work?
10. The Russians remain committed to achieving a democratic society.

When looking for the verb in a sentence, you should remember that they sometimes consist of more than one word. In such cases, they are called *verb phrases*, and they consist of a main verb and a helping verb, sometimes called an *auxiliary verb*. Any helping verbs in front of the main verb are part of the verb, as in the following examples:

may have disappeared

should be avoided

might stay

did guarantee

is speaking

could have objected

For a complete list of the words that serve as helping ("auxiliary") verbs, see page 5 in Chapter 1.

Exercise 2-3

Each of the following sentences contains one or more verbs with helping verbs. Circle both the main verb and its helping verb.

1. Termites have destroyed the floor of the toolshed.
2. Because of the change in the tax law, we can claim a deduction for our storm damage.

3. You should not run in a marathon until you have been running for about a year and can cover twenty to twenty-five miles a week comfortably.
4. Students in our chemistry class were assigned lab partners for the semester.
5. The ethics committee will present its report next Thursday.
6. Forrest has failed the driving examination three times.
7. The allergist had warned me that dairy products might provoke another asthma attack.
8. Many theories have been offered for the disappearance of dinosaurs.
9. Only a small percentage of the population is born with perfect pitch.
10. You should have been notified by now if you have won the lottery.

Exercise 2-4

Underline the verbs in the following sentences; be sure to include any helping verbs. Some sentences have more than one verb.

1. Normal red blood cells look round and plump, something like jelly doughnuts.
2. In about 8 percent of American blacks, however, some red blood cells are much smaller than normal and have a sickle, or crescent, shape.
3. Sickling of the red blood cells is an inherited trait that has been traced to a mutation in a single gene.
4. A person who has inherited two sickling genes has sickle-cell anemia.
5. Sickle cells carry much less oxygen than normal cells, and such a person frequently suffers from insufficient oxygen.
6. In addition, the cells often clog blood vessels, cause severe pain, damage tissue, and even cause death if vessels that supply the brain or lungs are blocked.
7. People with sickle-cell anemia frequently die at an early age.
8. Certain African populations contain a high incidence of the sickling gene.
9. These populations live in areas with a high incidence of malaria.
10. People with the sickle-cell trait (one sickling gene and one normal gene) have a substantially lower incidence of malaria than the rest of the population.
11. They concluded that having one sickle-cell gene improves a person's chances of surviving malaria.
12. Because having a single sickling gene is an advantage in areas with malaria, the gene remains in the population.
13. The sickling trait is destructive to blacks with two sickling genes, but it survives in many people with only one.
14. Malaria kills many individuals in Africa, but those with one sickle-cell gene are more likely to survive.
15. For American blacks, the sickling gene has no adaptive function because malaria is no longer a medical problem.

Words Mistaken for the Verb

You may sometimes be confused by two forms of the verb that may be mistaken for the main verb of the sentence. These forms are the *infinitive* and the *present participle*.

The *infinitive* is the "to" form of the verb: *to leave, to write, to start,* and so on. The infinitive is the base form of the verb—in other words, it merely names the verb. It does not give us any information about its person, its tense, or its number. The infinitive by itself is never the verb of the sentence. Note how the following word groups fail to make sense because they use only the infinitive form—the "to" form—of the verb:

Homeowners *to install* new roofs because of the damage from hail.

My reading comprehension *to improve* by fifteen percent.

Missionaries from Spain *to arrive* in California in the 1760s.

Ornithologists *to study* the mating habits of condors.

Contractors *to build* cheaper and smaller homes in the future.

These word groups are not sentences because they try to make an infinitive do the work of a main verb. They can be corrected by placing a verb before the infinitive:

Homeowners *had* to install new roofs because of the damage from hail.

I *wanted* to improve my reading comprehension by fifteen percent.

Missionaries from Spain *began* to arrive in California in the 1760s.

Ornithologists *plan* to study the mating habits of condors.

Contractors *plan* to build cheaper and smaller homes in the future.

Of course, these word groups could also have been converted to sentences merely by changing the infinitives to main verbs: *installed, improved, arrived, study,* and *will build.*

The other form of the verb that sometimes looks as though it is the main verb is the *present participle,* the "-ing" form of the verb. It is the result of adding *-ing* to the verb, as in the following: *leaving, starting, writing,* and so on. Like the infinitive, the present participle can never stand by itself as the verb in a sentence. Notice how the following groups of words fail to make sense because they attempt to use the present participle—the "-ing" form—as their verb:

Homeowners *installing* new roofs because of the damage from the hail.

My reading comprehension *improving* by fifteen percent.

Missionaries from Spain *arriving* in California in the 1760s.

Ornithologists *studying* the mating habits of condors.

Contractors *building* cheaper and smaller homes in the future.

These word groups can be corrected by placing a form of the verb *to be* in front of the present participle:

> Homeowners *were* installing new roofs because of the damage from the hail.
> My reading comprehension *has been* improving by fifteen percent.
> Missionaries from Spain *were* arriving in California in the 1760s.
> Ornithologists *have been* studying the mating habits of condors.
> Contractors *will be* building cheaper and smaller homes in the future.

A final warning: You will never find the verb of a sentence in a prepositional phrase. The reason for this rule is simple. Prepositional phrases are made of prepositions and their objects, which are either nouns or pronouns—never verbs. Therefore, a prepositional phrase will never contain the verb of a sentence.

TIPS ON FINDING THE VERB

1. Find the verb by asking what action takes place.
2. Find the verb by asking what word links the subject with the rest of the sentence.
3. If a word fits in the following slot, it is a verb:

   "I (or He or They) _____."

4. Remember that the verb in a sentence will never have "to" in front of it.
5. The *-ing* form (the present participle) can be a verb only if it has a helping verb in front of it.
6. The verb will never be in a prepositional phrase.

Exercise 2-5

Identify the italicized words by writing the appropriate letter in the space provided.

a. verb   *b. present participle*   *c. infinitive*

_____   1.   If you are a musician who dreams of fame and fortune, *making* an album is the first step.
_____   2.   Your own album *opens* avenues of publicity through radio airplay and record reviews.
_____   3.   It also offers a way *to make* money through off-stage sales, mail order, and retail outlets.
_____   4.   Most important, an album *is* more impressive than a demo tape when you are negotiating with clubs and getting good gigs.
_____   5.   *Producing* a marketable tape or CD is a multi-step process.

_____ 6. First, you *must decide* what percentage of your release is cassette or CD.

_____ 7. Most managers *recommend* a 50–50 mix, with an initial run of one thousand units.

_____ 8. Regardless of the format, you should *work* out the order of the cuts on the album.

_____ 9. It is important to try out tracks in different orders and *to pay* attention to the pacing of the cuts.

_____ 10. *Noticing* how the musical keys of songs blend together when they are back-to-back is also important.

_____ 11. On a cassette tape release, you *should try* to make both sides approximately the same length.

_____ 12. On a CD release, you should try *to keep* the total running time under seventy minutes and the total number of tunes under twenty.

_____ 13. Your next job *is* to locate a duplicator or replicator that suits your budget.

_____ 14. By *looking* in one of the many directories that list mastering, pressing, and duplication facilities that are available, you can find one that best suits your project.

_____ 15. After you receive the finished album, you are ready *to begin* the next stage of your journey to stardom: to make sure the right people hear your album.

Finding the Subject

A sentence is written about something or someone—the *subject* of the sentence. The verb, as you have learned, tells what the subject *is* or *does*. Every grammatically complete sentence has a subject. Sometimes, as in the case of commands, the subject is not directly stated but implied:

> *Please return all overdue library books by next Friday. (Although the subject* you *is not stated, it is implied.)*

The rule for finding the subject of a sentence is actually very clear. To find the subject of a sentence, first find the verb. Then ask, "Who?" or "What?" The answer will be the subject. Read the following sentences carefully to see how the rule works.

> *The invoice was paid on February 10. (By asking "What was paid?" you can easily determine the subject of this sentence:* invoice.*)*
> *Lou follows a strict diet because of his high blood pressure. (As in the sentence above, you can find the subject in this sentence by locating the verb and asking "Who?" or "What?" Lou follows a strict diet, and therefore is the subject.)*

Several cracks in the kitchen ceiling appeared after the last earthquake. (*What appeared?*
Cracks, *the subject.*)

Subjects and Other Words in the Sentence

Do not be confused if a sentence has several nouns or pronouns in it. Only the word that
answers "Who?" or "What?" before the verb can be the subject. In the following sentence
notice that only *mayor* answers the question, "*Who* blamed?"

(subject)
The mayor *blamed himself, not the city manager, the council, or the voters, for the defeat of
the bond issue.*

Do not mistake phrases beginning with such words as *along with, in addition to, including,
rather than, together with,* and similar terms for a part of the subject of the sentence. Note the
following sentences:

The summary, as well as the chapters, contains several important terms to memorize. (*Although*
chapters *might appear to be the subject because it is closer to the verb, the subject is* summary
because it answers the question "What contains?")

The basketball players, together with their coach, are featured in this week's sports special. (*The
subject is* players *because it answers the question* "Who are featured?")

Simple and Complete Subjects

The main noun or pronoun without any of its modifiers that answers the questions "Who?"
or "What?" before the verb is the *simple subject.* The *complete subject* is composed of the simple subject and its modifiers—the words and phrases that describe it.

In the sentence below, "waiter" is the *simple subject;* "A tall, gracious, smiling waiter" is
the *complete subject.*

A tall, gracious, smiling waiter seated us at our table.

In the sentence below, what is the simple subject? What is the complete subject?

The girl in the green dress and high heels is my sister.

When you are asked to identify the subject of a sentence, you normally name the simple
subject.

Compound Subjects

A sentence can have more than one subject, just as it can have more than one verb. Two
or more subjects are called *compound subjects.*

Athletes and celebrities are frequently seen on television endorsing products.

Polluted water and smog *made the city unattractive to tourists*.

Either hamburgers or hot dogs *will be served at the picnic*.

Exercise 2-6

Underline the simple subject of each sentence. Some sentences have two simple subjects.

1. The water in the oceans, as well as the gases in the atmosphere, came to the surface through volcanic activity.
2. Oceans and atmospheres are not an inevitable consequence of planet formation.
3. Smaller worlds, like Mercury and the moon, are too small to retain any surface fluids.
4. Neither volcano eruptions nor earthquakes can be predicted with accuracy.
5. Politicians, together with scientists, are now paying attention to the supply of water in the American West.
6. At one time New York and Los Angeles were under one hundred feet of water.
7. Air pollens, as well as smog, are included in most city weather reports.
8. Flowing from west to east, the jet stream often travels more than one hundred miles per hour.
9. The troposphere, rather than the stratosphere, is the warm layer of air next to the surface of the earth.
10. The "wind chill factor," together with the "comfort index," is often cited by television weathercasters.

Subjects in Inverted Sentences

Most sentences follow the subject-verb pattern. In *inverted sentences*, however, the pattern is reversed: the subject generally comes *after* the verb. Read the following inverted sentences carefully:

Across the street stood the abandoned schoolhouse. (*The abandoned* schoolhouse *stood across the street;* schoolhouse *is the subject, although* street *is in the subject position before the verb.*)

On her desk is a new word processor. (*What is the verb? What is the subject?*)

Questions are usually inverted, with the subject coming after the verb:

Was Charles Lindbergh the first man to fly across the Atlantic? (*The verb* Was *precedes the subject* Charles Lindbergh.)

Where are the keys to the car? (*The subject* keys *follows the verb* are.)

What is the best time to call you? (*The subject* time *follows the verb* is.)

© 1997 Addison-Wesley Educational Publishers Inc.

In sentences that begin with *here is*, *here are*, *there is*, or *there are*, the real subject follows the verb. To find the subject in such sentences, use the method you learned earlier. Ask "Who?" or "What?" before the verb.

> *Here is a map of the city. (What is here? The subject,* map, *is here.)*
> *There are several reasons to explain his refusal. (What are there? Several* reasons, *the subject.)*

Subjects with Verbs in Active and Passive Voice

The sentences that we have examined so far have contained subjects that performed actions indicated by action verbs, or they contained subjects that were connected by linking verbs to words that described or renamed them. Occasionally, however, we may encounter or write sentences in which the subjects receive the action.

If the subject of the sentence performs the act, the verb is in the *active voice*:

> Dale parked his car.
> Burl's dog attacked Bob.

In the *passive voice* the subject is replaced by the object:

> The car was parked by Dale.
> Bob was attacked by Burl's dog.

As you can see, in the active voice the emphasis is on the *subject*, which performs the action of the verb. In the passive voice the emphasis is shifted to the *object* instead of the subject, which is "passive" or acted upon. The passive voice of a verb always consists of a form of the helping verb *be* (such as *is*, *was*, *has been*, and so on) plus the *past participle* of the main verb. (The past participle of a regular verb is the form that ends in *-ed*. See pages 94–98 for more information.)

To change a sentence from active to passive voice, we turn the sentence around and use a form of *be* as a helping verb:

Active:	The intruder *surprised* the hotel guests.
Passive:	The hotel guests *were surprised* by the intruder.
Active:	The halfback *threw* the winning touchdown.
Passive:	The winning touchdown *was thrown* by the halfback.

To change a sentence from passive to active voice, we substitute a new subject for the previous one:

Passive:	Tides *are caused* by the moon.
Active:	The moon *causes* tides.

Passive: Three soldiers *were wounded* by the snipers.

Active: The snipers *wounded* three soldiers.

You will often be able to choose between active and passive voice when composing sentences. The active voice is usually more direct. For this reason you should use active verbs except in cases when you have good reason to use passive ones.

Exercise 2-7

Change the following sentences from passive to active voice to make them more emphatic.

1. Control gates were installed on the river by engineers and will be tested during the coming flood season.
2. It was decided by the judges that Tom's chocolate cake was the best in the fair.
3. The auto accident was witnessed by Esther as she was driving to work.
4. New evidence that brain damage can be caused by boxing was announced by a panel of physicians last week.
5. Spectators were warned by the police of the danger.
6. New safeguards were approved by the hospital administrator so that the chance of a mistaken dosage given by a nurse would be eliminated.
7. The changes in the election bylaws were approved by the committee.
8. The silken fiber that is spun by orb spiders is twisted into an endless variety of patterns.
9. The use of body language in communications has been studied by psychologists.
10. Your letter was postmarked last Thursday, and it was received yesterday, but it has been decided by the admissions committee that they are prohibited from making an exception.

Subjects and Prepositional Phrases

The subject of a sentence will never be in a prepositional phrase. The reason for this rule is simple. Any noun or pronoun in a prepositional phrase will be the object of the preposition, and the object of a preposition cannot also be the subject. Examine the following sentences, in which the subjects can be confused with objects of prepositions.

Thousands of tourists from countries throughout the world visit EPCOT Center near the city of Orlando in Florida. (*Tourists, countries,* and *world* are in the subject position before the verb *visit*, but they are all objects of prepositions, and therefore cannot be the subject. By asking "Who visits?" you can determine the subject: *Thousands* visit. *Thousands* is the subject.)

The author of *Adam Bede* was virtually ignored during her lifetime. (Although *Adam Bede* is in the subject position, it is the object of a preposition and therefore cannot be the subject of this sentence. Who was virtually ignored? The *author* of *Adam Bede*. The subject is *author*.)

One of the Beatles continues to produce records. (*Beatles* is the object of a preposition and therefore is not the subject. Who continues to produce records? The subject, *One*.)

By placing parentheses around the prepositional phrases in a sentence, you can more easily identify the subject and the verb. Examine the sentence below:

The warden (of a jail) (in the northern part) (of Minnesota) explained (in an interview) (on television) (during the past week) his position (on the death penalty.)

By discarding the prepositional phrases, we can easily see the subject ("The warden") and the verb ("explained").

TIPS FOR FINDING THE SUBJECT IN A SENTENCE

1. The subject will answer the questions *Who?* or *What?* before the verb.
2. In questions or inverted sentences the subject will usually come after the verb.
3. The subject of a sentence will never be "here" or "there."
4. The subject of the sentence will never be in a prepositional phrase.

Exercise 2-8

Underline the simple subject and circle the verb in these sentences.

1. Locating underground sources of water can be very expensive for farmers and contractors.
2. The traditional method has been to use a drill mounted on the back of a truck in the hope of finding water.
3. Many well drillers, however, prefer to use the ancient art of dowsing to find water.
4. Most water dowsers carry a pair of "L"-shaped rods, a pendulum, or a traditional "Y" stick cut from a tree.
5. They walk the property, asking questions silently about the location of the water, its depth, and its rate of flow.
6. According to dowsers, the device begins to twist and pull in response to their questions when passing over underground water.
7. Those building new houses in the countryside often use the services of a dowser to find the best sources of water on the land.
8. In a study in California, well drillers relying on dowsers found water eighty percent of the time at the specific location and depth indicated by the dowser.

9. Well drillers relying on test wells instead of dowsing were correct only forty percent of the time.
10. Further, dowsers can often find a decent water source at a comparatively shallow depth, thus reducing the costs of drilling.

Subjects and Verbs in Compound and Complex Sentences

You have seen that sentences may have more than one subject and more than one verb:

         (s)   (v)   (v)

a. *Mark Twain piloted a riverboat and later wrote several novels.*

         (s)   (s)   (v)

b. *Alexander Graham Bell and Thomas A. Edison are two of this country's most famous inventors.*

         (s)   (s)   (v)

c. *Dwight Eisenhower and Alexander Haig both rose to the rank of general and later entered politics.*

Sentence "a" above has one subject and two verbs; sentence "b" has two subjects and one verb; and sentence "c" has two subjects and two verbs. All three sentences are *simple sentences* because they each contain only one *independent clause*. An independent clause is a group of words with a subject and verb capable of standing alone. As we saw above, the subject and the verb may be compound. All of the sentences we have examined up to this point have been simple sentences—that is, they have consisted of one independent clause. We will now briefly look at two other kinds of sentences: the *compound sentence* and the *complex sentence*. Both kinds of sentences are discussed in detail in Chapter 7 ("Compound and Complex Sentences"). At this point we need to learn only enough to recognize their subjects and verbs.

A *compound sentence* consists of two or more independent clauses containing closely related ideas and usually connected by a coordinating conjunction. In other words, it is two or more simple sentences connected by one of the following conjunctions:

and, but, for, nor, or, so, yet

The following are simple sentences because each contains one independent clause:

The violin has only four strings.
It is difficult to play.

By combining these two simple sentences with the conjunction *but*, we can create a *compound sentence:*

© 1997 Addison-Wesley Educational Publishers Inc.

The violin has only four strings, but *it is difficult to play*.

Each of the independent clauses in the preceding sentence has its own subject (*violin* and *it*) and verb (*has* and *is*) and is capable of standing alone. A compound sentence, therefore, has at least two subjects and two verbs. Of course, a compound sentence can have more than two independent clauses. But regardless of the number of clauses, a compound sentence remains the same: two or more independent clauses usually connected by a coordinating conjunction. (In Chapter 7 you will see that semicolons may also connect independent clauses to form compound sentences.)

Notice that the conjunction *but*, which connected the two independent clauses in the compound sentence above, was preceded by a comma. In general, a coordinating conjunction linking two independent clauses in a compound sentence should be preceded by a comma. Chapter 7 will give you greater practice in the punctuation of compound sentences.

Exercise 2-9

In each of the following compound sentences, underline the simple subjects once and the verbs twice in each independent clause.

1. Acupuncture is a method of inhibiting or reducing pain impulses, but it is also used to abandon habits like smoking and nail-biting.
2. The word comes from two Latin words meaning "needle" and "to sting," but most acupuncture treatments are virtually painless.
3. Needles are inserted through selected areas of the skin, and then they are twirled by the acupuncturist or by a battery-operated device.
4. The location of the needle insertion depends on the patient's ailment, and each part of the body corresponds to certain illnesses.
5. To pull a tooth, one needle is inserted in the web between the thumb and the index finger; for a tonsillectomy, one needle is inserted about two inches above the wrist.
6. There is no satisfactory explanation to account for the effects of acupuncture; according to one theory, however, the twirling of the acupuncture needle stimulates two sets of nerves.
7. One very fine nerve is the nerve for pain, and the other, a much thicker nerve, is the nerve for touch.
8. The impulse passing along the touch nerve reaches the spinal cord first, and it "closes the gate" to the brain, keeping out the pain impulse and blocking the path.
9. Acupuncture is routinely used in China instead of anaesthesia; in an operation for the removal of a lung, one needle is placed in the forearm, midway between the wrist and the elbow.
10. Acupuncture still encounters much skepticism in the United States; nevertheless, increasing numbers of Americans, including medical doctors, are investigating its claims.

A *complex sentence* is a sentence containing a *dependent clause*. A dependent clause is a group of words containing a subject and verb but not capable of standing alone as a sentence. (An independent clause, you remember, has a subject and a verb and *can* stand alone to form a sentence.) A dependent clause always needs to be attached to an independent clause in order to complete its meaning. Examine carefully the following sentence:

Because a cure for cancer does not exist, some patients resort to bizarre diets and remedies.

This sentence is made up of two clauses, each containing a subject and a verb. The first clause ("Because a cure for cancer does not exist") will not stand alone to form a sentence, and therefore it is a *dependent* clause. The second clause ("some patients resort to bizarre diets and remedies") is capable of standing alone as a sentence, and therefore it is an *independent clause*. The entire sentence is a *complex sentence* because it contains a dependent clause.

You can recognize dependent clauses because they do not express complete thoughts. You can also spot them because they usually begin with a *subordinating conjunction*. Here are some of the most common subordinating conjunctions:

after, although, as, because, if, since, though, unless, until, when, while, why

In Chapter 7 you will learn how to recognize and form compound and complex sentences so that your writing will have variety and will not consist only of simple sentences.

Exercise 2-10

Place parentheses around the dependent clause in each of the following complex sentences. Then underline all of the subjects in the sentence once and the verbs twice.

1. Although autism is very rare, the disorder has been the subject of much research.
2. Because it appears in infancy, clinicians have used four major symptoms to identify autism.
3. Autistic infants do not seek social interaction, although they may respond to social situations.
4. The second symptom is prolonged repetitive behavior when they are alone, such as rocking in their cribs or spinning the wheels of a toy car for hours at a time.
5. The third symptom is a terrible temper tantrum if there is even a slight change in their environment.
6. The fourth characteristic of autistic children is their inability to communicate when they want or need something.
7. Although some autistic children do eventually use language, many never do it normally.
8. Autism is caused by some biological factor, although no one has yet been able to identify it.

9. If an autistic child has a nonverbal I.Q. score below 50, his or her future is very gloomy.
10. Those with more normal intelligence have a fair chance of overcoming many of their childhood deficits if they are shown appropriate social and conversational behavior.

Reviewing the Chapter: Writing Sentences

This review exercise asks you to identify the subjects and verbs in sentences that you write. When writing your sentences, do not hesitate to review the appropriate pages in this chapter as needed.

1. Write two original sentences; each sentence should contain a compound subject. Circle the subjects.
2. Write two inverted sentences. Circle the subject and verb in each sentence.
3. Write a sentence in which the verb is in the active voice. Circle the verb.
4. Using the same verb used in the preceding sentence, write a sentence with the verb in the passive voice. Circle the verb.
5. Write three compound sentences. Circle the subject and the verb in each independent clause.
6. Write three complex sentences. Circle the subject and the verb in each dependent (subordinate) and independent clause.

ddison-Wesley Educational Publishers Inc.

2-A

REVIEW EXERCISE

A. *Identify the italicized word or words by writing the appropriate letter in the space before each sentence.*

a. action verb   b. linking verb   c. helping verb   d. none of the above

_____ 1. Despite his injury, the quarterback *wanted* to remain in the game.
_____ 2. Cries of pain *could be* heard in the waiting room, frightening the patients.
_____ 3. The mob roamed the streets and *attacked* startled shoppers.
_____ 4. In addition to *collecting* old jukeboxes, he repaired old telephones.
_____ 5. Because membership in the United Nations *has* increased, several countries believe that the Security Council should be expanded.
_____ 6. If you *water* your roses frequently, they will begin to bloom almost immediately.
_____ 7. We decided *to accept* their offer, rather than wait for a higher bid.
_____ 8. Terri *announced* that she wanted to spend her weekend acquiring a suntan.
_____ 9. The directions for *assembling* the bicycle were not included.
_____ 10. Ralph painted the door with an old paint brush that his father *had* discarded.
_____ 11. What *do* the fans think about the increase in the price of tickets?
_____ 12. Some people *are* allergic to chocolate.

B. *In the space before each sentence, write the letter that corresponds to the simple subject of the sentence. Some sentences have more than one subject.*

_____ 13. Here are the compact discs that I have ordered.
   a. Here/I   b. compact discs/I   c. I/ordered   d. Here/discs

_____ 14. The navigator, not the pilot, was the only survivor of the crash.
   a. navigator   b. pilot   c. survivor   d. crash

_____ 15. Barking as he approached the cat, my dog pretended to be vicious.
   a. Barking   b. he/dog   c. cat/dog   d. dog/vicious

_____ 16. Patrick's recipe for corned beef was based on an old Irish tradition.
   a. Patrick's   b. recipe   c. corned beef   d. tradition

39

_____ 17. The price of new homes continued to rise, despite the decline in interest rates.

  a. price   b. homes   c. decline   d. rates

_____ 18. Overcoming the disadvantages of moving to a new country and learning a strange language, Joseph Conrad became a great English novelist.

  a. disadvantages   b. country   c. language   d. Joseph Conrad

_____ 19. Some of the French words spoken in Quebec are different from Parisian French.

  a. Some   b. words   c. Quebec   d. French

_____ 20. Abraham Lincoln, the sixteenth president, is admired by Americans of all political parties.

  a. Abraham Lincoln   b. president   c. Americans   d. parties

_____ 21. Anyone holding the winning lottery ticket would receive a lifetime income.

  a. Anyone   b. ticket   c. lifetime   d. income

_____ 22. Aren't you surprised at Jean's decision to move to Florida?

  a. you   b. Jean's   c. decision   d. Florida

_____ 23. Determined to improve his game, Mark practiced two hours a day in preparation for the tournament.

  a. game   b. Mark   c. hours   d. tournament

_____ 24. Trying to impress his girl friend, Clyde took accordion lessons and bought a tie with purple polka dots.

  a. girl friend   b. Clyde   c. lessons   d. tie

_____ 25. Trying to conceal her embarrassment at having been discovered eating the ice cream, Arlene covered her face with a napkin.

  a. embarrassment   b. ice cream   c. Arlene   d. napkin

Name _____   Date _____

2-B

REVIEW EXERCISE

A. *Identify the italicized word or words by writing the appropriate letter in the space before each sentence.*

a. action verb   b. linking verb   c. helping verb   d. none of the above

_____ 1. Walter *refused* to explain his decision or to talk to the reporters.
_____ 2. Clouds of smoke drifted across the sky, *obscuring* the sun.
_____ 3. The baby cried and *threw* toys out of its playpen.
_____ 4. After Doug graduated from high school, he *joined* the Navy.
_____ 5. Because some manufacturers *were* illegally sending computers to Iraq, all shipments of electronic equipment were searched.
_____ 6. If you add a bay leaf to the soup, you *will* enhance its flavor.
_____ 7. The owners decided *to close* the restaurant and move to Florida.
_____ 8. Here is the best place in the river for *catching* fish.
_____ 9. The reason for the cancellation of the concert *was* never given.
_____ 10. At certain times of the year, tornadoes *destroy* crops and homes in parts of the Midwest.
_____ 11. What *do* you want me to do now?
_____ 12. Some of the statements in the interview *were* false.

B. *In the space before each sentence, write the letter that corresponds to the simple subject of the sentence. Some sentences have more than one subject.*

_____ 13. Here is the book that I have been searching for.
    a. Here/I   b. book/I   c. I/searching   d. Here/book

_____ 14. The trainer, not the coach, was fired by the owner of the team.
    a. trainer   b. coach   c. owner   d. team

_____ 15. Smiling as he approached the podium, Luis waved to his family.
    a. Smiling   b. he/Luis   c. podium/family   d. Luis/family

_____ 16. My counselor's advice was to stay in the class until the end of the semester.
    a. advice   b. class   c. counselor   d. semester

_____ 17. The comedian's imitation of a drunk made the audience laugh.
a. comedian's   b. imitation   c. drunk   d. audience

_____ 18. Beyond the south edge of the park, the new theater will be built by the city.
a. edge   b. park   c. theater   d. city

_____ 19. One of the most popular restaurants in our town is a Thai restaurant.
a. One   b. restaurants   c. town   d. Thai

_____ 20. Jackson, the left end, played harder than any other player on the team.
a. Jackson   b. left end   c. player   d. team

_____ 21. Everyone knew the song because of its popularity on the radio.
a. Everyone   b. song   c. popularity   d. radio

_____ 22. Didn't your sister see me waving to her at the game last night?
a. sister   b. waving   c. game   d. night

_____ 23. Unwilling to listen to my explanation, my girlfriend called a taxicab and went home early.
a. explanation   b. girlfriend   c. taxicab   d. home

_____ 24. Refusing to learn the Library of Congress system, Sylvester wandered through the library stacks, unable to find the book.
a. Library of Congress system   b. Sylvester   c. stacks   d. book

_____ 25. Wilma's husband prepares breakfast for her, in addition to doing the laundry, mopping the floors, and washing the windows.
a. husband   b. breakfast   c. laundry   d. floors

Chapter 3

Making the Subject and Verb Agree

Mistakes in subject-verb agreement are among the most common writing and speaking errors, and they are particularly irritating to readers. The rule on subject-verb agreement is obvious:

The subject and the verb must agree in number and in person.

Agreement in number means that a singular subject takes a singular verb and a plural subject takes a plural verb. The singular form of all verbs except *be* and *have* is formed by adding *-s* or *-es: goes, takes, writes, fishes, brings, drives*. The singular forms of *be* and *have* are *is* and *has*. The singular form of the verb is used when the subject is *he, she, it,* a singular indefinite pronoun (such as *anyone* or *somebody*), or a singular noun. Plural verbs do not have these endings, and they are used when the subject is *I, you, we, they,* or a plural noun.

A *singular subject with a singular verb:*
Carol's mother teaches *at the local college.*
A *plural subject with a plural verb:*
Carol's parents play *tennis every Saturday.*

Notice that adding an *-s* or *-es* to a noun makes the noun *plural*, but adding *-s* or *-es* to a verb in the present tense makes the verb *singular*.

Agreement in person means that a subject and its verb must both be in the same person (*first, second,* or *third*). The following sentences illustrate this rule.

First person (I, we)

I work [*not* works] *during the summer to pay for the courses that I* take [*not* takes] *in the fall.*

We stay [*not* stays] *with my brother-in-law in San Jose when we* take [*not* takes] *a trip to northern California.*

Second person (you)

You are [*not* be *or* is] *too late for dinner.*

You students deserve [*not* deserves] *recognition for the fine work that all of you* have [*not* has] *done this semester.*

Third person (he, she, it, they)

Ken Griffey, Jr., reminds [*not* remind] *baseball fans of his father because he* plays [*not* play] *with the same enthusiasm.*

The blues and ragtime are [*not* is] *American contributions to music, and they* appeal [*not* appeals] *to listeners of all ages and races.*

Exercise 3-1

Circle the verbs that can be used with the following subjects. There may be more than one verb.

Example: *She   bring, (walks,) study, (plays)*

1. I   worries, smile, offers, own
2. You   leaps, keep, appeals, arrive
3. They   stay, feel, counts, sings
4. The skunk   smell, eats, run, sleeps
5. We   helps, hope, need, takes
6. The neighbors   accept, touch, ask, aims
7. She   knows, skate, sings, treat
8. He   goes, takes, believes, show
9. My parents   travels, tell, gives, drive
10. It   remain, wants, proves, mean

If the rule given above is so simple, why are there so many errors in subject-verb agreement? Probably because of the writer's uncertainty about the identity of the real subject of the sentence and confusion about whether the subject and verb are singular or plural.

Here are three steps to ensure subject-verb agreement. *First,* find the subject of the sentence. (You may want to review Chapter 2.) *Second,* determine whether the subject is singular or plural. *Third,* select the appropriate singular or plural form of the verb to agree with the subject. The suggestions below will help you follow these steps.

1. Remember that a verb must agree with its subject, not with any words that follow the subject but are not part of it. These include terms such as *as well as, including, such as, along with, accompanied by,* and *rather than.* If the subject is singular, use a singular verb; if the subject is plural, use a plural verb.

   A *taped confession by the suspects, as well as statements by eyewitnesses,* has [not have] *been read to the jury.*

   The color of the container, not the contents or advertising claims, usually determines [not determine] *the buyer's initial reaction to a product.*

   Plans for the convention center, together with a proposal for a tax increase, are [not is] *to be presented to the aldermen today.*

   The ambassadors from the South American countries, accompanied by a translator, intend [not intends] *to meet with the President this afternoon.*

2. Do not confuse the subject with words that rename it in the sentence.

   The police officer's only reward was [not were] *threats and taunts.*

   The cause of the accident was [not were] *the faulty brakes.*

   The attorney's secretaries are [not is] *the source of the news leak.*

3. Do not be confused by sentences that are not in the usual subject-verb pattern.

   Where is [not are] *the box of paper clips that were on my desk?*

   Are [not Is] *cumulus clouds a sign of rain?*

   Under the sofa were [not was] *found the missing cufflinks.*

   BUT: *Under the sofa* was [not were] *the set of missing cufflinks.*

   There are [not is] *many reasons for her success.*

   There is [not are] *one particular reason for her success.*

Exercise 3-2

Draw a line under the simple or compound subject. Then choose the correct verb and write the appropriate letter in the space provided.

_____ 1. The subject of the lecture (a. was   b. were) Israel, as well as its neighbors.
_____ 2. Goalies, rather than defensive players, often (a. receive   b. receives) most of the publicity.
_____ 3. In the newspaper (a. was   b. were) several stories about the famine in Africa.
_____ 4. On the curb (a. was   b. were) sitting several young men.
_____ 5. (a. Has   b. Have) the results of the election been announced yet?
_____ 6. A problem facing the area (a. was   b. were) killer bees.
_____ 7. Car alarms (a. are   b. is) a source of irritation for many.

_____ 8. Around the bend (a. was   b. were) seen the outlaws on their horses.

_____ 9. The expectations of the people (a. has   b. have) caused disappointment.

_____ 10. There (a. are   b. is) a good reason for the many divorces that occur among young people today.

4. Subjects connected by "and" or by "both . . . and" usually require a plural verb.

Following the proper diet and getting enough exercise are important for maintaining one's health.

Both Al Unser and his son have raced in the Indianapolis 500.

Exceptions: Use a singular verb when a compound subject refers to the same person or thing:

Vinegar and oil is my favorite salad dressing.

The secretary and treasurer of our class last year was Julie Patterson.

Use a singular verb when a compound subject is preceded by *each, every, many a,* or *many an:*

Each owner and tenant has been given a copy of the new zoning regulations.

Every cable and pulley receives a monthly inspection.

Use a plural verb when a compound subject is followed by *each:*

The tenor and the soprano each wear different costumes in the final act.

5. If the subject consists of two or more words connected by *or, either . . . or, neither . . . nor,* or *not only . . . but also,* the verb agrees with the subject that is closer to it. This rule presents few problems when both subjects are plural or singular:

Neither the politicians nor the voters show much interest in this year's election. (Both subjects are plural, and therefore the verb is plural.)

Not only the car but also the greenhouse was damaged by the hailstorm. (Both subjects are singular, and therefore the verb is singular.)

When one part of the subject is singular and the other is plural, the verb agrees with the part that is closer to it:

Either the frost or the aphids have killed my roses. (The plural noun aphids is closer to the verb, and therefore the verb is plural.)

Sentences with singular and plural subjects usually sound better with plural verbs. Notice the difference between the following sentences.

Neither the players nor the coach likes the new rules. (Although technically correct, this sentence would sound less awkward if the subjects were reversed and a plural verb used.)

Neither the coach nor the players like the new rules. (This version is less awkward and has not sacrificed the meaning of the sentence.)

© 1997 Addison-Wesley Educational Publishers Inc.

REMEMBER . . .

1. Adding an -s or -es to a *noun* makes the noun *plural.*
    Adding an -s or -es to a *verb* makes the verb *singular.*
2. If the subject is singular, the verb must be singular; if the subject is plural, the verb must be plural.
3. The verb must agree with its *subject,* not with any other words in the sentence. Do not be confused by sentences not in the usual subject-verb pattern.

Exercise 3-3

Write the letter of the correct verb in the space before each sentence.

_____ 1. Many a debt by Third World nations (a. has   b. have) been forgiven.
_____ 2. The pitcher and the relief hurler each (a. practice   b. practices) on the sidelines.
_____ 3. Every bank and savings institution (a. are   b. is) required to have depositor insurance.
_____ 4. Neither Chicago nor Los Angeles (a. has   b. have) a chance to win the pennant this year.
_____ 5. Either photographs or a painting (a. are   b. is) acceptable in the contest.
_____ 6. Salt and pepper (a. was   b. were) the only condiments available.
_____ 7. Stretching exercises and other forms of warmup (a. is   b. are) recommended before you begin to jog.
_____ 8. My sister's childhood model and favorite tennis player (a. was   b. were) Martina Navratilova.
_____ 9. Both high prices and high interest (a. stimulate   b. stimulates) inflation.
_____ 10. The Heisman Trophy winner, as well as several other college players, (a. has   b. have) been offered contracts worth millions of dollars.

6. Indefinite pronouns that are singular take singular verbs, and indefinite pronouns that are plural take plural verbs. Some pronouns may be either singular or plural in meaning, depending on the noun or pronoun to which they refer. An indefinite pronoun is one that does not refer to a specific thing or person.
    When used as subjects or as adjectives modifying subjects, the following indefinite pronouns are always singular and take singular verbs:

another	each
anybody	each one
anyone	either
anything	every

everybody	no one
everyone	nothing
everything	one
many	other
much	somebody
neither	something
nobody	someone

> *Everybody* is *eligible for the drawing tonight.*
>
> *Much of the work on the engine* has *been done.*
>
> *Something* tells *me that I am wrong.*
>
> *Each dismissed worker* receives *two weeks' pay.*

When used as subjects or as adjectives modifying subjects, the following indefinite pronouns are always plural and take plural verbs:

both	others
few	several
many	

> *Few of the passengers on the last cruise of the Titanic* are *living today.*
>
> *Many of the parts in an American car* are *manufactured in other countries; several* come *from Japan.*

When used as subjects or as adjectives modifying subjects, the following indefinite pronouns may be singular or plural, depending on the nouns or pronouns to which they refer:

all	most
any	none
more	some

> *Unfortunately, all of the rumors* were *true.*
>
> *All of the snow* has *melted.*
>
> *Most of the music* sounds *like country and western.*
>
> *Most of my freckles* have *disappeared.*
>
> **Note:**   *None* is *considered a singular pronoun in formal usage. According to informal usage, however, it may be singular or plural, depending on the noun to which it refers. Note the difference in the following sentences:*

| (formal usage) | *None of the roses* has *bloomed yet.* |
| (informal usage) | *None of the roses* have *bloomed yet.* |

Exercise 3-4

In the space before each sentence write the letter corresponding to the correct verb.

_____   1. Everyone, including the sponsors of the parade, (a. was   b. were) surprised at the size of the crowd.

_____   2. Anyone playing the drums (a. take   b. takes) a chance that his or her neighbors will complain.

_____   3. All of the herbs used by the chef (a. was   b. were) from his own garden.

_____   4. Some of the soil brought in by trucks (a. has   b. have) been washed away.

_____   5. The salesman claimed that everyone, even skeptics, (a. is   b. are) going to be surprised at the results of the spot-remover.

_____   6. Most of the young couples in the subdivision (a. attend   b. attends) monthly meetings of the neighborhood association.

_____   7. The taxpayers complained that none of the streets (a. has   b. have) been paved yet.

_____   8. Each of the jury members (a. vote   b. votes) according to the evidence.

_____   9. Everything in the store, including the fixtures, (a. was   b. were) for sale.

_____   10. Nobody except the judge (a. know   b. knows) the verdict.

___

REMEMBER . . .

Some indefinite pronouns always take *singular* verbs; some always take *plural* verbs; still other indefinite pronouns may be singular *or* plural, depending on the nouns or pronouns to which they refer. Look over the lists on pages 47–48 if you are not sure.

___

7. If the subject is *who, which,* or *that,* be careful: all of these relative pronouns can be singular or plural, depending on their antecedents. When one of them is the subject, its verb must agree with its antecedent in number.

> *Rick is one of those musicians* who are *able to play music at first sight.* (Who *refers to* musicians; *several musicians are able to play music at first sight, and Rick is one of them.*)

> *Lee is the only one of the musicians* who has *forgotten his music.* (Who *refers to* one. *Among the musicians, only one, Lee, has forgotten his music.*)

> *I ordered one of the word processors* that were *on sale.* (That *refers to* word processors *and therefore takes a plural verb.*)

> *I also bought a desk* that was *reduced 40 percent.* (That *refers to* desk *and therefore takes a singular verb.*)

Exercise 3-5

In the space before each sentence write the letter corresponding to the correct verb.

_____ 1. This restaurant is one of the few that (a. make b. makes) all of the desserts, cakes, and pies on the premises.

_____ 2. The English journalist was the only hostage held by the kidnappers who (a. was b. were) released to the Red Cross.

_____ 3. The California condor is one of the species that (a. are b. is) endangered in the United States.

_____ 4. Japan is one of the nations that (a. relies b. rely) on imported fuel.

_____ 5. Ralph Nader's report is the only study that (a. criticize b. criticizes) the advertiser's claims.

_____ 6. Las Vegas is a city that (a. derive b. derives) much of its income from gambling.

_____ 7. Boris Yeltsin was the first leader in one thousand years in Russia who (a. was b. were) elected directly by the people.

_____ 8. Nebraska is the only one of the fifty states that (a. has b. have) a unicameral legislature.

_____ 9. The tuba was one of the instruments that (a. was b. were) featured in the concerto.

_____ 10. Chess is one of the games that (a. require b. requires) concentration.

8. Collective nouns take singular verbs when the group is regarded as a unit, and plural verbs when the individuals of the group are regarded separately.

> A *collective noun* is a word singular in form but referring to a group of people or things. Some common collective nouns are *army, assembly, committee, company, couple, crowd, faculty, family, flock, group, herd, jury, pair, squad,* and *team.*

When the group is thought of as acting as one unit, the verb should be singular.

> *The faculty is happy that its request for additional secretarial help has been granted.*
> *The committee has published the list of witnesses who will appear.*
> *The couple was married last week.*

If the members of the group are thought of as acting separately, the verb should be plural.

> *The faculty have been assigned their offices and parking spaces.*
> *The committee are not able to agree on the winner.*
> *The couple constantly argue over their jobs and their children.*

9. Some nouns appear plural in form but are usually singular in meaning and therefore require singular verbs. The following nouns are used this way: *athletics, economics, electronics, mathematics, measles, mumps, news, physics, politics, statistics*.

> *Mathematics* frightens *many students*.
>
> *The news from the doctor* is *encouraging*.
>
> *Politics* is *the art of the possible*.

When the items they refer to are plural in meaning, these words are plural.

> The economics of your plan sound *reasonable*.
>
> *The statistics* indicate *that little progress has been made*.

10. Subjects plural in form that indicate a quantity or number take a singular verb if the subject is considered a unit but a plural verb if the individual parts of the subject are regarded separately. Such expressions include *one-half of* (and other fractions), *a part of*, *a majority of*, and *a percentage of*.
    If a singular noun follows *of* or is implied, use a singular verb:

> *Two-thirds of his fortune* consists *of real estate*.
>
> *Part of our intelligence, according to geneticists*, depends *on our genes*.
>
> *A majority of the herd of cattle* has *to be destroyed*.

If a plural noun follows *of* or is implied, use a plural verb:

> *Three-fourths of the students in the third grade* speak *a foreign language*.
>
> *A percentage of our individual characteristics* come *from our genes*.
>
> *A majority of the lawyers* want *to make the law exam more difficult*.

11. Words that refer to distance, amounts, and measurements require singular verbs when they represent a total amount. When they refer to a number of individual items, they require plural verbs.

> *Over fifty thousand dollars* was *spent on the renovation of the old house*.
>
> *Many thousands of dollars* were *lost in gambling*.
>
> *Two miles* is *the maximum range of his new rifle*.
>
> *The last two miles* were *paved last week*.
>
> *Six months* is *a long time to wait for an answer*.
>
> *Six months* have passed *since we last heard from you*.

12. When *the number* is used as the subject, it requires a singular verb. A *number* is always plural.

> *The number of students who work part-time* is *increasing*.
>
> *A number of students* receive *financial support from their parents*.

13. Some words taken from foreign languages, especially Greek and Latin, keep their foreign plural forms, but others have acquired English plural forms. As a result, it is not always obvious when to use the singular or the plural form of the verb. For example, "Data are available" is preferred to "Data is available." If you are not sure about their plural form, consult your dictionary. Here are some of the more common words from Greek and Latin and their plural forms.

singular	plural
alumnus	alumni
criterion	criteria
crisis	crises
medium	media
memorandum	memoranda
parenthesis	parentheses
phenomenon	phenomena
stimulus	stimuli
thesis	theses

REMEMBER . . .

Collective nouns take singular verbs if you consider the group as a unit; they take plural verbs if you regard the individuals in the group separately.

A number are, but *the number is.*

Exercise 3-6

In the space before each sentence write the letter corresponding to the correct verb.

_____ 1. The couple (a. was   b. were) awarded prizes for their costumes.

_____ 2. Every year the board of education in most school districts (a. recognize b. recognizes) the outstanding high school graduates.

_____ 3. Four miles (a. was   b. were) the distance that he ran every week last year.

_____ 4. Approximately $1,200 (a. remain   b. remains) in my bank account to pay my expenses next semester.

_____ 5. About half of the drivers on the road (a. has   b. have) no liability insurance.

_____ 6. The cab driver decided that fifteen minutes (a. was   b. were) long enough to wait for his fare.

_____ 7. Statistics (a. are   b. is) a required course for psychology majors.

_____   8.   Approximately two-thirds of last semester's graduates (a. has   b. have) been unable to find jobs.

_____   9.   Statistics (a. reveal   b. reveals) that women are still paid less than men for doing the same work.

_____   10.   The last two miles of the marathon (a. was   b. were) the most difficult.

_____   11.   The faculty at our college (a. tend   b. tends) to be very helpful to students who seek advice outside the classroom.

_____   12.   A number of scholarships available last fall (a. are   b. is) still available to students.

_____   13.   The number of representatives that a state may send to Congress (a. depend   b. depends) upon its population.

_____   14.   One-half of the questions on the test (a. was   b. were) on the previous chapter.

_____   15.   The freshman class (a. take   b. takes) a sequence of courses in Western civilization.

Reviewing the Chapter: Writing Sentences

In this exercise you are asked to write original sentences in which the subject and verb agree in number and person. Refer to the appropriate section of the chapter as needed.

1.   Write an original sentence with two subjects connected by "both . . . and" and requiring a plural verb.

2.   Write a sentence in which the subject consists of two or more words connected by "either . . . or," "neither . . . nor," or "not only . . . but also."

3.   Write two sentences that use an indefinite pronoun as a singular subject in each sentence. Circle the pronoun and the verb.

4.   Write two sentences that use an indefinite pronoun as a plural subject in each sentence. Circle the pronouns and the verbs.

5.   Select two of the following pronouns and use them as subjects of two sentences. Circle the pronouns and the verbs.

   all, any, more, most, none, some

6.   Write a sentence in which you use a collective noun as a singular subject. Circle the noun and its verb.

7.   Write a sentence in which you use a collective noun as a plural subject. Circle the noun and its verb.

3-A

REVIEW EXERCISE

Identify the correct verb by using the appropriate letter in the space provided.

_____ 1. The number of voters in the last several elections (a. continue   b. continues) to decline.

_____ 2. There (a. are   b. is), according to scientists, a strong probability that several severe earthquakes will occur within the next decade in Southern California.

_____ 3. Despite the defense attorney's arguments, there (a. was   b. were) solid evidence to convince the jury of the defendant's guilt.

_____ 4. One of the many causes responsible for the cracks in the walls (a. are   b. is) the shifting hillside.

_____ 5. Neither the sales clerk nor the customers (a. was   b. were) able to identify the suspect.

_____ 6. A fear of animals and bright lights (a. was   b. were) attributed to experiences in his childhood.

_____ 7. (a. Has   b. Have) either of your letters been answered?

_____ 8. At the back of the cave wrapped in blankets (a. was   b. were) found the missing container of gold coins.

_____ 9. There (a. are   b. is) many Native Americans who object to advertising that is based on stereotypes of their culture.

_____ 10. Not one of the veterans of World War I (a. was   b. were) able to attend the memorial service yesterday.

_____ 11. Neither the chairman nor the committee members (a. has   b. have) shown any interest in the proposal for the new park.

_____ 12. The pollen count and the sudden change in humidity (a. affect   b. affects) Reynaldo's asthma attacks.

_____ 13. Only one candidate from the hundreds of applicants (a. was   b. were) selected for an interview.

_____ 14. A long line of refugees (a. gather   b. gathers) every morning at the American embassy.

_____ 15. Both cotton and silk (a. has   b. have) been tested for the team uniform.

_____ 16. Every bride and groom (a. was   b. were) given a free souvenir.

_____ 17. Neither the oil nor the tires (a. has   b. have) been changed since I bought the car.

_____ 18. An orchestra without violins and cellos (a. play   b. plays) the first movement of the symphony.

_____ 19. Coffee with cream (a. are   b. is) usually all I have for breakfast.

_____ 20. Each visitor and guest (a. are   b. is) asked to initial the sign-in book.

_____ 21. Most of the destruction on these islands (a. was   b. were) caused by bombing raids during World War II.

_____ 22. Every quiz, oral report, and essay (a. receive   b. receives) equal credit.

_____ 23. Some of the rumors about the movie star (a. was   b. were) started by his ex-wife.

_____ 24. All of the work done by my brothers (a. are   b. is) going to be redone next week.

_____ 25. Most of the land in the Western states (a. are   b. is) owned by the Federal government.

3-B

REVIEW EXERCISE

Identify the correct verb by using the appropriate letter in the space provided.

_____   1.   My record of the conversations among the delegates (a. show   b. shows) that the resolution was defeated.

_____   2.   There (a. was   b. were), according to the weather bureau, several indications that the winter would be extremely cold.

_____   3.   Although I tried to smile, in my heart there (a. was   b. were) neither pleasure nor happiness.

_____   4.   One of the reasons for the many protests (a. are   b. is) the series of laws passed protecting the environment.

_____   5.   Either the President or the cabinet members (a. are   b. is) expected to attend the conference.

_____   6.   A disregard for the rights of tourists (a. give   b. gives) that country a bad reputation.

_____   7.   (a. Has   b. Have) either of your two brothers gone to college?

_____   8.   At the top of my list of goals to accomplish in the next several weeks (a. are   b. is) the improvement of my study habits.

_____   9.   There (a. are   b. is) many indications that young people are becoming more conservative in their political beliefs.

_____   10.   Not one of the football players drafted in the first round (a. play   b. plays) as a starter today.

_____   11.   Neither the referees nor his wife (a. influence   b. influences) his behavior on the tennis court.

_____   12.   The decision to close the military base and to lay off the civilian employees (a. affect   b. affects) the economy of the entire region.

_____   13.   Not one penny from the proceeds of the sales (a. was   b. were) used to pay expenses.

_____   14.   A long history of medical problems and complaints (a. cause   b. causes) Ted to be absent frequently from work.

_____   15.   Both India and England (a. has   b. have) had women prime ministers in this century.

_____   16.   Every subscriber and advertiser (a. receive   b. receives) a free issue of the magazine.

_____ 17. Neither the shirt nor the blue jeans (a. fit   b. fits) me now that I have lost weight.

_____ 18. A bagel with cream cheese (a. taste   b. tastes) great with a cup of coffee in the morning.

_____ 19. Cops and robbers (a. was   b. were) our favorite childhood game.

_____ 20. Each sentence and paragraph (a. contain   b. contains) several spelling errors.

_____ 21. Most of the forest on these islands (a. stand   b. stands) as it was when the white settlers first arrived.

_____ 22. Every essay, term paper, and quiz (a. receive   b. receives) a letter grade.

_____ 23. Some of the legends about Paul Bunyan (a. are   b. is) based on fact.

_____ 24. All of the medicine (a. were   b. was) paid for by her health insurance.

_____ 25. Most of the land (a. has   b. have) been subdivided into individual homesites.

Chapter 4

Using the Correct Form of the Pronoun

Most of us—unless we were just beginning to learn the English language or were babies—would not be likely to say or write sentences like "Me am tired" or "Her is my sister." We instinctively know that "I" is the subject for "am" and that "She" is used with "is." Unfortunately, the choices we face in our writing and speaking are not always so obvious. For example, do we say "between you and I" or "between you and me"? What about "he and myself"? Is there any way to keep "who" and "whom" separate? Pronouns can cause a great deal of uncertainty, even among the most educated writers and speakers.

One probable reason for confusion over pronouns is the existence of so many classes and forms to choose from. Unlike prepositions or conjunctions and most other parts of speech, pronouns have the distracting habit of changing their form or spelling depending on the way they are used in a particular sentence. To use them with confidence, therefore, it is important to recognize the various kinds of pronouns and to learn the specific way each kind is used in a sentence.

We will begin our study of this confusing part of speech with an overview of the most important classes of pronouns and then examine them more closely. The chart on page 61 gives a summary of the classes of pronouns, followed by a brief description of each class and then a detailed examination of the way they are used.

The Classes of Pronouns

Pronouns can be classified according to their form (the way they are spelled) and their function (the way they are used in a sentence).

1.   Personal Pronouns

Personal pronouns refer to specific individuals, and they are the pronouns most frequently used in writing and speaking. Personal pronouns can be singular or plural, and they can be classified by *gender* (*masculine*, *feminine*, or *neuter*) and by *function* or *case* (*subjective*, *possessive*, and *objective*).

2.   Indefinite Pronouns

Although they function as nouns, indefinite pronouns do not refer to specific individuals. Because of their importance in pronoun agreement and reference, they are treated in detail in Chapter 5 ("Common Errors in Pronoun Agreement and Reference").

3.   Demonstrative Pronouns

Demonstrative pronouns point out persons or things, as in the following:

This *is the house I was born in.* Those *are the trees my father planted.*

4.   Relative Pronouns

These pronouns connect or relate groups of words to nouns or other pronouns, as in the following sentences:

A *Vietnam veteran* who *is suffering from cancer testified* that *it was caused by chemicals* that *were used during the war.*

Because relative pronouns are used to introduce dependent clauses in complex sentences, they are discussed in Chapter 7 ("Compound and Complex Sentences").

5.   Intensive Pronouns

Intensive pronouns strengthen or intensify the subject of a verb:

I *did it* myself.
You yourself *are guilty.*

© 1997 Addison-Wesley Educational Publishers Inc.

CLASSES OF PRONOUNS

PERSONAL

I, you, he, she, it, we, they, me, her, him, us, them, my, mine, your, yours, hers, his, its, our, ours, their, theirs

INDEFINITE

all, another, any, anybody, anyone, anything, both, each, either, everybody, everyone, everything, few, many, more, most, much, neither, nobody, none, no one, nothing, one, other, several, some, somebody, someone, something, such

DEMONSTRATIVE

this, that, these, those

RELATIVE

who, whose, whom, which, what, that

REFLEXIVE AND INTENSIVE

myself, yourself, himself, herself, itself, ourselves, yourselves, themselves

INTERROGATIVE

who, whose, whom, which, what

6. Reflexive Pronouns

Reflexive pronouns are used to direct the action of a verb toward its subject:

He helped himself *to the cake.*
They let themselves *into the apartment.*

7.   Interrogative Pronouns

These pronouns introduce questions:

Who *can identify Norman Schwarzkopf?*
Whose *boomerang is this?*
What *is the anticipated population of the United States in 2000?*

Because personal pronouns are used most often—and because they cause most of the problems in pronoun usage—we will begin with them.

Personal Pronouns

The Subject Pronouns

Subject pronouns are used as the *subject of a verb*, as a *predicate pronoun*, or as an *appositive identifying a subject*.

AS THE SUBJECT OF A VERB

Donny and I [not me] rowed until we were exhausted.
Either she or I [not her or me] can explain the equation to you.

Note: *In some sentences a pronoun will be the subject of an implied verb. This occurs often in comparisons introduced by* than *or* as. *In such cases the subject form of the pronoun should be used. In the following sentences, the implied verbs are in parentheses.*

He is fourteen pounds heavier than I (am).
She is not as tall as he (is).
They work longer hours than we (do).

AS A PREDICATE PRONOUN   A pronoun that comes after some form of the verb *to be* and describes or renames the subject is called a *predicate pronoun*. It must be a subject pronoun.

That is she [not her] in the front row. (She is a predicate pronoun because it follows the linking verb is *and renames or identifies the subject* That.)
The last ones to cross the line were Larry and I [not me]. (I follows the linking verb were *and, with Larry, means the same as the subject* ones. *Therefore, the subject form* I *is needed.)*
Everyone knew that it was they [not them]. (Like the two sentences above, the pronoun following the linking verb identifies the subject and is therefore in the subject form.)

© 1997 Addison-Wesley Educational Publishers Inc.

Note: *Some exceptions to this rule are allowed.* It is me, It is her, *and* It is them, *for example, are widely used and accepted in informal situations. In formal speaking and writing, however, the preferred forms are* It is I, It is she, *and* It is they. *Follow the advice of your instructor.*

AS AN APPOSITIVE IDENTIFYING THE SUBJECT   An *appositive* is a word or group of words that renames or identifies an immediately preceding noun.

appositive
Cleveland, the city of my birth, *is the home of nine universities and colleges.*

appositive
Her brother Phil *was wounded in Vietnam.*

Occasionally a pronoun will serve as an appositive renaming the subject of a sentence or a predicate noun. In such cases the pronoun should be in the subject form. Note carefully the following sentences:

Only two members, Dean and *I* [not *me*] voted for an increase in dues. (*I*, a subject pronoun, is in an appositive phrase renaming the subject, *members*.)

The exceptions were the two new members, Ron and *she* [not *her*]. (*She* is in an appositive phrase renaming the predicate noun, *members*.)

TIPS FOR USING SUBJECT PRONOUNS

1. Memorize the subject pronouns; *I, you, he, she, it, who, whoever, we,* and *they.*
2. Remember that only subject pronouns can be subjects of verbs.
3. If a pronoun is part of a compound subject, break the sentence into two parts: "My brother and me get along well" is incorrect, as revealed by the following test: "My brother gets along well. I get along well. My brother and *I* get along well."

Exercise 4-1

In the following sentences underline every pronoun used as the subject of a verb and write "A" above it. Underline all pronouns used as a predicate pronoun and write "B" above them. Underline all pronouns used as an appositive identifying the subject and write "C" above them. Ignore all pronouns not used in these three ways.

1. As we watched in horror, the pit bull terriers ran toward us.
2. Because of Tony's gravelly voice, we knew it was he who answered the telephone.
3. They were startled to see themselves on videotape.

4. Will and I saw the guide ahead of us, but we were reluctant to follow him.
5. The three top students—Myra, you, and I—will not have to take the final examination.
6. It was Paul's father who taught him to play the cello when he was a child.
7. Frankly, it was you who disappointed me the most.
8. We reluctantly admitted that if we had worked as hard as they, we would have finished the job by now.
9. The three alumni who had come the farthest distance—Bernie, Emil, and Tom— were given prizes by the homecoming committee.
10. Laine has taken more data processing courses than Roberta or I.

The Object Pronouns

As their name suggests, object pronouns are used as objects: *objects of prepositions*, *objects of verbs*, and *indirect objects*.

AS THE OBJECT OF A PREPOSITION   In Chapter 1 you saw that a preposition is followed by a noun or pronoun, called the *object of the preposition*. When the object of the preposition is a pronoun, it must be from the list of object pronouns.

Between you and me [*not* I], *his singing is off-key.*

Her smiling parents stood next to her *at the capping ceremony.*

Solar energy is a possible answer to the energy problems faced by us [*not* we] *Americans.*

When the objects of a preposition are a noun *and* a pronoun, there is a mistaken tendency to use the subject form of the pronoun, as in the sentence below:

(Incorrect)   *Ruth's parents gave their concert tickets to her and* I. (I *is incorrect because it is a subject pronoun; after a proposition, an object pronoun should be used.*)

The best way to correct sentences like this is to break them up into separate sentences. Study the following carefully.

> *Ruth's parents gave their concert tickets to* Ruth.
>
> *Ruth's parents gave their concert tickets to* me.

(Correct)   *Ruth's parents gave their concert tickets to* Ruth and me.

AS DIRECT OBJECTS   A direct object is the word that receives the action of the verb. It can follow only an action verb, never a linking verb. When a pronoun is used as a direct object, it must be an object pronoun.

The falling tree missed him *by only a few feet.*
My big brother took me *with him on his first date.*
Please call us *if you get lost.*
Dick married her *before going to boot camp.*

As in the case of prepositions, when both a noun and a pronoun are the direct objects of the same verb, the object form for the pronoun is used. Notice the following:

(Incorrect)   *Sheila surprised* Bob *and* I *with her answer.*

By breaking up this sentence into two separate sentences, you can determine the correct form:

              Sheila surprised Bob *with her answer.*
              Sheila surprised me *with her answer.*
(Correct)   *Sheila surprised* Bob *and* me *with her answer.*

In some sentences a pronoun will be the object of an implied verb. This occurs frequently in comparisons introduced by *than* and *as*. In such cases the object form of the pronoun should be used. (Compare this construction with pronouns used as the subject and implied verbs, as explained on page 62.) In the following sentences, the implied subjects and verbs are in parentheses.

Lorraine knows my brother much better than (she knows) me.
The nurse said the shot would hurt her as much as (it hurt) him.

Using the correct pronoun after *than* and *as* is important, as the following sentences show. What is the difference in meaning between these sentences?

My girlfriend likes pizza more than I.
My girlfriend likes pizza more than me.

AS INDIRECT OBJECTS   An *indirect object* is the person or thing to whom or for whom something is done. The indirect object may be thought of as the recipient of the direct object, and it almost always comes between the action verb and the direct object. When a pronoun is used as an indirect object, the object form of the pronoun should be used.

The mail carrier gave me *a registered letter.*
The dealer offered Alex *and* her *a discount on the tires.*
Our neighbors sent us *a postcard from England.*

TIPS FOR USING OBJECT PRONOUNS

---

1. Memorize the object pronouns: *me, you, him, her, it, whom, whomever, us, them.*
2. Use object pronouns when they follow action verbs and propositions.
3. Never say or write "between you and *I*." The correct form is "between you and me."

Exercise 4-2

In the following sentences underline every object pronoun and above it write the letter appropriate to its use in the sentence:

a. object of preposition   b. direct object   c. indirect object

1. Because Mary Kay did not want to talk to the reporters, she ignored them.
2. Arlene married him despite the advice of her girlfriends and me.
3. The car dealer offered me a rebate if I bought a car from his inventory.
4. The social worker explained to us the consequences of alcoholism.
5. Between you and me, that paisley tie looks terrible on Fred.
6. I like that store because the clerks give me advice in selecting the best colors for me.
7. Jason moved from the farm because hard work and long hours did not agree with him.
8. The apartment manager told us that we would have to pay a cleaning deposit in order for us to move in.
9. Lou's former girlfriend sat behind him and me at the rock concert last night.
10. The pet shop owner gave Jim and me some advice for training our dogs.

Exercise 4-3

Write the letter corresponding to the correct pronoun in the space provided.

_____ 1. Ana and (a. I   b. me) have shared the same locker all semester.

_____ 2. The Bagbys and (a. us   b. we) have lived next door to each other for many years.

_____ 3. The woman in the jogging suit standing in front of Tom and (a. I   b. me) is Louise.

_____ 4. Ken was happy to do the favor for Kathy and (a. I   b. me).

_____ 5. Ms. Williams was proud of (a. us   b. we) staff members of the newspaper.

_____ 6. Juanita helped Caroline and (a. I   b. me) fill out the application forms for summer school.

_____ 7. The travel agency sent Brad and (a. I   b. me) some brochures describing Hawaii.
_____ 8. The responsibility for keeping the swimming pool clean will be shared by Carl and (a. I   b. me).
_____ 9. Because of the road conditions, Max will be arriving much later than (a. us   b. we).
_____ 10. The governor claimed that (a. us   b. we) voters were more prosperous than ever.
_____ 11. Everyone but Sharon and (a. he   b. him) thought the joke was funny.
_____ 12. It's difficult for strangers to tell the difference between Nell and (a. her   b. she).
_____ 13. I wish I were as confident as (a. her   b. she) about the results of the interview.
_____ 14. Please keep this a secret between you and (a. I   b. me).
_____ 15. The custodian left the door of the gymnasium unlocked for Pete and (a. I   b. me).

The Possessive Pronouns

The possessive pronouns are used to show ownership or possession of one person or thing by another. Most pronouns have two possessive forms:

my, mine, our, ours, his, her, hers, its, their, theirs, your, yours

Use *mine, yours, his, hers, its, ours,* or *theirs* when the possessive pronoun is separated from the noun that it refers to:

The decision was mine.
The problem became theirs.
The car keys that were found were hers.

Use *my, your, his, her, its, our,* or *their* when the possessive pronoun comes immediately before the noun it modifies:

It was my *decision.*
It became their *problem.*
She lost her *car keys.*

The possessive form is usually used immediately before a noun ending in -*ing*. (Such nouns are called *gerunds*, and they are formed by adding -*ing* to verbs: *walking, riding, thinking,* and so on.)

The team objected to his taking credit for the win.

Our bombing of the harbor was protested by the Cuban delegation.

Everyone was glad to hear of your winning a scholarship.

The possessive forms of *it, who,* and *you* cause problems for many writers. Remember that the apostrophe in *it's, who's* and *you're* indicates that these words are contractions, not possessive forms. In Chapter 10 we will look closely at the use of the apostrophe in contractions and possessive nouns. Notice the difference between the following pairs of words:

The dark clouds on the horizon suggests that it's [it is] going to rain tonight.

A cardiologist spoke to our physical education class on jogging and its effects on the cardiovascular system.

He thinks that he knows who's [who is] responsible for this mess.

Whose idea was this, anyway?

You're [You are] expected to be ready by five o'clock.

Have you memorized your account number?

TIPS FOR USING POSSESSIVE PRONOUNS

The possessive pronouns do not contain apostrophes.

It's *means* it is *or* it has.

Who's *means* who is *or* who has.

You're *means* you are.

Exercise 4-4

Write the letter corresponding to the correct word. Use the space provided.

_____   1.   Anyone (a. whose   b. who's) skiing for the first time should take some lessons.

_____   2.   The renters' committee was enraged at (a. us   b. our) painting the apartment building pink and purple.

_____   3.   According to my horoscope, (a. your   b. you're) going to give me a present today.

_____   4.   David Dravecky was a baseball pitcher (a. whose   b. who's) career was ended by a cancerous tumor in his throwing arm.

_____   5.   The gardenia bush needed fertilizer because (a. its   b. it's) leaves were yellow.

_____   6.   If you study hard, live an ascetic life, and marry the boss's daughter, (a. your   b. you're) going to go far in your career.

_____   7.   (a. Its   b. It's) probably true that I've been studying too hard.

_____   8.   When studying a foreign language, (a. its   b. it's) helpful to listen to tapes of native speakers.

_____   9.   (a. Whose   b. Who's) the author of _Doonesbury?_

_____   10.   Randy's roommate objected to (a. him   b. his) playing Grateful Dead tapes until three in the morning.

_____   11.   My wife laughed at (a. me   b. my) dancing the cha-cha while the band played a polka.

_____   12.   The "Elvis Is Alive" Society will have a surprise speaker at (a. its   b. it's) next meeting.

_____   13.   Whoever told me that (a. its   b. it's) possible to sleep through chemistry class obviously never took the course.

_____   14.   Professor Dwyer presented a slide lecture on Ireland and (a. its   b. it's) history.

_____   15.   Did the mayor give any excuse for (a. him   b. his) being late for the council meeting?

The Relative Pronouns

Relative Pronouns can be used in two ways in a sentence: they can connect one clause with another, and they can act as subjects or objects in their own clauses.

As connecting words:

Famine is one of the major problems that _Africa faces._

He usually accomplishes whatever _he tries to do._

As subjects or objects in their own clauses:

Bob Beamon's record for the long jump, which _has never been surpassed, was set in Mexico City in 1968._

Two pedestrians who _were walking near the curb were hit by flying glass._

A girl who _spoke French helped the couple from Paris._

Who, Which, and That: Special Uses

As relative pronouns, _who_, _which_, and _that_ each have particular uses. Use _who_ and _whom_ only for people:

Neil Armstrong was the first man who _set foot on the moon._

She is one of those natural athletes who _can play any sport._

Kate Smith was a singer whom *everyone admired.*
Muhammad Ali is an athlete whom *the whole world recognizes.*

Use *which* only for animals and things:

Her dog, which *is a dachshund, sleeps under her bed.*
The proposal which *I have offered will not cost more than the other plans.*

Use *that* for animals, people, and things:

A letter that *does not have sufficient postage will be returned to its sender.*
A desk that *belonged to Thomas Jefferson was sold recently for six thousand dollars.*
Every cat that *does not have a license will be put in the animal pound.*
A stranger that *claimed he was lost seized Joe's wallet and ran.*

Intensive and Reflexive Pronouns: Pronouns Ending in *-Self* and *-Selves*

Several pronouns end in *-self* or *-selves:*

myself, yourself, himself, herself, itself, ourselves, yourselves, themselves

As *reflexive pronouns,* these pronouns are used when the action of the sentence is done by the subject to himself or herself:

They helped themselves *to the cookies.*
I tried to bathe myself *despite my broken arm.*

As *intensive pronouns,* these words stress or emphasize another noun or pronoun:

She tuned the engine herself.
You yourself *are to blame.*
The President himself *awarded the medals to the members of the color guard.*

These pronouns should *not* be used in place of a subject or object pronoun:

(Incorrect)   *My wife and myself would be happy to accept your invitation.*
(Correct)   *My wife and I would be happy to accept your invitation.*
(Incorrect)   *On behalf of my family and myself, I would like to express our gratitude to all of you.*

© 1997 Addison-Wesley Educational Publishers Inc.

(Correct)   *On behalf of my family and* me, *I would like to express our gratitude to all of you.*

(Incorrect)   *Kevin helped Ray and* myself *install a new carburetor in my Chevrolet.*

(Correct)   *Kevin helped Ray and* me *install a new carburetor in my Chevrolet.*

Never use forms like *hisself, theirself, theirselves,* or *ourself.* These are nonstandard in both informal and formal speech and writing, and they should always be avoided.

MORE TIPS ON PRONOUNS

1. *Who* is the subject form; *whom* is the object form.
2. Do not use pronouns ending in *-self* or *-selves* as subjects or objects.
3. Never use *hisself, theirself, theirselves,* or *ourself.*

Some Problems with Pronouns: *Who* and *Whom*

The difference between *who* and *whom* is a trap into which some writers and speakers occasionally fall. "Whom" has nearly disappeared from informal English, whether spoken or written. In formal English, however, the differences between the two words are still important and should be learned.

The first step to take when selecting the correct form is to determine which word is the subject and which is the object. *Who* is the *subject* form:

Who *is at the door?* (Who *is the subject of* is.)

Who *did he say was at the door?* (*Notice that* "did he say" *does not affect the subject pronoun* Who *as the subject of the verb* was.)

Who *wants to help me wash the car?* (Who *is the subject of* wants.)

Who *do you think wants to help me wash the car?* (Who *is still the subject of* wants *and is not affected by the words that separate it from the verb.*)

Whom is the object form:

Whom *did you see?* (*If you turn this question around, you can see that* Whom *is the object of the verb* did see: "You did see whom?")

With whom *do you study?* (Whom *is the object of the preposition* With.)

Whom *you know sometimes seems to be more important than what you know.* (Whom *is the object of the verb* know.)

If you are uncertain about the correct form, substitute a personal pronoun (*he, him; they, them*). If *he* or *they* fits, use *who*; if *him* or *them* fits, use *whom*. Study the following examples:

I don't know (who, whom) *he wanted.* (*Substitute* him: *He wanted* him.) *The correct form: I don't know* whom *he wanted.*

(Who, Whom) *shall I say is calling?* (*Substitute* he: *He is calling.*) *The correct form:* Who *shall I say is calling?*

Don't be misled by expressions like "he said" and "I think" that can follow *who* when it is the subject of a verb.

My grandfather is the person who *I think has been most influential in my life.* (Who *is the subject of the verb* has been, *not the object of* think.)

By deleting or omitting the interrupting words you can easily decide whether the pronoun is the subject or the object.

Many people use *who* at the beginning of a question in cases when *whom* would be the grammatically correct form, as in the following:

Who *did he ask for?*

Who *should I send the thank-you note to?*

Such usage is a matter of debate, however, and many careful writers and speakers would object to such a construction. Follow the advice of your instructor in this matter.

Exercise 4-5

In the space before each sentence write the appropriate letter.

_____ 1. (a. Who b. Whom) does he think will win the American League championship this year?

_____ 2. It is not possible to predict (a. who b. whom) will benefit by the new tax laws passed this year.

_____ 3. Norman helped Mitchell and (a. me b. myself) to move into our new apartment.

_____ 4. The President (a. himself b. hisself) greeted the astronauts.

_____ 5. By the gestures you used, I knew (a. who b. whom) you were imitating.

_____ 6. The villagers (a. who b. whom) were living in the earthquake area were left homeless.

_____ 7. I will speak to the person (a. who b. whom) answers the telephone.

_____ 8. We have no one to blame but (a. ourself b. ourselves).

_____ 9. Sylvia was the only person (a. who b. whom) the children trusted.

_____ 10. Patrick helped (a. himself b. hisself) to more dessert.

_____ 11. Manuel and (a. I b. myself) dressed up as clowns for the party.

_____ 12. A cousin (a. who b. whom) she has not seen for twenty-five years is coming to visit her.

_____ 13. (a. Who   b. Whom) the President will name as ambassador to Ukraine is difficult to predict.

_____ 14. (a. Who   b. Whom) is brave enough to wear this tie?

_____ 15. Mr. Gradgrind, (a. who   b. whom) you all know, will be our supervisor.

Reviewing the Chapter: Writing Sentences

Choosing the correct form of the pronoun can be confusing. This exercise lets you demonstrate that you know how to use the right form of the pronoun when you have to make a choice.

1. Write a sentence in which you use "you and I" correctly.
2. Write a sentence using "you and me" correctly.
3. Write a sentence using "who" correctly.
4. Write a sentence using "whom" correctly.
5. Write a sentence using "you" as the subject of a verb.
6. Write a sentence using "you" as the predicate pronoun.
7. Write a sentence using "me" in an appositive.
8. Write a sentence using "us" as the object of a preposition.
9. Write a sentence using "whom" as a direct object.
10. Write a sentence using "them" as an indirect object.

4-A

REVIEW EXERCISE

A. *Write the appropriate letter corresponding to the use of the italicized pronoun in each sentence. Use the space provided.*

a. object of a preposition   b. direct object   c. indirect object

   _____   1.   Julie decided to give her extra concert tickets to Norm and *me*.

   _____   2.   The real-estate agent showed *us* houses that cost over a million dollars.

   _____   3.   The district attorney charged *him* with spousal rape and battery.

   _____   4.   While he was in Paris, Nicholas sent postcards to Denise and *me*.

   _____   5.   Because of the rain, my father gave *me* an umbrella.

B. *Write the appropriate letter corresponding to the use of the italicized pronoun in each sentence. Use the space provided.*

a. subject of a verb   b. predicate pronoun   c. an appositive identifying the subject

   _____   6.   Because our father died when *we* were infants, my sister and I do not remember him.

   _____   7.   To the surprise of his estranged son, the sole heir to the estate was *he*.

   _____   8.   The committee decided to award the prize to *whoever* gave the best impromptu performance.

   _____   9.   Three unsuspecting contestants—Maria, Lois, and *I*—were asked to come up to the stage.

   _____   10.   Emil watches much more television than *I*.

C. *Write the appropriate letter corresponding to the correct pronoun. Use the space provided.*

   _____   11.   The quarterback was distracted by the fans because of (a. their   b. them) taunting.

   _____   12.   Although I had studied longer than Chris and Earl, they received higher grades than (a. I   b. me).

   _____   13.   The nurse explained to Eva and (a. I   b. me) the benefits of a low-fat diet.

_____ 14. Professor Douglass described the experiments that Dr. Cohen and (a. her b. she) had performed while in Australia.

_____ 15. The beneficiaries of the new regulations are Roberta and (a. I   b. me).

_____ 16. The insurance agent offered my brother and (a. I   b. me) a discount on our car insurance.

_____ 17. The losing candidate blamed (a. himself   b. hisself) for his defeat.

_____ 18. As every planner of a picnic knows, (a. its   b. it's) impossible to predict the weather with complete accuracy.

_____ 19. That was Luis and (a. her   b. she) in the front row of the auditorium.

_____ 20. Raymond and (a. I   b. myself) will be leaving for Chicago tomorrow morning.

_____ 21. They should have been ashamed of (a. theirselves   b. themselves) for their behavior.

_____ 22. Scientists claim that tests taken in childhood can predict (a. your   b. you're) chances of suffering from certain diseases in old age.

_____ 23. (a. Its   b. It's) a good idea to know what you will use a computer for before you buy one.

_____ 24. The peace treaty between Jordan and Israel pleased Michael and (a. I b. me).

_____ 25. A chef (a. whose   b. who's) recipe won first prize admitted that it was based on his mother's idea.

© 1997 Addison-Wesley Educational Publishers Inc.

4-B

REVIEW EXERCISE

A. *Write the appropriate letter corresponding to the use of the italicized pronoun in each sentence. Use the space provided.*

a. object of a preposition   b. direct object   c. indirect object

_____ 1. Rafael prefers to play tennis with George rather than with *me*.
_____ 2. Tamara sent *us* some postcards while she was in London.
_____ 3. The housemother at the dorm caught Tina, Jennifer, and *me* as we were climbing through the window.
_____ 4. As he passed our car, the driver made an obscene gesture at Sheila and *me*.
_____ 5. After the clothing drive, Mr. Goddard thanked *us* volunteers for our help.

B. *Write the appropriate letter corresponding to the use of the italicized pronoun in each sentence. Use the space provided.*

a. subject of a verb   b. predicate pronoun   c. an appositive identifying the subject

_____ 6. For years Patrick and *I* have been in love with the same girl.
_____ 7. The most confident couple on the dance floor was Elton and *she*.
_____ 8. *Whoever* told you that was wrong.
_____ 9. Three students—Fred, Mark, and *you*—have been selected to represent us.
_____ 10. Katie plays chess much better than *I*.

C. *Write the appropriate letter corresponding to the correct pronoun. Use the space provided.*

_____ 11. It was difficult to concentrate because of (a. their   b. them) whispering.
_____ 12. Although Charlotte is older than (a. I   b. me), she is not as tall.
_____ 13. Dentists try to make (a. us   b. we) patients relax before they examine us.
_____ 14. While driving to New Orleans, Arnold and (a. her   b. she) stopped in Lafayette to visit their parents.

_____ 15. The only students who were able to interview the mayor were Paul and (a. I b. me).

_____ 16. Will offered my wife and (a. I b. me) a chance to invest in his company.

_____ 17. Mr. Andrews did most of the work (a. himself b. hisself), although he is eighty years old.

_____ 18. I found out the hard way that (a. its b. it's) better to review each night rather than at the last minute.

_____ 19. The last ones to leave the playing field—Jess and (a. I b. me)—were the first to leave the locker room.

_____ 20. Gilbert and (a. I b. myself) have looked forward to this moment for many months.

_____ 21. When the hostess wasn't looking, the children helped (a. themselves b. theirselves) to the soda.

_____ 22. What are (a. your b. you're) chances of receiving a scholarship?

_____ 23. (a. Its b. It's) not always easy to predict my father's behavior.

_____ 24. Calvin offered Naomi and (a. I b. me) a piece of his birthday cake.

_____ 25. A runner (a. whose b. who's) shoe came off had to drop out of the race.

Chapter 5

Common Errors in Pronoun Agreement and Reference

In the last chapter we noted that even the most educated speakers and writers are occasionally uncertain about the correct form of the pronoun to use. Another area of usage that causes confusion is pronoun agreement and reference.

Pronouns should agree with the words to which they refer. In other words, if a pronoun refers to a plural antecedent, the pronoun should be plural; if the antecedent is singular, the pronoun should also be singular; and if the antecedent is a pronoun in the third person, the pronoun should also be in the third person. (An *antecedent* is the word or term referred to by the pronoun.)

The rules for pronoun agreement and reference are usually easy to follow. However, there are several situations when the choice of pronoun is not clear or when the antecedent is not obvious. Such cases can result in confusion or ambiguity on the part of the reader as well as the writer. Because pronoun agreement and reference are necessary if your writing is to be logical and effective, this chapter will examine the situations when they are most critical.

Agreement in Number

A pronoun must agree with its antecedent *in number*. If the antecedent is singular, the pronoun is singular. If the antecedent is plural, the pronoun is plural. This rule poses no problems in sentences in which the pronoun and its antecedents are close, as in the following examples:

Elizabeth *wanted a new* car, *but* she *did not want to pay more than eight thousand dollars for* it. (*This sentence has two singular pronouns, each matched with its singular antecedent:* she [Elizabeth] *and* it [car].)

Her *parents* told Elizabeth *that* they *would be willing to lend her an additional two thousand dollars.* (*The plural pronoun* they *matches its plural antecedent* parents. *Do you see another pronoun in this sentence? What is its antecedent?*)

Richard *purchased* his *tickets yesterday for the Beach Boys concert.* (*The singular pronoun* his *matches its singular antecedent* Richard.)

Problems in pronoun agreement occur when the writer loses sight of the antecedent or confuses it with other nouns in the sentence, as in the following sentence:

(Incorrect) *The faculty committee presented* their *recommendations for graduation requirements to the deans and chancellor of the college.*

This sentence is incorrect because the plural pronoun *their* does not agree with its singular antecedent *committee*. How many committees were there? Only one. Therefore, the pronoun referring to it should be singular: *its*. The writer of this sentence may have been thinking of the individuals on the committee or of the recommendations that were submitted, or even of the deans and chancellor, and therefore wrongly selected *their*, a plural pronoun.

Here, then, is the correct version:

(Correct) *The faculty committee presented* its *recommendations for graduation requirements to the deans and chancellor of the college.*

The following rules will help you to use pronouns in your sentences that will agree with their antecedents in number:

1. In general, use a *singular pronoun* when the antecedent is an *indefinite* pronoun. (For a review of indefinite pronouns, see Chapter 4.) Some indefinite pronouns present exceptions to this rule—they are always plural, or they can be singular or plural depending on the kind of noun they represent.
   a. The following indefinite pronouns are always *singular*, which means that other pronouns referring to them should be singular:

   another, anybody, anyone, anything, each, each one, either, every, everybody, everyone, everything, many a, much, neither, nobody, no one, nothing, one, other, somebody, someone, something

   Notice that in the following sentences the indefinite pronouns are accompanied by singular pronouns:

© 1997 Addison-Wesley Educational Publishers Inc.

Anyone planning a trip to Russia should apply for a visa before he *leaves this country.*

Each of the girls told me her *name.*

When I returned, everything *was in* its *place.*

Many a son belatedly wishes he *had listened to* his *father's advice.*

Everyone was asked to contribute as much as he *could.*

Everybody is responsible for making his *own bed.*

Neither of the girls wanted her *picture taken.*

You probably noticed the use of masculine pronouns (*he* and *his*) in the first, fifth, and sixth sentences preceding. Many writers and readers object to the exclusive use of masculine pronouns with indefinite pronouns such as *anybody, everyone, someone,* and *everybody.* Note carefully the following sentence:

Everyone took his *seat.*

This is traditional usage, with *his* used to refer to humanity in general. To avoid the sole use of masculine pronouns, some writers would word the sentence like this:

Everyone took his or her *seat.*

Because this form can be awkward, some writers prefer the following method to avoid only masculine pronouns:

Everyone took their *seats.*

While avoiding the exclusive use of the masculine pronoun, this sentence combines a plural pronoun (*their*) with a singular antecedent (*Everyone*). Those who prefer this version should be aware that it is not yet accepted in formal written English.

What is the answer to this dilemma? An increasingly popular solution is to re-word the sentence, making the subject plural:

The members of the audience took their *seats.*

b.   The following indefinite pronouns are always *plural*:

both, few, many, others, several

When they are used as antecedents, pronouns referring to them are always *plural.* Note their use in the following sentences:

Many of his customers transferred their *accounts to another company.*

A few of the students admitted they *had not studied.*

Several of the golfers said they *wanted to bring* their *own caddies.*

Both of the cars had their *mufflers replaced.*

c.   The following indefinite pronouns can be either singular or plural:

all, any, more, most, none, some

Antecedents referring to them will be either singular or plural, depending on their meaning and the noun they represent:

(Plural)	Most *fast-food customers want less fat in* their *hamburgers*.
(Singular)	Most *of the hamburger has less fat in* it.
(Plural)	All *of the leaks have been traced to* their *sources*.
(Singular)	All *of the water has leaked from* its *container*.
(Plural)	Some *of the customers want* their *money refunded*.
(Singular)	Some *of the money was found in* its *hiding place*.

Exercise 5-1

In the space before each sentence, write the letter indicating the correct pronoun.

_____ 1. Some of the acid rain in Canadian cities has been traced to (a. its   b. their) source in northern New England.

_____ 2. Some of the immigrants from Ethiopia are learning Hebrew in (a. his   b. their) new homeland.

_____ 3. Anyone who buys a used car in California must get a smog certificate be-fore (a. he   b. they) can purchase new license plates.

_____ 4. At a recent public meeting of battered wives in Baltimore, each woman told (a. her   b. their) story.

_____ 5. Many of the early settlers passed laws as intolerant as those (a. he   b. they) had previously suffered.

_____ 6. When dialing a 900 number, one should realize that (a. he   b. they) will be charged for the call.

_____ 7. Each of the band members was responsible for bringing (a. his   b. their) instrument and music.

_____ 8. Some members of the band complained about (a. his   b. their) living conditions and salaries.

_____ 9. Every player on the girls' lacrosse team must furnish (a. her   b. their) own uniform and shoes.

_____ 10. Both laws were modified in (a. its   b. their) language and intent.

2. Antecedents joined by *and* usually take plural pronouns:

Joe DiMaggio and Ted Williams *are remembered for* their *batting averages*.

West Germany and East Germany *voted to unite* their *peoples in 1990*.

When the antecedents are joined by *and* but refer to a single person or thing, the pronoun may be singular:

The physicist and Nobel Prize winner was able to present her *ideas in terms that the students could understand.*

The largest tree and oldest living thing on earth, the Sequoiadendron giganteum, *is better known by* its *familiar name, the Giant Sequoia.*

When the compound antecedent is preceded by *each* or *every*, a singular pronoun should be used:

Each *team player and substitute received a certificate recognizing* her *participation.*

Every *father and son was assigned to* his *table.*

3. Collective nouns (see Chapter 3) usually take singular pronouns if the group is regarded as a unit:

The couple was honored for its *contribution to the church.*

The faculty was renowned for its *research and scholarship.*

If the members of the group are acting separately, a plural pronoun should be used:

The couple disagreed over the amount of money they *should pay for a new car.*

The faculty were paid various amounts, depending on their *education, experience, and publications.*

4. When two or more antecedents are joined by *or* or *nor*, the pronoun should agree with the nearer antecedent:

Neither Millard Fillmore nor James Polk is remembered for the brilliance of his *presidency.*

Neither the defendant nor the witnesses changed their *testimony.*

Neither the roofers nor the carpenters finished their *work on schedule.*

When the antecedent closer to the pronoun is singular, the result can sometimes be awkward:

Neither the sopranos nor the tenor could sing his *part without looking at* his *music. (Though technically correct, this sentence is confusing.)*

Such a sentence should be revised:

Neither the tenor nor the sopranos could sing their *parts without looking at* their *music.*

5. Pronouns that are used as *demonstrative adjectives (this, that, these, those)* must agree in number with the nouns they modify. Do *not* say or write "these kind," "these sort," "those kind," "those type," and so on. The correct forms are "these kinds," "these sorts," "this kind," "this sort," "that kind," "those kinds," and so on.

The following sentences illustrate the use of pronouns as demonstrative adjectives:

(Incorrect)   These kind of trees are common throughout the South.

(Correct)   This kind of tree is common throughout the South. [**Or:** These kinds of trees are common throughout the South.]

(Incorrect)   These type of ball bearings never need lubrication.

(Correct)   This type of ball bearings never needs lubrication. [**Or:** These types of ball bearings never need lubrication.]

TIPS ON PRONOUN AGREEMENT

Pronouns should agree in number with the nouns for which they stand.

1. Determine which noun is the real antecedent.
2. Determine whether the antecedent is singular or plural in meaning.
3. Remember that singular pronouns must refer to singular antecedents and that plural pronouns must refer to plural antecedents.

Exercise 5-2

In the space before each sentence, write the letter corresponding to the correct pronoun.

_____   1.   Neither of the twin daughters looked like (a. her   b. their) father.

_____   2.   Every cassette tape and compact disc was labeled according to (a. its   b. their) recording artist and kind of music.

_____   3.   The Olympic prize winner and swimmer was greeted by (a. her   b. their) coach and parents.

_____   4.   (a. These   b. This) kind of social problem does not have a quick or easy solution.

_____   5.   The Popov family received (a. its   b. their) passports from the American embassy.

_____   6.   Neither the witness nor the policemen (a. was   b. were) able to recall the color of the car.

_____   7.   The company released (a. its   b. their) annual report to the stockholders.

_____   8.   Each major religion and its history (a. was   b. were) discussed in the class.

_____   9.   The Mexican soccer team surprised everyone by (a. its   b. their) victory over the Sudanese team.

_____   10.   The family was forced to sell (a. its   b. their) shares in the corporation in order to raise money.

Agreement in Person

You have seen that pronouns agree in number with their antecedents. If the agreement breaks down, the reader is distracted and confused. Agreement in *person* is equally important. *Person* refers to the difference between the person speaking (first person), the person spoken to (second person), and the person or thing spoken about (third person).

First person pronouns:	*I, me, my, mine, we, us, ours, our*
Second person pronouns:	*you, your, yours*
Third person pronouns:	*he, him, his, she, her, hers, it, its, they, them, theirs*

When you make a mistaken shift in person, you have shown that you have lost your way in your own sentence—that you have forgotten what you were writing about. Here are some examples of confusing shifts in person:

(Shift)   *Swimmers in the ocean should be very careful because* you *can get caught in riptides. (This sentence shifts from third person "Swimmers" to second person "you.")*

(Revised)   *Swimmers in the ocean should be very careful because* they *can get caught in riptides.*

(Shift)   *When* you *fly to St. Louis,* passengers *can see the arch on the bank of the Mississippi River from miles away. (This sentence shifts from second person "you" to third person "passengers.")*

(Revised)   *When* you *fly to St. Louis,* you *can see the arch on the bank of the Mississippi River from miles away.*

(Shift)   *When* I *entered the room,* you *could smell the fresh paint.*

(Revised)   *When* I *entered the room,* I *could smell the fresh paint.*

The best way to avoid such shifts is to decide in advance whom you are talking about—and stick with that point of view.

Exercise 5-3

Correct any errors involving needless shift of person in the following sentences. If a sentence is correct, mark it "C."

1. When someone does not exercise or follow a proper diet, it is likely that you will gain weight.
2. If you want to become a good chess player, you should read articles about the game and enter tournaments.
3. When you first study a foreign language, it is difficult for the student to remember all of the rules of pronunciation.

4. When we left the hotel to go shopping, you had to turn in your key to the clerk.
5. Alberto complained that if he wanted something done right, you had to do it yourself.
6. Once you have heard her distinctive voice, the listener will never forget it.
7. The foreign visitor first seeing Mt. Rushmore does not always recognize the faces of the presidents that tower above him.
8. Americans driving for the first time in Ireland should remember that you have to drive on the left side of the road.
9. If a student does not do homework or attend class regularly, you cannot expect a good grade at the end of the semester.
10. Everyone should vote intelligently and be informed about the issues so that you can make intelligent choices at the polls.

Pronoun Reference

Pronouns depend on other words—their antecedents—for their meaning. If their relationship to their antecedents is unclear, their meaning or identity will be confusing. For this reason, you should make certain that every pronoun in your writing (except for indefinite pronouns like *anyone* and *somebody*, and idioms like "*It* is two o'clock") refers specifically to something previously named—its antecedent. In doing so, you will avoid the two most common kinds of problems in pronoun reference: *vagueness* because the writer did not furnish a specific antecedent, and *ambiguity* because the writer supplied too many antecedents.
    Here is an example of each kind of error:

(Vague)   *Several minor political parties nominate presidential candidates every four years. This is one of the characteristics of the American political system. (What is one of the characteristics of the American political system?)*

(Ambiguous)   *Gore Vidal wrote a biography of Abraham Lincoln that demonstrates his knowledge and sensitivity. (Who demonstrates his knowledge and sensitivity: Gore Vidal or Abraham Lincoln?)*

By following the rules given below, you can make clear the relationship between pronouns and their antecedents:

1. The antecedent of a pronoun should be specific rather than implied. Avoid using *that, this, which,* and *it* to refer to implied ideas unless the reference is unmistakably clear.

(Vague)   *Juana was so impressed by the lecture given by the astronomer that she decided to major in it. (Major in what? It has no antecedent in this sentence.)*

(Revision)	*Juana was so impressed by the lecture given by the astronomer that she decided to major in astronomy.*
(Vague)	*Brad consumes huge quantities of potatoes, spaghetti, and ice cream every day, and it is beginning to be noticeable. (What is beginning to be noticeable?)*
(Revision)	*Brad consumes huge quantities of potatoes, spaghetti, and ice cream every day, and the increase in his weight is beginning to be noticeable.*
(Vague)	*Helen enjoys singing with music groups at school, and she would like to be a professional one someday. (A professional what?)*
(Revision)	*Helen enjoys singing with music groups at school, and she would like to be a professional singer someday.*

Such vague sentences are corrected by supplying the missing antecedent. Some sentences, however, are confusing because they have more than one possible antecedent, and the result is ambiguity.

2. To avoid ambiguity or confusion, place pronouns as close as possible to their antecedents. Revise sentences in which there are two possible antecedents for a pronoun.

(Confusing)	*Connie's new car has leather seats, a sunroof, a digital dash with graphic readouts, a vocal warning system, power windows, and an eight-speaker stereo. It is power-driven. (What does It refer to? What is power-driven?)*
(Revision)	*Connie's new car has leather seats, a sunroof that is power-driven, a digital dash with graphic readouts, a vocal warning system, power windows, and an eight-speaker stereo.*
(Confusing)	*Spanish cooking and Mexican cooking should not be confused; it is not as spicy. (What is not as spicy?)*
(Revision)	*Spanish cooking is not as spicy as Mexican cooking.*
(Confusing)	*The dish has been in our family for one hundred years that you dropped.*
(Revision)	*The dish that you dropped has been in our family for one hundred years.*

TIPS ON PRONOUN REFERENCE

1. Don't shift pronouns unnecessarily from one person to another.
2. Learn the pronouns for first, second, and third person.
3. Make sure that every *that, this, which,* and *it* in your sentences has a clear antecedent.
4. Place pronouns as close as possible to their antecedents.

Exercise 5-4

Rewrite the following sentences to make clear the vague or ambiguous pronoun references. You may add, omit, or change words as necessary.

1. Margaret plays the piano very well, but she keeps it hidden.
2. Ray's secret ambition is to be a chef, but he has never studied it.
3. At registration time they check your record and transcript.
4. After having been an executive of a large bank for many years, Anne has taken a job at a small company which has created several problems.
5. Mel has been taking tap-dancing lessons but still can't do it very well.
6. As Burl and Conn talked, his voice began to rise in anger.
7. Unemployment continues to rise and the recession is still felt throughout the country. That is why Maxine and Bob delayed their marriage.
8. Luciano Pavarotti is a great tenor who claims that he has practiced it every day since he was a child.
9. Many companies use lie detectors when interviewing job applicants because they believe it is effective.
10. Although Vince has never been there, he likes Mexican food.

Reviewing the Chapter: Writing Sentences

As you saw in this chapter, writing can be confusing and readers can be confused if pronouns do not agree with the words to which they refer. In this exercise you will be writing sentences demonstrating the correct use of pronoun agreement and reference.

1. Write two sentences using a collective noun in each as the subject requiring a singular pronoun as its antecedent.
2. Use the collective nouns from the preceding sentences as the subjects of two sentences, each requiring a plural pronoun as its antecedent.
3. Write two sentences that contain mistaken shifts in person. Then revise each sentence correctly.
4. Write two sentences that contain unclear pronoun references. Then revise each sentence correctly.
5. Write two sentences in which you illustrate your solution to the exclusive use of masculine pronouns with indefinite pronouns.

5-A

REVIEW EXERCISE

A. *In the space provided, write the letter corresponding to the kind of error in pronoun usage each sentence contains. If the sentence is correct, write "d."*

a. shift in person   b. unclear pronoun reference   c. failure to agree in number   d. correct

_____ 1. Neither of the two suspects could afford their own attorney.

_____ 2. When the typical male watches television, they jump from one channel to another.

_____ 3. Rollie painted his garage and installed new garage doors, which surprised his wife.

_____ 4. Anyone who claims that they overpaid their bill may file a claim with the manager.

_____ 5. The loggers complain that the new regulations have harmed their industry, which is controversial.

_____ 6. Both Jay and Tim agree that he was cheated.

_____ 7. I was surprised to discover that you have to present two forms of identification before cashing a check at my bank.

_____ 8. Many students who watched the television series on astronomy were better able to understand the theories of Galileo and Kepler as explained by their professor.

_____ 9. Con plays golf five days a week, which angers his wife.

_____ 10. Anne's ability to solve difficult mathematical problems is partly due to the fact that her father had been one.

_____ 11. The identity of the witness was concealed in order to protect them.

_____ 12. Beginning skiers who have not taken lessons run the risk of injury if they try to ski on the expert ski runs and trails immediately.

_____ 13. Statistics have clearly demonstrated that drivers who do not use their seatbelts are more likely to suffer an injury if you have an accident.

_____ 14. The new sales clerk did not know how to use a cash register, but he denied it.

_____ 15. The oboe is a member of the woodwind family, and many beautiful concertos have been written for it.

B. In the space before each number write the letter corresponding to the correct pronoun.

_____ 16. Every new drug must pass rigorous tests before (a. it   b. they) can be approved by the Food and Drug Administration.

_____ 17. (a. These   b. This) kind of rose will not bloom in cold climates.

_____ 18. Both the painter and the carpenter have submitted (a. his   b. their) estimates.

_____ 19. Many an inexperienced mountain climber has lost (a. his   b. their) life attempting to reach the top of Kilimanjaro.

_____ 20. Jangling your car keys or constantly looking at your wristwatch can be signs that (a. one is   b. you are) impatient.

_____ 21. Each magazine and book was catalogued according to (a. its   b. their) subject.

_____ 22. When you visit a foreign country for the first time, (a. Americans   b. you) should prepare by studying travel books and learning a few appropriate phrases.

_____ 23. Mrs. Alvarez said that each of us was responsible for preparing (a. his or her   b. our) own meals.

_____ 24. Senator Carlson told the panel that (a. that   b. those) kind of proposed federal regulation would discourage individual savings.

_____ 25. The cast of the play was praised by the director for (a. its   b. their) performance on opening night.

5-B

REVIEW EXERCISE

A. In the space provided, write the letter corresponding to the kind of error in pronoun usage each sentence contains. If the sentence is correct, write "d."

a. shift in person   b. unclear pronoun reference   c. failure to agree in number   d. correct

_____ 1. Neither of his two daughters has their own telephone.

_____ 2. The first time an American drives a car in England, they are likely to be confused by the movement of traffic.

_____ 3. Laverne worked hard and saved her money, which surprised her parents.

_____ 4. Everyone is entitled to their own opinion with respect to the best candidate.

_____ 5. Many people in this country are alcoholics, which is unfortunate.

_____ 6. Both Jerry and Rudy were upset with his semester grade.

_____ 7. Ralph was disappointed to learn that you have to take a course in calculus in order to major in engineering.

_____ 8. Many refugees from Vietnam have succeeded in maintaining their ancient traditions while adjusting to their new homes in the United States.

_____ 9. Richard has been transferred to the night shift, which pleases his wife very much.

_____ 10. The reason that Constance is such an expert at gardening is that she had once been one.

_____ 11. A beginning reporter on a newspaper is assigned important stories after they demonstrate their ability.

_____ 12. Drivers who listen to music and do not pay attention to the traffic run the risk of causing an accident.

_____ 13. People with fair skin should not stay in the sun too long, or you will risk developing skin cancer.

_____ 14. Lester was too shy to ask Marilyn for a date, and he was teased about it.

_____ 15. Norman bought a bowling ball and a baseball bat and then returned it.

B. In the space before each number write the letter corresponding to the correct pronoun.

_____   16.   Every airline passenger must walk through a metal detector before (a. he b. they) may board the airplane.

_____   17.   (a. That   b. Those) kinds of puzzles drive me crazy.

_____   18.   Both Scott and Tony have completed (a. his   b. their) homework.

_____   19.   Many a speculator in the stock market has lost (a. his   b. their) entire fortune.

_____   20.   Cracking your knuckles or tapping your fingers is often a sign that (a. one is   b. you are) nervous.

_____   21.   Each dog and cat was classified according to (a. its   b. their) breed.

_____   22.   When studying a foreign language, one should avoid translating each word separately into (a. his   b. your) own language.

_____   23.   Each of the workers was responsible for furnishing (a. his   b. their) own tools.

_____   24.   (a. That   b. Those) kind of television program tends to glamorize violence.

_____   25.   The faculty of the engineering school was praised by the president for (a. its   b. their) dedication to the college.

Chapter 6

Common Errors Involving Verbs

One reason why many mistakes are made in verb usage is that every sentence contains at least one verb, and consequently there are more chances to go wrong. Furthermore, the verbs most often used in the English language are irregular, which means that they change in a variety of ways that makes any kind of generalization about them impossible. This also means that they must be memorized. To make matters even worse, verbs change their forms and appearance more often than any other part of speech, offering us a series of choices and snares that force us to pick our way through them carefully and deliberately.

Is the case hopeless, then? Is it impossible to learn to use verbs correctly and confidently? Not at all; despite the difficulties mentioned above, problems with verbs fall into a few manageable categories. A common problem, for instance, is not knowing the correct form of the verb needed to express when a particular action is taking place. Another difficulty is not knowing the correct form of an irregular verb. This chapter will present solutions to these and other common problems that many writers and speakers have in using verbs.

Before we begin, however, look at the following sentences to see whether you use the correct verb form. Each sentence contains a verb that is often used incorrectly. The incorrect verb is in brackets.

Araceli watched in horror as the dog dragged [not drug] *her new silk blouse across the floor.*

Although I saw [not seen] *Madonna at the restaurant, I was too shy to ask for an autograph.*

We got lost in the museum and then discovered that the bus had gone [not went] *without us.*

93

ticiple forms of the irregular verbs. Fortunately, irregular verbs form their present participles in the same way as regular verbs: by adding -ing to the present form.

To understand why it is difficult to make any generalization about irregular verbs, let us examine the verbs *sing* and *bring*. From our familiarity with the English language we know that *sing* is present tense ("I *sing* in church every Sunday"), *sang* is the past tense ("I *sang* last Sunday"), and *sung* is the past participle ("I have *sung* every Sunday this month"). Imagine the confusion of someone learning English who, having mastered *sing*, applies the same changes by analogy to the verb *bring*. He logically concludes that the past tense of *bring* is *brang* ("I *brang* my lunch yesterday") and that the past participle is *brung* ("I have *brung* my lunch"). To native speakers of English these forms are humorous; to others who have not mastered the inconsistencies of our verbs, there is nothing within the verb *bring* to suggest that the past tense and past participle are *brought* ("I *brought* my lunch yesterday" and "I *have brought* my lunch").

The English language contains over two hundred irregular verbs, and they are the verbs most often used. Consult your dictionary if you are not sure about the past tense and past participle forms of irregular verbs. Don't trust your ear; what "sounds right" may only be the result of having repeatedly heard, said, and written the incorrect form. The "piano" you have been playing all these years may be out of tune.

Below is a list of some of the most common irregular verbs, as well as a few regular verbs that often present problems. Practice their correct forms by putting "I" in front of the present and past tense forms, "I have" in front of the past participle form, and "I am" in front of the present participle form: "I *begin*. I *began*. I have *begun*. I am *beginning*." Practice saying them correctly until they sound correct and natural.

Present Tense	Past Tense	Past Participle	Present Participle
arise	arose	arisen	arising
awake	awoke (or awaked)	awaked, awoken	awaking
bear	bore	born (pertaining to birthdate) borne (carried)	bearing
begin	began	begun	beginning
blow	blew	blown	blowing
break	broke	broken	breaking
bring	brought	brought	bringing
burst	burst	burst	bursting
catch	caught	caught	catching
choose	chose	chosen	choosing
come	came	come	coming

dig	dug	dug	digging
dive	dived, dove	dived	diving
do	did	done	doing
drag	dragged	dragged	dragging
draw	drew	drawn	drawing
drink	drank	drunk	drinking
drive	drove	driven	driving
drown	drowned	drowned	drowning
eat	ate	eaten	eating
fly	flew	flown	flying
freeze	froze	frozen	freezing
give	gave	given	giving
go	went	gone	going
grow	grew	grown	growing
hang	hung	hung	hanging
hang (executed)	hanged	hanged	hanging
hide	hid	hidden	hiding
know	knew	known	knowing
lay	laid	laid	laying
lead	led	led	leading
leave	left	left	leaving
lie	lay	lain	lying
light	lighted, lit	lighted, lit	lighting
ride	rode	ridden	riding
ring	rang	rung	ringing
rise	rose	risen	rising
run	ran	run	running
see	saw	seen	seeing
set	set	set	setting
shake	shook	shaken	shaking
shine (glow)	shone	shone	shining
shine (polish)	shined	shined	shining

© 1997 Addison-Wesley Educational Publishers Inc.

5. To no one's surprise, the bill was _____ an overwhelming vote of approval. (*give*)
6. After the Congressional clerk had _____ the revised bill to the Senate, a separate committee there also voted its approval. (*bear*)
7. Finally, the bill had _____ to the President for his approval. (*come*)
8. He had _____ how eagerly the public and politicians supported the bill, but he still thought carefully about it. (*see*)
9. Although conflicting opinions about the bill had _____ his party apart, he soon approved it. (*tear*)
10. Finally, the bill which Jorge and many others supported had _____ a law. (*become*)

Using the Correct Tense

You have noticed in your study of verbs that they can show different tenses or times by the ending -*ed* or -*d*, by a change in spelling, and by the helping verbs that go with them. The forms of the verb change according to the time expressed—when the action or state of being occurs. Each tense has a specific purpose, and careful speakers and writers select the appropriate tense according to that purpose.

Here is a list of the six common tenses in English and their uses.

Present	*I sail (am sailing).*
Past	*I sailed (was sailing).*
Future	*I will¹ sail (will be sailing).*
Present Perfect	*I have sailed (have been sailing).*
Past Perfect	*I had sailed (had been sailing).*
Future Perfect	*I will* have sailed (will have been sailing).*

¹*Shall* is often substituted for *will* in the future and future perfect tenses.

The following list shows the six common tense forms of *take*. Showing all of the forms of a verb in this way is called conjugating a verb.

Conjugation of Take

Present Tense

Singular	**Plural**
I take	we take
you take	you take
he, she, or it takes	they take

Past Tense

Singular	**Plural**
I took	we took
you took	you took
he, she, or it took	they took

Future Tense

Singular	**Plural**
I will (shall) take	we will (shall) take
you will take	you will take
he, she, or it will take	they will take

Present Perfect Tense

Singular	**Plural**
I have taken	we have taken
you have taken	you have taken
he, she, or it has taken	they have taken

Past Perfect Tense

Singular	**Plural**
I had taken	we had taken
you had taken	you had taken
he, she, or it had taken	they had taken

Future Perfect Tense

Singular	**Plural**
I will (shall) have taken	we will (shall) have taken
you will have taken	you will have taken
he, she, or it will have taken	they will have taken

Each of the six tenses has an additional form called the *progressive form*, which expresses continuing action. The progressive is not a separate tense but an additional form of each of the six tenses in the conjugation. It consists of a form of the verb *be* plus the present participle of the verb.

Progressive Forms

Present Progressive:	am, are, is taking
Past Progressive:	was, were taking
Future Progressive:	will (shall) be taking
Present Perfect Progressive:	has, have been taking
Past Perfect Progressive:	had been taking
Future Perfect Progressive:	will (shall) have been taking

The present tense is used in the following situations:

a.   To express a condition or an action that exists or is going on now.

> *Her car* is *fast.*
> *But she* is driving *under the speed limit.*

b.   To express an action that is habitual.

> *He* plays *in the charity tournament every summer.*
> *He always* beats *his opponents.*

c.   To express a truth or an idea that is always true.

> *There* is *no game like baseball.*
> *St. Louis* is *the home of the Cardinals baseball team.*

The past tense expresses an action or a condition completed in the past.

> *The Coalition forces* bombed *Iraq on January 17, 1991.*
> *Sheldon* visited *his mother last night.*

The future tense expresses an action that will take place in the future.

> *Javier* will race *in the next Olympics.*
> *Uncle Jim* will be *fifty years old next August.*

The present perfect tense is used for an action that began in the past and continues into the present:

> I *have gone* to many of the Mets games. [And I still go.]
> I *have lived* in Atlanta since 1991. [And I still live in Atlanta.]
> Our neighbor's dog *has barked* for two days now. [And he's still barking.]

The present perfect tense can also be used for an action that started in the past and has been completed at some indefinite time:

> The fire in the warehouse *has been extinguished.*
>
> My grandfather *has been* to a doctor only once in his lifetime.

The past perfect tense is used for an action that began and ended in the past. In other words, it describes an action that was completed before something else happened.

> I *had lived* in Mobile before I moved to Atlanta. [NOT: I lived in Mobile before I moved to Atlanta.]
>
> Everyone knew that Clark's father *had been* a member of President Nixon's cabinet. [NOT: Everyone knew that Clark's father was a member of President Nixon's cabinet.]
>
> Muriel asked us if we *had watched* the Rose Bowl Parade on television. [NOT: Muriel asked us if we watched the Rose Bowl Parade on television.]

The future perfect tense is used for an action that begins and will end in the future before a particular time.

> Her parents *will have been married* forty years next Thanksgiving.
>
> I *will have used up* all of my vacation time by the time your visit ends next week.

A Few Suggestions for Using the Correct Tense

1. Do not use the past tense of a verb when it should be in the present tense.

    > *Margie took a course in anthropology last year. She said that it was an interesting subject that studied cultures and societies throughout the world.* (**Incorrect.** *"Was" and "studied" imply that anthropology no longer is interesting and does not study other societies and cultures. The correct verbs are "is" and "studies."*)

2. Use the present infinitive (*to write, to invent, to leap,* and so on) unless the action referred to was completed before the time expressed in the governing verb.

    > *Helen and her husband planned* to stay [not to have stayed] *awake for "Saturday Night Live."*
    >
    > I am fortunate to have had [*not* to have] *my life jacket during the stormy boat trip.*

3. When a narrative in the past tense is interrupted by a reference to a preceding event, use the past perfect tense.

    > *No one could believe that I* had known *her before she became a movie star.*
    >
    > *The film's ending made no sense to me because I* had missed *the beginning.*

© 1997 Addison-Wesley Educational Publishers Inc.

A FEW REMINDERS ABOUT TENSES

1. Use the past tense only if the action referred to took place at a specific time in the past.
2. Use the past perfect tense ("had" plus the past participle) only when you want to place a completed action *before* another action in the past.

Exercise 6-3

In the space before each sentence, identify the tense of the italicized verb by writing past, present, future, present perfect, past perfect, or future perfect.

_____   1.   The average American *watches* television for about seven hours every day.

_____   2.   Some media analysts *have described* some patterns in the programs many of us watch on television.

_____   3.   For example, the typical number of violent acts shown on television *has remained* fairly stable.

_____   4.   Six to eight violent incidents *occur* per hour in average adult programming.

_____   5.   That figure *will have jumped* to twenty to thirty-five per hour, however, if you turn to children's cartoons.

_____   6.   The professions which *had been featured* until recently are law enforcement officers and health professionals.

_____   7.   In addition, more than half of the people who *appeared* on television were middle-aged white males.

_____   8.   Most studies *will show* that men outnumber women on television by three to one.

_____   9.   Researchers also *had noticed* that most of the programs were about power, danger, and threats.

_____   10. Because violence on television is so prevalent, researchers say that heavy viewers often *will perceive* the world as more dangerous than it really is.

Exercise 6-4

In the space before each sentence, write the verb shown in parentheses in the tense indicated.

_____   1.   There (*be*—present) some simple steps you can take to prepare your mind and body for an exam.

_____   2.   First, you should (*sleep*—present perfect) at least eight hours the night before the test.

_____   3.   The best students always (*eat*—past) a healthy breakfast before they took their exams.

_____ 4. I (*drink*—present perfect) orange juice for an energy boost before tests this semester.

_____ 5. Some students said their concentration (*grow*—past) stronger after they had drunk a cup of coffee.

_____ 6. Once you (*sit*—present perfect) down at your desk, relax your body and mind.

_____ 7. (*Draw*—present) in a deep breath, hold it for a few seconds, and then release it.

_____ 8. My brother reported that his tension (*leave*—past) his body when he tried this breathing technique.

_____ 9. Make sure you (*lay*—present perfect) your pencils, calculators, and other needed supplies on the desk ahead of time.

_____ 10. Most important, read all of the instructions; don't (*speed*—present) through the test.

Shifts in Tense

Having learned the uses of the six common tenses, you should use them consistently, avoiding unnecessary shifts from one tense to another. If, for example, you begin an essay using the past tense to describe events in the past, do not suddenly leap to the present tense to describe those same events. Similarly, don't abruptly shift to the past tense if you are narrating an incident in the present tense. This does not mean that you can't use more than one tense in a piece of writing. It does mean, however, that you must use the same tense when referring to the same period of time.

In the paragraph below, the writer uses past tense verbs to describe events that occurred in the past, and then shifts correctly to the present tense to describe events occurring in the present.

> *I learned to respect fine craftsmen when I was a young boy helping my father build the house that I lived in until I married. My father had an exact, precise air about him that could make sloppy people like me somewhat nervous. When he laid out the dimensions of the house or the opening of a door he did it with an exactness and precision that would not allow for the careless kind of measurements that I would settle for. When he measured a board and told me to cut it, I knew that it would have to be cut in an unwavering line and that it would fit exactly in the place assigned to it. Doors that he installed still fit tightly, drawers slide snugly, and joints in cabinets and mortices can scarcely be detected. Today, when I measure a piece of new screenwire to replace the old or a fence to put around the rose bushes, I can still hear the efficient clicking of his six-foot rule as he checks my calculations.*

This passage is correct in its use of tenses. The events of the past are recalled by the author and narrated in the past tense ("I learned," "My father had," "he laid out," and so on). When he shifts to the present, he changes his tense accordingly ("Today, when I measure," "I can still hear," and so on). The paragraph below, on the other hand, is confusing because

© 1997 Addison-Wesley Educational Publishers Inc.

of its inconsistent use of tenses, shifting from the past to the present tense to refer to the same time.

America's journey to the moon began on the morning of July 16, 1969, when three American astronauts lifted off in Apollo II. Neil Armstrong, Mike Collins, and Buzz Aldrin are on their way to the moon. They will travel at a speed of 24,300 miles per hour. When they were thirty-four hours into the flight, the astronauts begin a live broadcast in color of their activities. Over 500 million people throughout the world have watched. The astronauts report they were impressed by the sight of the earth as they pull away from it. Aldrin said, "This view was out of this world." As they neared the moon's surface, the propulsion system was fired and the spacecraft's velocity goes from 6,500 mph to 3,700 mph as it went into elliptical orbit around the moon. After undocking Eagle, the Lunar Module, they brought it closer to the moon's surface until they are close enough to see a sheet of moon dirt blow by the rocket exhaust. Armstrong shut off the engine and reports, "Tranquility Base here. The Eagle has landed."

You probably noticed that the first sentence is in the past tense ("America's journey to the moon *began*. . ." and "three American astronauts *lifted off*. . ."), signaling the reader that the paragraph will be related in the past tense. Therefore, we are not prepared for the shift to the present tense in the second sentence ("They *will travel*. . ."), the return to the past tense and subsequent jump to the present tense in the third sentence, and so on, through a series of scrambled tenses that continue to jerk the reader from past to present to future without warning. The writer of this paragraph could not decide (or perhaps forgot) when the events he or she was writing about took place. To avoid such confusion, keep in mind the tense forms you are using.

Exercise 6-5

Some of the following sentences contain confusing tense shifts. Rewrite them so that the tenses are consistent. If a sentence is correct, mark it "C."

1. Most people know that cigarettes were bad for their health, but many don't know exactly how cigarettes affect their bodies.
2. First, the nicotine speeds up the heartbeat and the blood pressure rose.
3. The tar found in cigarettes is even more harmful because it bore ingredients that cause cancer.
4. Tar also brings breathing problems such as shortness of breath or a chronic cough.
5. Your lungs also took in carbon monoxide when you smoke.
6. It then became more difficult for your blood to bring oxygen to vital tissues.
7. People who hang onto their smoking habits took chances with their health.
8. But they enjoy sitting down and lighted up a cigarette.
9. People now began their smoking habits at a younger age than ever before.
10. Most smokers know they should quit, but this is easier said than did.

Two Pairs of Irregular Verbs: *Lie* and *Lay; Sit* and *Set*

Four irregular verbs cause more trouble than most of the others: *lie* and *lay*, and *sit* and *set*. Unwary speakers and writers can easily confuse them, but careful speakers and writers observe their differences.

Lie and Lay

"To lie" means "to remain in position or be at rest." (We are ignoring the other meaning—"to tell a falsehood"; when *lie* carries this meaning, it is a regular verb.) *Lie* never takes an object—that is, you never *lie* anything down. *Lie* is usually followed by a word or phrase that tells where (*lie* down, *lie* on the grass, and so on).

The principal parts of *lie* are *lie* (the present tense form), *lay* (the past tense), and *lain* (the past participle). The present participle is *lying*. Because our ear tells us that a "d" sound is usually the sign of the past tense, we are tempted to say or write *laid* for the past tense, instead of the correct form *lay*.

Present:	*Our dog often* lies *by the fire on cold nights.*
Past:	*Roberta* lay [not laid] *by the pool for hours yesterday.*
Present Perfect:	*The dishes have* lain [not laid] *in the sink all day.*

The present participle *lying* is used with helping verbs; it should not be confused with *laying*.

The children have been lying [not laying] *on the porch and telling ghost stories.*
Your soccer ball is lying [not laying] *in the middle of the street.*

"To lay" means to place or put something somewhere, and it is a *transitive verb*—that is, it requires an object to complete its meaning: lay the *package* down, lay your *head* down, and so on. The principal parts of *lay* are *lay* (present tense), *laid* (past tense), *laid* (past participle), and *laying* (present participle).

Present:	*Please* lay *your essay on my desk.*
Past:	*Paul* laid *his Red Sox cap on the floor under his chair.*
Present Perfect:	*We have* laid *over two hundred bricks in the new driveway.*

The present participle *laying* is used with helping verbs; it is followed by an object.

We were laying *bricks in uneven lines and had to remove them.*
As planes flew overhead, the President was laying *a wreath at the Vietnam War Memorial yesterday.*

The most effective way of mastering *lie* and *lay* is to memorize their forms: *lie, lay, lain, lying; lay, laid, laid, laying.*

Sit and Set

"To sit," meaning "to occupy a seat," is an *intransitive verb*—it never takes an object. This means that you never "sit" anything down, for example. The principal parts are *sit* (the present tense), *sat* (the past tense), and *sat* (the past participle). The present participle is *sitting*. Study the following sentences carefully:

Jack Nicholson sits *in the front row at many Lakers games. (present tense)*

We always sat *in the back row at movies. (past tense)*

My sister has sat *next to us in Spanish class all year. (past participle)*

Have you been sitting *in the balcony for all of the performances this season? (present participle)*

"To set" resembles "to lay" in meaning. "To set" means "to put in place," and, like *lay*, it is a *transitive* verb and is followed by another word (a direct object) to complete its meaning.* Its principal parts remain the same in all forms: *set* (present tense), *set* (past tense), and *set* (past participle). The present participle is *setting*. Study the following sentences carefully.

Jin-Sun always sets *the compact disc player for "Continuous Play." (present tense)*

Last night I set *the volume control too high and almost blew the speakers. (past tense)*

I have set *your Run DMC disc back on the shelf. (past participle)*

Setting his old records near the heater was careless. (present participle)

As in the case of *lie* and *lay*, the most effective way of mastering *sit* and *set* is to memorize their forms: *sit, sat, sat, sitting; set, set, set, setting.*

TIPS FOR USING "LIE AND LAY" AND "SIT AND SET"

1. "To lie" means "to be at rest"; you don't *lie* anything down. The forms are *lie, lay, lain,* and *lying*.
2. "To lay" means "to place or put somewhere"; an object must always follow this verb. The forms are *lay, laid, laid,* and *laying*.
3. "To sit" means "to occupy a seat"; you don't *sit* anything down. The forms are *sit, sat, sat,* and *sitting*.

---

*In a few idioms such as "The hen *sets* on her nest" and "The sun is *setting*," set does not require a direct object. In most other cases, however, it is followed by a direct object.

4. "To set" means "to put in place," and except for idioms like "The hen sets" and "The sun sets," it is always followed by an object. The forms do not change in the present and past tenses or the past participle: *set, set,* and *set.* The present participle is *setting.*

Exercise 6-6

A. *Use the correct form of "lie" and "lay" in the following sentences.*

1. Yesterday afternoon I _____ at the beach.
2. It was my favorite stretch of sand, and I have _____ there every summer since childhood.
3. Because the sky was overcast, not many people were _____ nearby.
4. My radio _____ by my head, playing my favorite tunes.
5. I had _____ my new pink volleyball in the sand beside me.
6. After _____ in the sun for a few minutes, I fell asleep.
7. When I woke up, the ball was not where I had _____ it.
8. This was no time to _____ around in the sand; I decided to find it.
9. After _____ the radio and towel next to my ice cooler, I began searching for the ball.
10. I asked everyone who _____ on the beach if they had seen the ball.
11. After looking everywhere on the beach, I _____ down by the pier and became very despondent.
12. It was all my fault because I had _____ the ball near me, but I had not kept my eye on it.
13. Soon a big but friendly dog _____ down next to me.
14. I caught a glimpse of something pink _____ in the sand by his head.
15. And there _____ my prized volleyball—with a few teeth marks but still good as new.

B. *Use the correct form of "sit" and "set" in the following sentences.*

16. Everything was finally _____ for our Super Bowl party.
17. Trenton and I had _____ in the kitchen for hours last night, deciding which refreshments to serve.
18. We worried whether there would be room for all of our friends to _____ on the couch.
19. We _____ out some extra folding chairs, just in case there weren't enough.
20. "Some of them will _____ on the floor," Trenton said.
21. I already had _____ a tray of cups and plates on the coffee table.

22. I asked Trenton to _____ our new flower vase in the other room so that it would not be broken.
23. Everyone _____ down as soon as they arrived.
24. The children were _____ in front so that they could see the television.
25. Trenton _____ the correct channel and soon the ball game began.
26. We didn't notice that our cat had _____ down by my cousin Rita.
27. Rita began sneezing violently and overturned a bowl of popcorn which _____ nearby.
28. I _____ a box of tissues near her and she recovered from her attack.
29. The cat, meanwhile, was now _____ on the television and had somehow disconnected the antenna.
30. Although several people had _____ by the television set trying to repair the antenna, the picture disappeared—and so did our party.

Reviewing the Chapter: Writing Sentences

Two common problems when using verbs are dealt with in this chapter: not knowing the correct form of the verb needed to express when a particular action is taking place, and not knowing the correct form of an irregular verb. This writing exercise will give you an opportunity to show that you do not suffer from either problem.

1. Using two of the verbs listed on pages 95–97, write two sentences showing the correct use of the present perfect tense.
2. Using two additional verbs listed on pages 95–97, write two sentences showing the correct use of the past perfect tense.
3. Using two other verbs on pages 95-97, write two sentences showing the correct use of the future perfect tense.
4. Write a sentence correctly using *sit* in the past tense.
5. Write a sentence correctly using *set* in the past tense.
6. Write a sentence correctly using *lie* in the present perfect tense.
7. Write a sentence correctly using *lay* in the present perfect tense.

6-A

REVIEW EXERCISE

A. Identify the tense of the italicized verb in each sentence by using the appropriate letter. Use the space provided.

a. present perfect tense   b. past tense   c. past perfect tense   d. present tense

_____ 1. Herb's driver's license *had expired* before he bought his new car.
_____ 2. The tunnel connecting France and England *began* operating in 1994.
_____ 3. The dog Virgil *lies* at my feet while I watch television.
_____ 4. Many swimmers *have tried* to swim from Santa Monica to Catalina Island.
_____ 5. Before the cement *sets*, I will carefully set a tile in place.
_____ 6. The mood of the voters *depends* on how their own lives are affected.
_____ 7. The stock market *has plummeted* each Friday for the last month.
_____ 8. Too much exposure to sunlight *causes* skin cancer, according to my doctor.
_____ 9. Paul's dirty laundry *lay* in a heap next to his bed.
_____ 10. Ten writers *had participated* in the preparation of the movie script.

B. Using the correct letter, select the correct form of the verb in the following sentences. Use the space provided.

_____ 11. Because Sharon was driving too fast, she did not notice the box that was (a. laying   b. lying) in the road ahead of her.
_____ 12. The mob stormed the police station and (a. dragged   b. drug) the murderer away.
_____ 13. The tomatoes had (a. laid   b. lain) in the field for a week before they could be gathered.
_____ 14. Each side claimed that the other had (a. broke   b. broken) the treaty.
_____ 15. After the clock in the tower had (a. rang   b. rung) three times, the troops rushed to the city square.
_____ 16. None of the guests at the dude ranch had (a. ridden   b. rode) a horse before.
_____ 17. During the timeout the players (a. drank   b. drunk) a few sips of water.
_____ 18. After he had (a. began   b. begun) to play his piano solo, Richard started to feel nauseous.

111

_____ 19. The salesman claimed that the car had been (a. driven   b. drove) only three thousand miles.

_____ 20. Although Marcus lost the match, he knew that he had (a. did   b. done) his best.

_____ 21. In her senior year at college, Loretta realized that she had (a. chose   b. chosen) the wrong major.

_____ 22. When Charles was still living at home, he (a. gave   b. give) his parents a trip to Europe for their wedding anniversary.

_____ 23. Three paintings by Picasso that (a. hanged   b. hung) in the museum were stolen over the weekend.

_____ 24. In the Wild West days, cattle thieves were often (a. hanged   b. hung).

_____ 25. After my sister had (a. sat   b. set) in the dentist's waiting room for forty-five minutes, she decided to leave.

6-B

REVIEW EXERCISE

A. *Identify the tense of the italicized verb in each sentence by using the appropriate letter. Use the space provided.*

a. *present perfect tense*   b. *past tense*   c. *past perfect tense*   d. *present tense*

_____ 1. The police found the money that the thief *had buried*.
_____ 2. The waiter *sets* the tables for four people, unless a large party is expected.
_____ 3. The bubbles *burst* when the temperature exceeds 90 degrees.
_____ 4. Members of the veterans' organization *laid* flowers at the Tomb of the Unknown Soldier.
_____ 5. One obstacle *lies* in her path before she can achieve her goal.
_____ 6. The price of gasoline *has varied* from one week to the next.
_____ 7. Letters of introduction *have been given* to each ambassador.
_____ 8. Hardy *spends* money as if it were water.
_____ 9. The village *lay* in a valley three miles east of the battlefield.
_____ 10. Although they *had done* a number of experiments, they finally admitted that their theory was inconclusive.

B. *Using the correct letter, select the correct form of the verb in the following sentences. Use the space provided.*

_____ 11. I have (a. sat   b. set) at the desk for hours trying to solve this math problem.
_____ 12. The papers (a. laid   b. lay) on the desk, forgotten by their owner.
_____ 13. Because of his complicity in the atrocities of World War II, Adolf Eichmann was (a. hanged   b. hung).
_____ 14. In response to the reporters' questions, the mayor (a. gave   b. give) a series of vague and confusing responses.
_____ 15. Members of the emergency team were (a. chose   b. chosen) on the basis of their scores on the physical examination.
_____ 16. Although Nancy was disappointed, she knew she had (a. did   b. done) her best in the competition.
_____ 17. Clem bought a used car that had been (a. driven   b. drove) more than 150,000 miles.

_____ 18. Guests continued to arrive even after the band had (a. began   b. begun) to play the national anthem.

_____ 19. Their throats parched with thirst, the survivors (a. drank   b. drunk) the water eagerly.

_____ 20. Because Marcia was from Manhattan, she had never (a. ridden   b. rode) a horse.

_____ 21. The children ran from the room when the fire alarm (a. rang   b. rung).

_____ 22. Someone had (a. broke   b. broken) the window during the night.

_____ 23. The wounded soldier had (a. laid   b. lain) on the battlefield for seven hours before he could be removed.

_____ 24. The dog (a. dragged   b. drug) its injured paw painfully along the ground.

_____ 25. Fred (a. lay   b. laid) on his back for three days after his operation.

Chapter 7

Compound and Complex Sentences

One of the marks of a good writer is the ability to use a variety of sentence types. The *simple* sentence is an important weapon to have in your writing arsenal, but it is limited in the ways it can be used and in the jobs it can perform. *Compound* and *complex* sentences give you additional alternatives for expressing your ideas, usually in more precise ways.

In Chapter 2 you were given a brief introduction to compound and complex sentences. In this chapter you will learn more about them, including how they are formed and punctuated and how they can make your writing more exact and interesting.

Compound Sentences

You will recall from Chapter 2 that a simple sentence has a single subject-verb combination:

The Beatles performed dozens of songs.
The Beatles performed and recorded dozens of songs.
The Beatles and the Rolling Stones performed dozens of songs.
The Beatles and the Rolling Stones performed and recorded dozens of songs.

A *compound sentence* consists of two or more simple sentences (or *independent clauses*) containing closely related ideas and usually connected by a comma and a coordinating conjunction (*and, but, so, for, nor, or, yet*). Below are some examples of compound sentences. Notice how each sentence consists of two independent clauses with related ideas joined with a comma and a coordinating conjunction:

> *Real estate prices in California have declined,* but *most young couples cannot afford to buy a home.*
>
> *Jack Nicholson is my favorite actor,* and *Chinatown is my favorite movie.*
>
> *Vincent volunteered to help cook dinner,* so *Janet asked him to make the salad.*

If these sentences were divided into halves, each half could stand as an independent clause or simple sentence:

> *Real estate prices in California have declined. Most young couples cannot afford to buy a home.*
>
> *Jack Nicholson is my favorite actor. Chinatown is my favorite movie.*
>
> *Vincent volunteered to help cook dinner. Janet asked him to make the salad.*

By combining these simple sentences with commas and coordinating conjunctions, the results are longer, smoother compound sentences. But remember: the independent clauses in a compound sentence must contain a closely related idea, and they are usually joined with a coordinating conjunction. Never try to combine two independent clauses with *only* a comma. The result will be a *comma-splice,* a serious sentence fault. (See Chapter 8 for ways to avoid and to correct comma-splices.)

Exercise 7-1

Below is a series of independent clauses, each followed by a comma. Change each clause into a compound sentence by adding a second independent clause containing a related idea and combining the two clauses with a coordinating conjunction (and, but, so, for, nor, or, and yet). Try to use each of the coordinate conjunctions at least once.

1. Nonfat foods are increasingly popular with today's shoppers, _____

   _____.

2. Left-handed people encounter several disadvantages daily, _____

   _____.

3. Most people do not pay the entire balance on their credit-card account every

   month, _____

   _____.

4. Everyone has trouble spelling certain words, _____

    _____ .

5. An airport in southern California is named after the actor John Wayne, _____

    _____ .

6. Most colleges require SAT or ACT scores from applicants, _____

    _____ .

7. The Hubble telescope ran into several technical problems, _____

    _____ .

8. Nearly everyone can remember a very embarrassing moment, _____

    _____ .

9. The singer Placido Domingo was born in Madrid and educated in Mexico

    City, _____

    _____ .

10. Automobiles built in the United States have improved in quality within the past

    few years, _____

    _____ .

Most independent clauses are connected by coordinating conjunctions. You may, however, use a *semicolon* (;) to connect the clauses if the relationship between the ideas expressed in the independent clauses is very close and obvious without a conjunction. In such cases the semicolon takes the place of both the conjunction and the comma preceding it. For example:

> *Robert Penn Warren was this country's first official Poet Laureate; he was named on February 26, 1986.*
>
> *I love tacos and enchiladas; they are my favorite kinds of Mexican food.*

When using a semicolon, be certain that a coordinating conjunction would not be more appropriate. Using a semicolon in the following sentence would be confusing because the relationship between the two clauses would not be clear:

> **(Confusing)**   *I have never played hockey; I like to watch hockey games on television.*

By substituting a coordinating conjunction for the semicolon, you can make clear the relationship between the clauses:

(Revised)   *I have never played hockey*, but *I like to watch hockey games on television.*

Tips for Punctuating Compound Sentences

1. If the clauses in a compound sentence are connected by a coordinating conjunction, place a comma in front of the conjunction. Do not try to combine independent clauses with only a comma—the result would be a *comma-splice*, a serious sentence error. Notice the following:

(Comma-splice)   *Calcium is important in one's diet, it is particularly important for pregnant women.*

(Correct)   *Calcium is important in one's diet, and it is particularly important for pregnant women.*

2. Do *not* place a comma before a coordinating conjunction if it does not connect independent clauses.

(Incorrect)   *Herbs add flavor to salads, and are easy to grow.*

(Correct)   *Herbs add flavor to salads and are easy to grow.*

(Incorrect)   *My cousin Phil was born in Syracuse, but later moved to Buffalo.*

(Correct)   *My cousin Phil was born in Syracuse but later moved to Buffalo.*

In both sentences above, the conjunctions do not connect independent clauses, and therefore they should not be preceded by commas. In Chapter 10 you will learn the rules for using the comma, including its use before *and* when it connects items in a series.

Exercise 7-2

Place a comma before any conjunction connecting independent clauses in the following sentences. Some sentences do not need commas.

1. The St. Louis Cardinals used to play in Sportsmen's Park but now they play in Busch Stadium.
2. The musical sonata was pioneered by Haydn and transformed by Beethoven.
3. Either she is from Italy or she has an incredible ability to imitate foreign accents.
4. The mayor won by a landslide but later was recalled while still in office.
5. Arlene graduated with honors from college yet she was unable to find a job in her hometown.
6. Bruce was afraid of the dog but continued to play with it.
7. Many people do not vote yet complain about their elected officials.
8. The savings and loan scandal caused many small investors to lose their life savings and to file for bankruptcy.

9. The Knicks lost the first two games but they won the playoffs.
10. My Aunt Sylvia has five children and works on the railroad.

REMINDERS FOR COMPOUND SENTENCES

1. A compound sentence consists of two or more independent clauses connected by a semicolon or a coordinating conjunction (a word like *and, but,* and *or*).
2. If the clauses in a compound sentence are connected by a coordinating conjunction, place a comma in front of the conjunction.
3. Independent clauses must never be combined with a comma *only.* You must use a comma *and* a coordinating conjunction.

Complex Sentences

Because their ideas can be shifted around to produce different emphases or rhythms, *complex* sentences offer the writer more variety than do simple sentences. Complex sentences are often more precise than compound sentences because a compound sentence must treat two ideas equally. Complex sentences, on the other hand, can establish more exact relationships. In Chapter 2 you learned that there are two kinds of clauses: *independent* and *dependent*. An independent clause can stand alone and form a complete sentence. A dependent clause, however, cannot stand alone. Even though it has a subject and a verb, it fails to express a complete thought. It must be attached to an independent clause in order to form a grammatically complete sentence.

You can recognize dependent clauses by the kinds of words that introduce them, making them dependent. The technical terms for these introducing words are *subordinating conjunctions* and *relative pronouns*. Notice that each of the following dependent clauses begins with such a word:

After *we reached our motel that night*.

If *you speak a foreign language*.

Because *baldness is inherited*.

Who *collected heavy metal music cassettes*.

Which *shocked everyone*.

Although these clauses contain subjects and verbs, they do not express complete ideas; therefore, they are dependent clauses. By adding an independent clause to each, however, you can change them into complete, grammatically correct *complex* sentences:

After we reached our motel that night, we called our parents.

If you speak a foreign language, you have an advantage when applying for many jobs.

Because baldness is inherited, Steve and his brothers lost their hair while in their late twenties.

Our guide in Moscow was a young man who collected heavy metal music cassettes.

The graduation speaker made a vulgar gesture which shocked everyone.

> **Note:** *A dependent clause is usually followed by a comma when it begins a sentence. If an independent clause comes first, no comma is needed.*

The following list contains the most common dependent clause introducing words. Whenever a clause begins with one of them (unless it is a question), it is a dependent clause in a complex sentence.

after	than
although	that
as, as if	though
as though	unless
because	what, whatever
before	when, whenever
how	where, wherever
if	whether
in order that	which, whichever
once	while
since	who, whose, whoever
so that	whom

Exercise 7-3

If the italicized clause in each sentence is a dependent clause, write "dep"; if it is an independent clause, write "ind." Use the space provided on the left.

_____ 1. *When the war was over,* parades honoring the troops were held throughout the United States.

_____ 2. If you take out a large life insurance policy, *you will have to pass a physical examination.*

_____ 3. The men *who wrote the Constitution* could not have foreseen the debate over electronic eavesdropping.

© 1997 Addison-Wesley Educational Publishers Inc.

_____ 4. *The word* euphemism *is from a Greek word* that means "to use words of good omen."

_____ 5. *Before he became a famous writer,* Mark Twain was a boat pilot on the Mississippi River.

_____ 6. *As we sailed into the harbor,* we could see the remains of the old dock.

_____ 7. The bass fiddle and the violin both have four strings, *and the names of the strings are the same.*

_____ 8. My history professor wrote a magazine article about the President *which is very unflattering.*

_____ 9. *Paul wisely invested the inheritance* that his father had left him.

_____ 10. *The movie was in French,* and therefore I didn't understand all of the humor.

Exercise 7-4

Add an independent clause to each of the following dependent clauses, thereby creating a complex sentence.

1. Because the amendment did not pass, _____

   _____.

2. _____ before I realized it.

3. Although the coach had wanted to complete the season, _____

   _____.

4. If plants are not watered or fed regularly, _____

   _____.

5. _____ that it would not be possible.

6. Unless the laws are enforced fairly, _____

   _____.

7. _____ until a truce had been declared.

8. _____ when the solar eclipse was occurring.

9. Because she confused "astrology" with "astronomy," _____

   _____.

10. _____ after a loud explosion was heard shortly after

   midnight.

Three Kinds of Dependent Clauses

Now that you can recognize dependent clauses in complex sentences, it is time to take a closer look at them so that you will know how to use them correctly and make your own sentences more interesting and mature.

All dependent clauses share three traits: they all have a subject and a verb, they begin with a dependent clause introducing word, and they must be combined with independent clauses to form a complete sentence. So much for the similarities; let us now consider the differences among them.

Dependent clauses can be used in sentences in three different ways: as adverbs, as adjectives, and as nouns. Consequently, we label them *adverb clauses*, *adjective clauses*, and *noun clauses*.

REMINDERS FOR COMPLEX SENTENCES

1. Dependent clauses begin with words like "after," "if," "although," and other words on the list on page 120. A dependent clause cannot stand alone—it must be combined with an independent clause in order to be complete.
2. When a dependent clause begins a sentence, it is followed by a comma. If the independent clause comes first, no comma is needed.
3. A complex sentence is one that contains a dependent clause.

ADVERB CLAUSES   Adverb clauses act as adverbs in a sentence—they modify verbs, adjectives, and adverbs. Like single-word adverbs, they can be recognized by the questions they answer. They tell *when, where, why, how,* or *under what conditions something happens.* They can also be recognized because they begin with subordinating conjunctions. In the following sentences the adverb clauses are italicized:

When I was a senior in high school, I broke my arm playing basketball. (The adverb clause tells *when.*)

Jack's dog follows him *wherever he goes.* (The adverb clause tells *where.*)

Because she could speak Spanish fluently, Edith was hired as an interpreter at the court-house. (The adverb clause tells *why.*)

She threw the shot put *as if it were a tennis ball.* (The adverb clause tells *how.*)

I would help you *if I could.* (The adverb clause tells *under what conditions.*)

Adverb clauses can usually be moved around in a sentence. In the first sentence above, for example, the adverb clause can be placed at the end of the sentence without affecting its basic meaning: I broke my arm playing basketball *when I was a senior in high school.* Notice that an adverb clause is followed by a comma when it comes at the beginning of a sentence; when it comes at the end of a sentence, it is not preceded by a comma.

Exercise 7-5

Underline all of the adverb clauses in the following sentences and supply any missing commas.

1. Although interest rates on credit cards are high many cardholders do not mind paying hundreds of dollars a year in interest.
2. Because credit cards are a profitable business for banks the competition for new customers is heating up.
3. More than ten million consumers applied for cards when AT&T introduced its Universal card.
4. Because more than six thousand financial institutions issue cards many issuers of cards are trying to stand out from the competition.
5. They offer such benefits as travel discounts, contributions to charities, and other features when cardholders use their cards to charge anything from meals to vacations.
6. Studies have shown that the use of charge cards stimulates spending because it is not necessary to have cash at hand.
7. Fast-food customers, for example, spend twice as much on average when they use a credit card.
8. Although most U.S. consumer spending is by cash and checks the use of plastic cards is increasing.
9. Though economists talk about the cashless society it will be a few years before such a phenomenon occurs.
10. If the card companies have their way the cashless society will come about sooner rather than later.

ADJECTIVE CLAUSES   Adjective clauses modify nouns and pronouns in a complex sentence. Like all clauses, they have subjects and verbs. But as dependent clauses, they must be attached to independent clauses to express complete ideas and to form grammatically complete sentences.

Most adjective clauses begin with the relative pronouns *which, whom, that, who,* and *whose,* but a few are introduced by *when, where, why,* and *how.* Adjective clauses usually follow immediately the noun or pronoun they modify. In the following sentences the adjective clauses are italicized:

Anne Frank's diary, *which she began in 1942,* was terminated by her capture and death in 1945. (The adjective clause modifies *diary.*)

Angela's father, *whom you met last night,* is from Baltimore. (The adjective clause modifies *father.*)

Many of the monuments *that have survived in ancient Egypt through thousands of years* were built at a terrible cost in human suffering and death. (The adjective clause modifies *monuments.*)

Any pitcher *who deliberately hits a batter* will be ejected. (The adjective clause modifies *pitcher.*)

Drivers *whose cars are left unattended* will receive citations. (The adjective clause modifies *Drivers.*)

Exercise 7-6

Underline the adjective clauses in the following sentences. In the space before each sentence, write the noun or pronoun modified by the clause.

_____ 1. An orange crate that served as a bookcase stood in one corner of the room.

_____ 2. The Nobel Prize for Peace is an award whose recipients have often been the subjects of controversy.

_____ 3. Jimmy Carter is an ex-President who has become more admired since leaving office.

_____ 4. A clause in the insurance policy which was not clearly stated was explained by the salesman.

_____ 5. A missionary from Ethiopia told the congregation about conditions that have caused starvation and poverty in that country.

_____ 6. Margaret Thatcher, who was the first woman Prime Minister of England, resigned at the insistence of her fellow politicians.

_____ 7. The driver whom I argued with turned out to be my girlfriend's father.

_____ 8. The baseball game that had been rained out was finally canceled.

_____ 9. The chemistry lab, which had inadequate ventilation, was closed by the health inspector.

_____ 10. Letters that do not have ZIP codes will be arriving after the deadline.

Punctuating Adjective Clauses Perhaps you noticed that the adjective clause in sentences 6 and 9 in Exercise 6 and those in the first two examples on page 123 (*which she began in 1942* and *whom you met last night*) were set off by commas. That is because they are *nonessential* (or *nonrestrictive*) adjective clauses. Nonessential clauses merely give additional information about the nouns or pronouns they modify. If we were to omit the adjective clauses in the two examples on page 123 cited above, they would still convey their central idea:

Anne Frank's diary, *which she began in 1942*, was terminated by her capture and death in 1945. (The adjective clause provides nonessential information.)

© 1997 Addison-Wesley Educational Publishers Inc.

Anne Frank's diary was terminated by her capture and death in 1945. (Although the adjective clause has been removed, we still can identify the subject.)

Angela's father, *whom you met last night,* is from Baltimore. (The fact that you met her father last night is nonessential.)

Angela's father is from Baltimore. (By identifying the subject as *Angela's father,* the writer is able to delete the nonessential clause without destroying the sentence.)

The punctuation rule for *nonessential* adjective clauses is easy: they should be set off by commas. Essential clauses—those needed to identify the subject—should not be set off by commas. In the first example on page 124, the omission of the adjective clause would be confusing:

Many of the monuments were built at a terrible cost in human suffering and death.

This is a complete sentence, but the adjective clause is essential because it tells the reader *which* monuments the writer is referring to. Therefore, it is needed to identify the subject and is not set off with commas:

Many of the monuments that have survived in ancient Egypt through thousands of years *were built at a terrible cost in human suffering and death.*

The punctuation rule for essential adjective clauses, therefore, is simple: they should *not* be set off by commas. Chapter 10 gives additional examples concerning the punctuation of essential and nonessential clauses.

REMINDERS FOR PUNCTUATING ADJECTIVE CLAUSES

1. If the adjective clause is essential to the meaning of the sentence, do *not* set it off with commas.
2. If the adjective clause is *not* essential to the meaning of the sentence, set it off with commas.

Exercise 7-7

Underline all adjective clauses in the following sentences and supply any missing commas.

1. Charles Dickens who wrote the novel *Bleak House* wrote a book about his experiences while traveling in the United States.

2. Oil paintings which are worthless during the painter's lifetime are sometimes valuable many years later.
3. People who have fair skin should protect themselves from excessive exposure to the sun.
4. The volcano that erupted in the Philippines did millions of dollars of damage.
5. Sunspots that can be observed only by astronomers can affect weather patterns throughout the earth.
6. Women who conduct major symphony orchestras are a rarity in the music world.
7. Leonard Bernstein who conducted the New York Philharmonic Orchestra was a composer and pianist as well.
8. The Chicago Cubs baseball fans who are long-suffering hope that this year will bring a championship to the Windy City.
9. An applicant whose parents graduated from a prestigious college has an advantage when applying for admission to that institution.
10. The poet T. S. Eliot who was born in St. Louis spent his adult life in England.
11. Anyone who hopes to be a chess grand master must spend hours of study and practice every day.
12. Robert Redford who is known by most people as an actor and a director is also an active environmentalist in Utah.
13. Television programs that are criticized by the critics are sometimes very popular with viewers.
14. Heart attack victims who embark on a vigorous exercise program should first consult with their physicians.
15. California which has a state income tax uses a tax form that is similar to the federal form.

NOUN CLAUSES   Noun clauses do the same things in sentences that single nouns do: they function as subjects, objects, or subject complements. Unlike adjective clauses and adverb clauses, noun clauses do not join independent clauses to form complete sentences. Instead, they replace one of the nouns in independent clauses. As a result, they function as subjects, objects, or subject complements of independent clauses. They are usually introduced by such words as *that, who, what, where, how,* and *why.*

As a subject:	*Why a particular material reacts with light in a particular way requires a complicated explanation.*
As a direct object:	*I have just finished a book that promises that the reader can improve his or her I.Q. by following its suggestions.*
As the object of a preposition:	*When selecting your courses, you should be guided by what your counselor recommends.*
As a subject complement:	*The sticker price of the car was more than I expected.*

Exercise 7-8

Underline the noun clauses in the following sentences.

1. Everyone was surprised to learn that the algebra test was canceled.
2. Whatever he does is overlooked by those who know him.
3. The senator stated that the problem of the homeless requires the cooperation of all segments of society.
4. Professor Neill mentioned that Mozart liked to play billiards.
5. I will always remember when I heard that President Kennedy had been assassinated.
6. My grandmother taught me how to make Irish soda bread.
7. Most people learn ethics by how others act, rather than by what they are told.
8. What Lincoln said that afternoon at Gettysburg will always be remembered.
9. I was surprised to learn that Reno is farther west than San Diego.
10. The crowd was pleased by what the speaker said.

Exercise 7-9

In the space before each sentence identify the italicized noun clause according to the way it is used in the sentence, using the following letters:

a. subject   *b. direct object*   *c. object of preposition*   *d. subject complement*

1. _____ Even the veteran detectives were shocked by *what they found.*
2. _____ Roy's cheerful smile was *what we missed most about him.*
3. _____ *How Donny can eat a quart of ice cream every night and not gain weight* amazes me.
4. _____ Because of his deafness, Beethoven could not hear *how many of his compositions sounded.*
5. _____ With his attorney's help, the defendant remembered *where he was on the night of the crime.*
6. _____ Sales of real estate in our city are affected by *what happens to interest rates.*
7. _____ *That I would not be selected for the squad* had not even occurred to me.
8. _____ By the look on his face we could tell *what had happened to Glenn.*
9. _____ Most chefs sample *what they are preparing* as they work in the kitchen.
10. _____ *How gender affects the workplace* was the topic of Ms. Wallace's speech.

Reviewing the Chapter: Writing Sentences

As you saw in this chapter, one of the marks of a good writer is the ability to use a variety of sentence types. This exercise asks you to try your hand at writing exact and interesting sentences.

1. Write a compound sentence in which the independent clauses are combined with a comma and a coordinating conjunction.
2. Write a compound sentence in which the independent clauses are combined with a semicolon.
3. Write two complex sentences each containing an independent and an adverb clause. Underline the adverb clause in each.
4. Write two complex sentences containing an independent and a noun clause in each. Underline the noun clause in each.
5. Write two complex sentences containing essential (restrictive) adjective clauses. Underline the adjective clause in each.
6. Write two complex sentences containing nonessential (nonrestrictive) adjective clauses. Underline the adjective clause in each, and be sure to punctuate them correctly.

7-A

REVIEW EXERCISE

A. *If the italicized group of words in each of the following sentences is an independent clause, write "a"; if it is a dependent clause, write "b"; if it is not a clause, write "c." Use the space provided on the left.*

_____ 1. In a unanimous decision expanding the "in plain view" doctrine, the Supreme Court decided *that no warrant is needed for the seizure of certain items.*

_____ 2. *Michael Jordan announced his retirement from basketball in 1993,* but he did not sever his relationship with athletics.

_____ 3. *Eggplant is a vegetable* that I have never been able to eat.

_____ 4. Janet Reno, *who became the first woman to serve as attorney general of the United States,* had previously served as a Florida state attorney.

_____ 5. Toni Morrison won the Novel Prize for literature, *the first African-American to do so.*

B. *Using the appropriate letter, identify the structure of the following sentences.*

a. simple sentence   b. compound sentence   c. complex sentence

_____ 6. No one knows for certain who designed the American flag.

_____ 7. In the worst accident in the history of the nuclear power industry, an explosion at the Chernobyl nuclear plant near Kiev spread radioactive material over much of Europe.

_____ 8. The National Invitational Tournament was first played in 1938, and it is the nation's oldest basketball tournament.

_____ 9. When the Census Bureau announced its results last year, our state lost two Congressional representatives.

_____ 10. I gave away the wrong pair of shoes to the charity drive.

C. *Each of the following sentences contains one or two blanks. If a comma should be inserted in one or both blanks, write "a" on the line in front of the sentence; if no commas should be inserted, write "b."*

_____   11.   New Jersey _____ which was the scene of nearly one hundred battles during the American Revolution _____ has over one hundred miles of beaches.

_____   12.   Several professional athletes _____ who left college early to play football _____ have returned in order to complete their degrees.

_____   13.   Although he has been in this country only four years _____ Tran speaks English fluently.

_____   14.   Most of the offenders admitted _____ that they knew that they were violating the law.

_____   15.   The workers _____ who had children _____ were able to purchase health insurance for their families.

_____   16.   Musicians _____ who attended the audition _____ were asked to bring their own music and instruments.

_____   17.   Keith sent me a birthday card _____ but I never received it.

_____   18.   William Shakespeare who was born in 1564 _____ died in 1616.

_____   19.   The pianist slammed down the lid of the piano _____ and stormed off the stage.

_____   20.   Pete quit his job at the restaurant _____ but soon regretted his decision.

_____   21.   The news _____ that the messenger brought _____ was not very encouraging.

_____   22.   When Brian heard the hisses and boos during the opening scene _____ he knew that his play was doomed to failure.

_____   23.   Anyone _____ who wants to be a chess champion _____should start practicing early in life.

_____   24.   I have been playing chess for several years _____ but I am not very good.

_____   25.   Art's compact disc collection _____ which consisted primarily of jazz _____ was destroyed in the fire.

Name _____   Date _____

7-B

REVIEW EXERCISE

A. *If the italicized group of words in each of the following sentences is an independent clause, write "a"; if it is a dependent clause, write "b"; if it is not a clause, write "c." Use the space provided on the left.*

_____ 1. Many Indian tribes in the United States *operate gambling casinos*, but some tribe members complain that their new-found prosperity is changing their ancient ways.

_____ 2. *Bob Hope relies on his writers*, but Jay Leno depends on his quick wit.

_____ 3. Cricket is a game *that I have never understood*.

_____ 4. Last week I received a telephone call from a friend *who has been living in Quebec for the past two years*.

_____ 5. *To everyone's surprise, including the owner's*, the horse came in first.

B. *Using the appropriate letter, identify the structure of the following sentences.*

a. *simple sentence*   b. *compound sentence*   c. *complex sentence*

_____ 6. Sheila carefully packed her camera and film, but she forgot them when leaving for the airport the next morning.

_____ 7. Ms. Francis claims that it is unwise to eat a heavy meal immediately before jogging.

_____ 8. Boasting of his ability to hit the ball out of the park, Tim strode to the plate and promptly struck out.

_____ 9. Mr. Wiggins watered the cabbage while Mrs. Wiggins slept.

_____ 10. Interviewed on television last night, the senator announced that he was not going to run for reelection.

C. *Each of the following sentences contains one or two blanks. If a comma should be inserted in one or both blanks, write "a" on the line in front of the sentence; if no commas should be inserted, write "b."*

_____ 11. Willa Cather _____ who was from Nebraska _____ wrote several novels about first-generation Americans.

131

_____   12. The mayor fired his press secretary _____ and refused to be interviewed by the television reporters.

_____   13. When Mark visited Italy last summer _____ he stayed with his sister in Milan.

_____   14. Your offer to help is appreciated _____ but I have solved the problem.

_____   15. I had studied hard and long _____ but failed the test.

_____   16. Earl angrily quit his job _____ but regretted his decision later.

_____   17. The news _____ that he brought to me _____ was very discouraging.

_____   18. Anyone _____ who really wants to lose weight _____ must exercise as well as eat properly.

_____   19. Although they angrily denied it _____ the boys had forgotten their father's birthday.

_____   20. The taxi driver claimed that he had not been drinking _____ but he could not pass the sobriety test.

_____   21. The old hotel was torn down _____ and replaced by a parking lot.

_____   22. A group of Scouts _____ who had bicycled across the state _____ discussed their trip at our meeting last night.

_____   23. Our class was given eight weeks in which to write our term papers _____ but several students were unable to complete it on time.

_____   24. We tend to forget that Babe Ruth _____ who is remembered for his hitting _____ was an excellent pitcher before he played the outfield.

_____   25. Because they were concerned about the increase in teenage alcoholism _____ the legislature raised the minimum age for drinking.

Chapter 8

Correcting Sentence Fragments, Run-on Sentences, and Comma-Splices

The purpose of writing is to communicate facts, ideas, and feelings in a clear and effective manner. If we make serious mistakes in sentence structure or grammar, our readers are confused and irritated, and communication fails. This chapter deals with ways to remedy three serious kinds of errors a writer can make: *sentence fragments*, *run-on sentences*, and *comma-splices*.

Sentence Fragments

A *sentence* is a group of words containing at least one independent clause. It has a subject and a verb, and it conveys a certain sense of completeness. A *sentence fragment*, on the other hand, is a group of words lacking an independent clause. Although it looks like a sentence because it begins with a capital letter and ends with a period or other end punctuation, it leaves the reader "hanging," waiting for more to follow.

Sentence fragments are common in conversation, particularly in responses to what someone else has said or as additions to something we have just said. Their meanings and missing parts are usually clear because of the context of the conversation and the speaker's gestures. In writing, however, it is best to avoid sentence fragments. Although professional writers occasionally use them for special effects, fragments usually suggest that the writer is careless and unable to formulate a complete thought.

One of the best ways to avoid sentence fragments is to read your written work *aloud*. Your voice will often detect an incomplete sentence. Another tip: Don't be fooled by the length of a so-called sentence. A long string of words without an independent clause is still a sentence fragment, despite its length. Here is an example of such a fragment:

The freeing of Nelson Mandela and other political prisoners, an end to news censorship, abolition of executions, and powersharing talks with black leaders, among other dramatic changes for South Africa.

At first glance this "sentence" is complete—after all, it begins with a capitalized word and concludes with a period. Despite its length, however, it is a sentence fragment because it does not contain an independent clause and therefore cannot convey a complete thought.

The following list contains the most common types of fragments that people write:

1. *Prepositional phrase fragments*
2. *Infinitive fragments*
3. *Participle fragments*
4. *Noun fragments*
5. *Dependent clause fragments*

By understanding each type of fragment, you can eliminate them from your writing. Now we will look at the various types of sentence fragments and the ways to correct them.

Phrases as Fragments

One of the most common kinds of sentence fragments is the *phrase*. (A *phrase*, you recall, is a group of words lacking a subject and a verb and acting as a single part of speech within a sentence.) *Prepositional phrases, infinitive phrases,* and *participle phrases* are often confused with complete sentences.

THE PREPOSITIONAL PHRASE AS A FRAGMENT   A prepositional phrase never contains a subject and a verb. Therefore, it can never stand alone as a sentence. The following sentences are followed by prepositional phrases masquerading as sentences:

(Fragment)   *Some of the world's fastest boats raced for the cherished America's Cup.* Off the coast of southern California.

(Fragment)   *Whitey Ford won a record ten World Series games.* During his career as a pitcher for the New York Yankees.

(Fragment)   *After delaying it several weeks, Jeff finally began his term paper.* On the subject of religious cults in America.

Because prepositional phrases are parts of sentences, the best way to correct this kind of fragment is to join it with the sentence to which it belongs. Notice how the fragments above are eliminated when they are joined to the preceding sentences:

(Sentence)	*Growing up in a large, poor family in the Appalachian Mountains, he realized that a college education would be an impossibility.*
(Sentence)	*Madame Tussaud's Wax Museum is a popular tourist attraction in London, featuring likenesses of historical personages reproduced in lifelike poses.*
(Sentence)	*Exercising every day, cutting down on calories, and avoiding ice cream and other desserts, I was able to lose twenty pounds last summer.*

Another way to correct fragments like these is to supply them with their missing subjects or verbs (or both):

(Sentence)	*He grew up in a large, poor family in the Appalachian Mountains, and he realized that a college education would be an impossibility.* (Supplying the missing subject and verb and combining the fragment with another sentence)
(Sentence)	*Madame Tussaud's Wax Museum is a popular tourist attraction in London. It features likenesses of historical personages reproduced in lifelike poses.* (Supplying the missing subject and verb and creating two separate sentences)
(Sentence)	*Because I exercised every day, cut down on calories, and avoided ice cream and other desserts, I was able to lose twenty pounds last summer.* (Changing the fragment into a dependent clause and changing the sentence into a complex sentence)

Exercise 8-1

Some of the following word groups contain sentence fragments. Underline the fragment, writing on the line the kind of fragment it is. Then correct the fragment by one of the methods explained above. If the group does not contain a fragment, write "C."

1. _____ Kite-flying has been a popular pastime. Throughout much of human history.
2. _____ Kites were invented in China about three thousand years ago.
3. _____ The earliest kites must have been very lightweight and elegant. Consisting of silk sails stretched across bamboo frames.
4. _____ Simple and convenient, kites were often used. To perform a variety of tasks.
5. _____ Measuring weather, delivering love notes, and carrying signals. Kites proved to be accurate, multi-purpose tools.
6. _____ In fact, one of the Wright brothers' earliest flights was conducted in a sort of motorized kite.
7. _____ Modern kite-builders are able to make kites that have a special ability. To fly in stunt formations or even hover.
8. _____ Instead of silk, most kites are now made of rip-stop nylon which was originally used. To make parachutes for American soldiers in World War II.

_____ 9.   It is called "rip-stop" because holes and tears will not spread. Throughout the fabric after the kite is accidentally punctured.

_____ 10. Coming in a variety of complex styles and costing as much as a hundred dollars or more. Kites aren't just child's play anymore.

Noun Fragments

Another type of fragment is a noun followed by a modifier with no main verb:

(Fragment)   *The planet Venus, known to have a rough surface scarred by volcanoes and quakes.*

(Fragment)   *A newly invented crib, comforting babies by imitating movements of the womb.*

(Fragment)   *The annual Candace Awards, given for leadership and achievement by the National Coalition of 100 Black Women.*

Most noun fragments can be corrected by supplying the missing verbs:

(Sentence)   *The planet Venus* is *known to have a rough surface scarred by volcanoes and quakes.*

(Sentence)   *A newly invented crib* comforts *babies by imitating movements of the womb.*

(Sentence)   *The annual Candace Awards* are *given for leadership and achievement by the National Coalition of 100 Black Women.*

Dependent Clauses as Fragments

Dependent clauses cannot stand alone as complex sentences. But because they contain subjects and verbs, they often end up as fragments. Dependent clauses can be spotted by the kinds of words that introduce them: subordinating conjunctions like *after, although, as, because,* and *if* or relative pronouns like *who, which,* and *that* (see page 120 for a list of words that introduce dependent clauses).

A dependent clause set off as a complete sentence can be corrected by combining it with the independent clause preceding or following it. Another method is to delete the subordinating conjunction or relative pronoun, thereby converting it to an independent clause.

(Fragment)   *The world's oldest living trees are the bristlecone pines.* Which grow in California.

(Revised)   *The world's oldest living trees are the bristlecone pines which grow in California.*

(Fragment)   *Slave importation was outlawed in 1808.* Although 250,000 more were imported illegally in the next fifty years.

(Revised)   *Slave importation was outlawed in 1808, although 250,000 more were imported illegally in the next fifty years.*

SOME TIPS FOR AVOIDING SENTENCE FRAGMENTS

1. Read your paper aloud. You will usually be able to hear whether or not you have written a fragment.
2. Be sure that every word group has a subject and a verb.
3. Look for the most common types of fragments:
   - Phrase fragments (prepositional phrases, *to* and *-ing* phrases)
   - Noun fragments (a noun followed by modifiers but without a verb)
   - Dependent-clause fragments

Exercise 8-2

Correct any sentence fragments in the following word groups, using any of the methods explained above. If the sentence is correct, write "C" in front of it.

1. Believe it or not, there is a set of rules about how to display the American flag. Which the War Department wrote in 1923.
2. Citizens may display their flags any time they want to. Although it is traditional to fly them only from sunrise to sunset.
3. The White House, unusual because its flag flies both day and night.
4. The awesome sight of the flag above Baltimore's Fort McHenry inspired Francis Scott Key to write "The Star Spangled Banner."
5. No other flag may be flown above or to the right of the U.S. flag. Except at the United Nations headquarters in New York City.
6. A rule that most Americans are familiar with, that the flag should never touch the ground or floor.
7. A flag may cover the casket of military personnel or other public officials. If it is not permitted to touch the ground or be lowered into the grave.
8. Disposal of a worn or damaged flag in a dignified way, preferably by burning.
9. The U.S. Supreme Court's recent decision to allow destruction of the flag as a means of political protest.
10. Politicians still debate whether American schoolchildren should be required to pledge their allegiance to the flag. Although reciting that oath is not mandatory now.

Run-on Sentences

A *run-on sentence* is just the opposite of a sentence fragment. It is a group of words that *looks* like one sentence but is actually two sentences run together without punctuation. Normally, of course, two or more independent clauses are separated by a coordinating conjunction or a semicolon. But if the conjunction or the semicolon is omitted, the result is a run-on sentence.

© 1997 Addison-Wesley Educational Publishers Inc.

Run-on sentences can be corrected in four ways:

1. *By inserting a comma and a conjunction* (and, but, for, or, yet, nor, so) *between the independent clauses.*

(Run-on)   *Years ago I took calculus I have forgotten practically all I once knew about the subject.*

(Revised)   *Years ago I took calculus, but I have forgotten practically all I once knew about the subject.*

2. *By changing one of the independent clauses into a dependent clause.*

(Run-on)   *In the first inning the Cubs were losing six to two three innings later they were winning twelve to eight.*

(Revised)   *Although the Cubs were losing six to two in the first inning, three innings later they were winning twelve to eight.*

3. *By inserting a semicolon between the two independent clauses.*

(Run-on)   *St. Augustine, Florida, is America's oldest city it was settled by Spain in 1565.*

(Revised)   *St. Augustine, Florida, is America's oldest city; it was settled by Spain in 1565.*

4. *By using a period or other end punctuation between the independent clauses, making them two separate sentences.*

(Run-on)   *The Gideon decision is one of the landmark cases of the U.S. Supreme Court it grants all poor defendants the right to counsel.*

(Revised)   *The Gideon decision is one of the landmark cases of the U.S. Supreme Court. It grants all poor defendants the right to counsel.*

SOME TIPS FOR AVOIDING RUN-ON SENTENCES

1. Read your paper aloud. Listen for a break marking the end of each thought.
2. Be sure that every independent clause is followed by a period or other end punctuation, a semicolon, or a comma and a coordinating conjunction.

Exercise 8-3

Using any of the methods explained above, correct any run-on sentences in the following word groups. If a sentence is correct, mark it "C."

1. Most people are concerned about how much they weigh some people are even obsessed with it.

2. Americans spend millions of dollars each year on dieting gimmicks the best method of weight control doesn't cost a penny.
3. Nearly anyone can lose weight and feel healthier by following two simple rules: eat right and exercise.
4. Reducing the fat in your diet is one key to losing weight some experts even say that watching fat is more important than watching calories.
5. Aerobic exercise is very effective for weight loss it raises your metabolism, which is the rate at which your body burns fat and calories.
6. Too much exercise may do more harm than good consult a fitness expert or physician before you start an exercise program.
7. Many people say they are too tired at the end of the day to exercise however, exercising can restore their energy and vigor.
8. Some dieters are so desperate to lose weight that they skip meals altogether this actually slows down their metabolism.
9. It is more sensible to eat three meals just make sure that they are balanced.
10. Although I have tried many types of diets and diet products, common sense works the best it's also much less expensive.

Comma-Splices

A common-splice consists of two independent clauses connected ("spliced") by only a comma instead of being joined with a comma *and* a coordinating conjunction or with a semicolon. A comma-splice is only slightly less irritating to a reader than the run-on sentence: the writer made some attempt (although mistakenly) to separate two independent clauses. Nevertheless, a comma-splice is a serious error in sentence construction because it is difficult to read. Furthermore, it suggests, like the fragment and run-on sentence, that the writer cannot formulate or recognize a single, complete thought.

Comma-splices can be corrected in the same ways as run-on sentences:

1. *By using a period or other end punctuation between the independent clauses, making them two sentences.*

(Comma-splice)   *For many years sociologists referred to the United States as a "melting pot," that term has been replaced by the term "pluralistic society."*

(Revised)   *For many years sociologists referred to the United States as a "melting pot." That term has been replaced by the term "pluralistic society."*

2. *By inserting a comma and a conjunction between the independent clauses.*

(Comma-splice)   *Dennis enrolled in a course in hip-hop dancing, now all of the women want to dance with him.*

© 1997 Addison-Wesley Educational Publishers Inc.

(Revised) *Dennis enrolled in a course in hip-hop dancing, and now all of the women want to dance with him.*

3. *By inserting a semicolon between the two independent clauses.*

(Comma-splice) *Sue told me I'd like the new Randy Travis album, she was right.*
(Revised) *Sue told me I'd like the new Randy Travis album; she was right.*

4. *By changing one of the independent clauses into a dependent clause.*

(Comma-splice) *Miguel studied classical music at a conservatory in New York, he plays drums in a rock group.*

(Revised) *Although Miguel studied classical music at a conservatory in New York, he plays drums in a rock group.*

SOME TIPS FOR AVOIDING COMMA-SPLICES

1. Do not use a comma alone to separate your sentences.
2. Read your sentence aloud. When you signal a new thought, use a period or other end punctuation, a semicolon, or a comma *and* a coordinating conjunction.

Exercise 8-4

Using any of the methods explained above, correct any comma-splices in the following word groups. If a sentence is correct, mark it "C."

1. California is earthquake country, the state has hundreds of faults that produce a thousand or more tremors annually.
2. Fortunately, half of them go unnoticed except by animals, birds, and the seismograph, and only thirty are capable of minor damage.
3. A major earthquake occurs about once every 100 years, like the one that devastated San Francisco without warning one spring morning in 1906, killing 600 people.
4. This earthquake was far more severe than the earthquake that jolted Los Angeles in 1993, in terms of property loss and death toll.
5. In minutes, buildings and homes were piles of rubble, then fires broke out turning San Francisco into a flaming funeral pyre.
6. Half-awake citizens stumbled into the buckling streets to be bombarded by chunks of concrete and brick.
7. Broken gas lines and water pipes jutted into the air and sewer pipes erupted, adding an awful stench to the destruction, everywhere fire was consuming the fallen city.

8. Thousands tried to sleep in the parks, others, too tired to run anymore, lay down in the path of the fire to sleep soundly.
9. In twenty-four hours, San Francisco was rubble and ashes, 300,000 homeless people wore a mask of blank despair.
10. From the ashes of destruction, a new San Francisco rose to even greater heights.

Comma-Splices and Conjunctive Adverbs

Some comma-splices are the result of the writer's confusing a *conjunctive adverb* with a co-ordinating conjunction. A conjunctive adverb is a kind of connecting word that looks like a conjunction but is actually an adverb. Conjunctive adverbs are words like the following:

accordingly, also, besides, consequently, furthermore, hence, however, moreover, nevertheless, nonetheless, otherwise, therefore

When one of these words appears *within* an independent clause, it is usually set off by commas:

(Correct)	*It was obvious from her face,* however, *that she was disappointed.*
(Correct)	*I believe,* nevertheless, *that Vince will continue to play.*
(Correct)	*Iran and Iraq,* moreover, *also plan to sign the treaty.*

When a conjunctive adverb appears *between* main clauses, it must be preceded by a semicolon (and often followed by a comma) or a period. If the semicolon or period is omitted, the result is a comma-splice:

(Comma-splice)	*Hershey is famous for its chocolate,* however, *the company also makes pasta.*
(Correct)	*Hershey is famous for its chocolate;* however, *the company also makes pasta.*
(Correct)	*Hershey is famous for its chocolate.* However, *the company also makes pasta.*
(Comma-splice)	*The Internal Revenue Service has been forced to lay off thousands of its employees,* consequently, *it has audited fewer income-tax returns in recent years.*
(Correct)	*The Internal Revenue Service has been forced to lay off thousands of its employees;* consequently, *it has audited fewer income-tax returns in recent years.*
(Correct)	*The Internal Revenue Service has been forced to lay off thousands of its employees.* Consequently, *it has audited fewer income-tax returns in recent years.*

Remember: Conjunctive adverbs are not conjunctions and can never be used by themselves to link clauses or sentences.

Exercise 8-5

Correct any comma-splices in the following groups of words. Use any of the methods presented above. If a sentence is correct, mark it "C."

1. The easiest way to become an American citizen is to have been born here, however, natives of other countries may become citizens through the process of naturalization.
2. To begin this process, aliens must first obtain application forms from a local office of the Immigration and Naturalization Service, or from the clerk of a court which handles naturalization cases.
3. There are several requirements for those who seek citizenship, nevertheless, it is not altogether impossible.
4. Applicants must be at least eighteen years old, moreover, they must be able to prove at least five years of lawful residence in the United States.
5. For spouses of U.S. citizens, on the other hand, the required residence period is usually only three years.
6. Applicants must also show an understanding of the English language, therefore, many aspiring citizens take night classes in English.
7. Knowledge of America's history and government is also required, in fact, the applicants will take a test on these subjects.
8. A fee must be paid by the applicants when they turn in their citizenship application, consequently, they receive an appointment for a hearing.
9. Applicants may bring attorneys with them to the hearing, however, it is optional.
10. There is a thirty-day waiting period after the hearing, eventually the court may approve the applicant's application and finally administer the official oath of citizenship.

Reviewing the Chapter: Writing Sentences

This writing exercise requires that you can recognize and correct three of the most serious kinds of errors a writer can make: sentence fragments, run-on sentences, and comma-splices.

1. Write a prepositional phrase fragment. Next, correct it by using one of the methods recommended in this chapter.
2. Write an infinitive fragment. Next, correct it by following the suggestions in this chapter.
3. Write a participle fragment. Next, correct it by one of the methods explained in this chapter.

4. Write a dependent clause fragment. Next, correct it by following one of the suggestions in this chapter.
5. Write a run-on sentence. Correct it by inserting a comma and a conjunction between the independent clauses.
6. Write a run-on sentence. Correct it by changing one of the independent clauses into a dependent clause.
7. Write a run-on sentence. Correct it by inserting a semicolon between the two independent clauses.
8. Write a comma-splice. Correct it by using a period or other end punctuation between the independent clauses, making them two sentences.
9. Write a comma-splice. Correct it by inserting a comma and a conjunction between the independent clauses.
10. Write a comma-splice. Correct it by changing one of the independent clauses into a dependent clause.

8-A

REVIEW EXERCISE

In the space before each sentence, write the letter corresponding to the kind of error each sentence contains. If a sentence is correct, write "d" in front of the sentence.

a. sentence fragment   b. run-on sentence   c. comma-splice   d. correct

_____ 1. Steven King's latest book was published last month to no one's surprise it is already on the best-seller list.

_____ 2. You may take as much time as you need to reach a decision, however, there are advantages to acting immediately.

_____ 3. My wife has read the novel she did not like the movie.

_____ 4. Either our expenses will have to be reduced, or I'll have to get a weekend job.

_____ 5. The committee, after hearing arguments on the proposed tax increase and unable to reach a decision.

_____ 6. Employees are eligible for early retirement at age fifty, however, most workers choose to continue working.

_____ 7. I asked for seven copies of the report to my surprise I received seventy copies.

_____ 8. Most high schools in our state offer courses in computer sciences, and several offer three years of Russian.

_____ 9. Colorado Springs was founded in 1859, it is at the foot of Pikes Peak.

_____ 10. Important facts about the condition or plans of a corporation that have not been released to the general public.

_____ 11. Esperanto is an artificial language invented in 1887 by a Polish physician.

_____ 12. The Coast Guard shield, which is worn on both sleeves of officers and on the right sleeve of all enlisted personnel.

_____ 13. Astronomers recognize eighty-eight constellations that cover the entire celestial sphere many of their names have their origins in medieval days.

_____ 14. Arnie complained that the newspaper carrier often failed to deliver his paper, occasionally it was thrown onto the porch roof.

_____ 15. Golf tournaments were the only sports entertainment available on television last weekend, my father complained.

_____ 16. Julie was advised by her doctor to limit her salt intake to 2000 milligrams a day, this means that she had to give up eating entire bags of potato chips.

_____ 17. The referee constantly warning both boxers about low blows and head butts.

_____ 18. Margaret received her pilot's license when she was twenty-four, however, she has never flown as a passenger in a commercial airliner.

_____ 19. Many grocery stores that offer discount coupons and special promotions in order to boost their sales.

_____ 20. Our pastor said that he had enrolled in college as a biology major before transferring to a seminary.

_____ 21. In certain cultures and countries to be left-handed is to suffer discrimination and prejudice.

_____ 22. The popularity of self-help books in our society was discussed by the panel, however, they were unable to agree on the value of the books.

_____ 23. Scoliosis, a disease occurring more often among women than among men, according to my physician.

_____ 24. The city of New York is divided into five boroughs, each with its own identity and personality.

_____ 25. Cruise ships, popular with passengers who do not want to fly or drive to far-off destinations.

8-B

REVIEW EXERCISE

In the space before each sentence, write the letter corresponding to the kind of error each sentence contains. If a sentence is correct, write "d" in front of the sentence.

a. sentence fragment   b. run-on sentence   c. comma-splice   d. correct

_____ 1. Nell was happy; she had just received a promotion.

_____ 2. Years ago, everyone read or studied by candlelight no one had electricity.

_____ 3. The linebacker tackled the quarterback, the ball dropped from the quarterback's grasp.

_____ 4. After locking her doors, Lois realized that she had left her keys in the ignition.

_____ 5. Sylvia had never studied a foreign language; nevertheless, she became fluent in Spanish after living in Guadalajara only six months.

_____ 6. Donny loves to dance to any kind of music, however, he is shy and waits until others are on the dance floor before he ventures out.

_____ 7. Many shops along the United States–Mexico border accept pesos as well as dollars, because the exchange rate varies, prices in pesos may change from day to day.

_____ 8. Jules attempted to drill a hole into a metal door frame, after investigating he found that he was using a drill bit designed for wood.

_____ 9. A recent study revealed that many air traffic controllers often suffer from hypertension and ulcers, according to some experts these ailments result from their working conditions.

_____ 10. Identifying features such as freckles, tattoos, and moles which are used by police to identify suspects.

_____ 11. A loud, continuous wail of the siren, interrupting the calm Sunday afternoon and bringing many occupants of the neighborhood into the street.

_____ 12. Carol, remembering while standing in the checkout line at the grocery store that she had forgotten her purse and not having any money or credit cards in her wallet.

_____ 13. Grace's physician recommended that she exercise on a regular basis in an effort to reduce her blood pressure she was also given a diet to follow.

_____ 14. In graphics class we learned the meanings of many technical terms our instructor took us on tours of printing houses and a newspaper plant.

_____ 15. The police officer yelling at the crowd to stand behind the ropes and allow the fire fighters room to bring in their equipment.

_____ 16. Summer television seems to consist solely of reruns it is almost enough to make me look forward to the opening of school.

_____ 17. Burl shaved off his beard after having worn it for six years he was surprised to discover that he had developed a double chin.

_____ 18. Julie visited Phoenix last summer to meet a pen pal she had been writing to since the sixth grade.

_____ 19. Mac attended the state university for two years, later, after working and saving his money, he returned and eventually earned his degree.

_____ 20. The birth of the quadruplets created a sensation, everyone wanted to see them.

_____ 21. A black Labrador dog, straining at the end of its leash and barking at passersby.

_____ 22. Bob's parents sued the doctor and the staff of the hospital. Because they believed that he was given incorrect treatment.

_____ 23. Diabetics should not eat certain foods they should follow the diet given them by their doctors.

_____ 24. Professional football began in the early decades of this century, today it is a highly successful sport followed by millions of fans.

_____ 25. Hilda complained that the newspaper contained nothing but stories of violence, stories featuring good news are hidden in the back of the paper.

Chapter 9

Confused Sentences

To write sentences that are not confusing, we have to make certain that they are grammatically correct. This means, for example, that their subjects and verbs agree and that their pronouns and antecedents are linked without confusion. But clarity and correctness depend on other considerations as well. In this chapter we will look at some of the other ways to avoid illogical, inexact, or confused sentences.

Misplaced and Dangling Modifiers

Modifiers are words that describe other words in sentences. They may be single words, phrases, or clauses; they may come before the word they modify, or they may follow it. In either case, a modifier should appear near the word it modifies, and the reader should not be confused about which word it modifies.

A *misplaced modifier* is one that is not close to the word it modifies, and as a result it modifies the wrong word. Sentences with misplaced modifiers are usually confusing and often humorous because of the unintended meaning. But by placing the modifier next to the word it modifies or by rewording the sentence, we can make the meaning of such sentences clear.

Notice the unintended meanings in the following sentences; in each sentence, the modifier has been misplaced.

Yoko Ono will talk about her husband John Lennon who was killed in an interview with Barbara Walters.

Two cars were reported stolen by the Midvale police yesterday.

For sale: Mixing bowl set designed to please a cook with round bottom for efficient beating.

An event that appears every seventy-six years, Professor Silver showed us slides of Halley's Comet.

You probably had little difficulty in trying to unscramble the intended meaning in these sentences. As we will see in this chapter, however, not all sentences can be revised as easily.

Exercise 9-1

Rewrite any of the following sentences that contain misplaced modifiers. If a sentence is correct, write "C" in front of it.

 1. Morris ate a hamburger at a restaurant that was full of grease and fat.
2. My neighbors argued while I tried to study in a loud voice.
3. Laura read a novel written by Danielle Steele while she waited for her appointment with the dentist.
4. The tourists waited for the bus in front of the hotel that was to take them to the airport.
5. Ms. Mather discussed the high cost of living with her neighbor.
6. The pizza was placed in the refrigerator that was not eaten.
7. Marlene served strawberries to her guests covered in whipped cream.
8. Ralph bought a motorcycle for his wife with five speeds.
9. Most colleges in the United States report an increase in the enrollment of minority students.
10. Last night I heard about the earthquake on television.

A variation of the misplaced modifier is the *squinting modifier,* a modifier that usually appears in the middle of a sentence so that it can modify either the word that precedes it or the one that follows it. As a result, the squinting modifier makes the sentence ambiguous. The following sentences contain squinting modifiers:

Applicants who can already dance normally are placed in an advanced class. (Who are placed in the advanced class? Applicants who dance normally? More probably, they are normally placed in an advanced class.)

Senator Warner decided during the Christmas holiday to announce her opposition to the bill. (While she was on her Christmas holiday, did Senator Warner decide to announce her opposition to the bill? Or did she decide to announce her opposition as soon as the holiday began?)

As you can see, sentences with squinting modifiers have two possible meanings. Therefore they can be revised in two ways, depending on the meaning:

Applicants who can dance are normally placed in an advanced class.

Applicants who dance normally are usually placed in an advanced class.

During the Christmas holiday Senator Warner decided that she would announce her opposition to the bill.

Senator Warner decided that during the Christmas holiday she would announce her opposition to the bill.

Exercise 9-2

Rewrite any of the following sentences that contain squinting modifiers. If a sentence is correct, write "C" in front of it.

1. Those who gamble secretly take chances with their finances.
2. Hugh's story about his vacation in Hawaii that he told slowly put us to sleep.
3. Anyone who sings occasionally hits a wrong note.
4. The tax lawyer advised his clients early in the year to establish a trust fund.
5. Donna reminded her husband regularly to get a physical examination.
6. Gail's brother promised every week to call her.
7. As he approached the cashier, Sam realized he had forgotten his wallet.
8. The nurse who was assisting quietly removed the sponge from the open wound.
9. The building that had been painted last week burned down.
10. During the intermission the master of ceremonies announced a change in the cast.

A *dangling modifier* is a modifier that has no word in the sentence for it to modify. It is left "dangling," and as a result it ends up accidentally modifying an unintended word, as in the following example:

After reviewing my lecture notes and rereading the summaries of each chapter, the final examination was easier than I had thought.

According to this sentence, the final examination reviewed the lecture notes and reread the summaries of each chapter. But this is obviously not the meaning intended. To correct this sentence, we must first determine *who* was doing the action. By supplying the missing subject, we can then improve the sentence:

After reviewing my lecture notes and rereading the summaries of each chapter, I found that the final examination was easier than I had thought.

or: *After I reviewed my lecture notes and reread the summaries of each chapter, the final examination was easier than I had thought.*

Here are some more sentences with dangling modifiers:

Sound asleep, the alarm clock was not heard by Fred.
Arriving home after midnight, the house was dark.
Frightened by the noise, the barks of the dog woke us up.

By supplying subjects and rewording these sentences, we can make their meanings clear:

Sound asleep, Fred did not hear the alarm clock.
When we arrived home after midnight, the house was dark.
Frightened by the noise, the dog woke us up by its barking.

TIPS FOR CORRECTING MISPLACED AND DANGLING MODIFIERS

1. Place every modifier close to the word it modifies.
2. If the word meant to be modified is not in the sentence, insert it close to its modifier.
3. Reword or punctuate the sentence so that the intended meaning is clear.

Exercise 9-3

Rewrite any of the following sentences that contain dangling modifiers. If a sentence is correct, write "C" in front of it.

1. Unable to get the book accepted by a publisher, paying a local printer seemed a good idea.
2. After removing what seemed to be tons of trash, the room was finally neat and tidy.
3. As a young boy my mother told me stories of her childhood in Mexico.
4. Careening from side to side, the skier picked up speed as she reached the finish line.
5. Stirring the sour constantly, the aroma filled the room.
6. To avoid cavities, flossing daily is recommended.
7. Planning for months and reading about the countries to be visited, Helen's vacation was unforgettable.
8. Having painted over the graffiti, the wall regained its former beauty.
9. Standing on the bridge, the water flowed rapidly in its journey south.
10. If ordered before July 1, a 10 percent discount will be credited to your account.

Illogical Comparisons

A comparison is a statement about the relation between two or more things:

Wal-Mart is larger than any other retailer in the United States.
My father's 1982 Chevrolet runs as well as my new Honda.
Carl Lewis won more gold medals at the 1984 Olympics than any other athlete.

When making a comparison, be certain that the things being compared are similar and that your comparison is complete. Omitted words often make the comparison unclear, illogical, or awkward.

(Unclear)   *Tulsa is closer to Oklahoma City than Dallas.*

This sentence is not clear because the comparison is not stated fully enough. Be sure that the comparisons are full enough to be clear.

(Revised)   *Tulsa is closer to Oklahoma City than* it is to *Dallas.*

(Illogical)   *The population of Mexico City is growing at a faster rate than that of any major city in the world.*

This sentence is illogical because it compares its subject with itself. When comparing members of the same class, use *other* or *any other.*

(Revised)   *The population of Mexico City is growing at a faster rate than that of any* other *major city in the world.*

(Unclear)   *The average hourly wage for a woman is lower than a man.*

This sentence is unclear because it compares an hourly wage with a man. Be sure that items being compared are comparable.

(Revised)   *The average hourly wage for a woman is lower than a* man's.

Exercise 9-4

Revise any of the following sentences that contain illogical comparisons. If a sentence is correct, write "C" in front of the number.

1. Detroit reported that this year's total sales are lower than last year.
2. According to the Census Bureau, Americans seventy and older are increasing more than any age group in the country.
3. Prices at the Blue Shoe restaurant are cheaper than the Albatross.

4. Seismologists say that southern California is more likely to experience an earthquake than us.
5. Although she had never previously studied French, her grades were better than anyone in the class.
6. Magic Johnson had more assists than any basketball player in the NBA when he retired.
7. The average woman has more body fat than a man.
8. Cats are more difficult to train than any other animal.
9. Her allergist told Lois that ragweed caused reactions more powerful than other pollen.
10. Stephen King's novels are more frightening than Kingsley Amis.

Confusing Adjectives and Adverbs

Adjectives and adverbs are modifiers; they limit or describe other words.

Adjective: Moderate *exercise suppresses the appetite.*
Adverb: *The surgeon* carefully *examined the sutures.*

Many adverbs end in *-ly (hurriedly, graciously, angrily)*; some of the most common, however, do not *(here, there, now, when, then, often)*. Furthermore, some words that end in *-ly* are not adverbs *(silly, manly, hilly)*.

Using Adjectives after Linking Verbs

You will recall from Chapter 1 that the most common linking verbs are *be, appear, become, grow, remain, seem,* and the "sense" verbs *(feel, look, smell, sound,* and *taste)*. Words that follow such verbs and refer to the subject are *adjectives*—never adverbs. In the following sentences, the adjective (called a *predicate adjective* because it follows the verb and modifies the subject) comes after a linking verb:

Pat's ideas are exciting. (Exciting *modifies* ideas.)
Their wedding reception was expensive. (Expensive *modifies* wedding reception.)
That detergent makes my hands feel rough. (Rough *modifies* hands.)

The rule for deciding whether to use an adjective or an adverb after a verb, therefore, is simple: if the verb shows a condition or a state of being, use an adjective after it. Here are some additional examples that illustrate the rule:

The hamburger smells tantalizing.
Mike's girlfriend appeared nervous.

The math final seemed easy.

Marvin looked handsome *in his new suit.*

Most of us would not write or say, "This soup is warmly," or "She is beautifully." In both cases we would instinctively use an adjective rather than an adverb. The choice is not so obvious with "bad" and "well," however. Study carefully the use of these words in the sentences below.

(Incorrect):	*He had some of my homemade soup and now he feels* badly. (Badly *is an adverb following a linking verb; it cannot modify the pronoun* He.)
(Correct):	*He had some of my homemade soup and now he feels* bad. (Bad *is an adjective modifying* He.)
(Incorrect):	*I feel* badly *about that.* (As in the first example above, badly *is an adverb and therefore cannot modify the pronoun* I.)
(Correct):	*I feel* bad *about that.* (Bad *is an adjective modifying* I.)
(Incorrect):	*That hat looks very* well *on you.* (Looks *is a linking verb, and therefore we need an adjective after the verb to modify the noun* hat. Well *is an adverb except when it means "to be in good health.")*
(Correct):	*That hat looks very* good *on you.* (Good *is an adjective modifying the noun* hat.)
(Correct):	*Although she has been sick, she looks* well *now.* (Well, *as noted above, is an adjective when it means "to be in good health." In this sentence it follows the linking verb* looks *and modifies* she.)

Using Adverbs to Modify Verbs

When a verb expresses an *action* by the subject, use an *adverb* after it—not an adjective. Study the following sentences:

(Incorrect):	*Because Jack was unfamiliar with the city, he drove* careful.
(Correct):	*Because Jack was unfamiliar with the city, he drove* carefully.
(Incorrect):	*Lorraine spoke very* quiet *of her many accomplishments.*
(Correct):	*Lorraine spoke very* quietly *of her many accomplishments.*
(Incorrect):	*Sharon picked up the expensive glass* delicate.
(Correct):	*Sharon picked up the expensive glass* delicately.

Verbs that sometimes show condition or state of being in one sentence but an action by the subject in another sentence can be troublesome:

The dog smelled the meat carefully. (Smelled *is an* action *verb.*)

The meat smelled rotten. (Smelled *is a* linking *verb.*)

The alarm sounded suddenly. (Sounded is an action verb.)

His cries sounded pitiful. (Sounded is a linking verb.)

Claire appeared tired. (Appeared is a linking verb.)

Claire appeared abruptly. (Appeared is an action verb.)

TIPS FOR CHOOSING ADVERBS OR ADJECTIVES

The choice of an adverb or an adjective depends on the kind of verb in the sentence:

1. If the verb is *linking* and you want to describe the subject, an *adjective* is correct.
2. If you want to modify a verb that shows *action,* an *adverb* is correct.

Exercise 9-5

Write the letter of the correct word on the line preceding the sentence.

_____   1.   Frank felt (a. bad   b. badly) about smashing up his girlfriend's new car.

_____   2.   Frank was (a. bad   b. badly) hurt in the accident.

_____   3.   Despite her inexperience, Melissa played the cymbals (a. loud   b. loudly) and confidently in the concert.

_____   4.   Although the sauce tasted (a. delicious   b. deliciously), it contained excessive calories and grams of fat.

_____   5.   The economy of Hungary is doing (a. good   b. well), despite the years of Soviet repression.

_____   6.   The music and costumes matched the play (a. perfect   b. perfectly).

_____   7.   Jeff tied his tie too (a. tight   b. tightly) and became uncomfortable during the concert.

_____   8.   I thought I could pass the driving test (a. easy   b. easily), but I was surprised.

_____   9.   Horace claimed that he was not treated (a. fair   b. fairly) by his supervisor.

_____   10.   The herd of cows moved (a. slow   b. slowly) across the meadow.

Parallel Structure

When writing about items in a series, be sure that you present each item in the same grammatical form. In other words, each item should be an adjective or a prepositional phrase or an infinitive, and so on. When all items in a series are in the same grammatical form, the sentence or passage is said to have *parallel structure*.

© 1997 Addison-Wesley Educational Publishers Inc.

Notice the use of parallel structure in the following sentences:

Mike approached *the plate*, tugged *at his belt*, adjusted *his grip*, *then* swung *the bat*. (*parallel verbs*)

Tanya sang softly, confidently, *and* seductively. (*parallel adverbs*)

To lose weight, to study conscientiously, *and* to spend less time on the telephone—*these were Ken's New Year's resolutions*. (*parallel infinitive phrases*)

Paul quit smoking because it was an expensive habit, because his wife had quit, *and* because his doctor had urged him. (*parallel dependent clauses*)

Parallel structure is a writing technique worth acquiring because it makes sentences smoother and shows the connection between ideas. For these reasons, professional writers and public speakers often make use of parallel structure. It helps to "bind up" a sentence, making its parts and meaning much easier to grasp.

Study carefully the following excerpt from Abraham Lincoln's second inaugural address. It has been arranged so that the parallelism can easily be seen.

> *With malice toward none,*
> *with charity for all,*
> *with firmness in the right, as God gives us to see the right,*
> *let us strive on*
> > *to finish the work we are in;*
> > *to bind up the nation's wounds,*
> > *to care for him who shall have borne the battle,*
> > > *and for his widow and his orphan,*
> > *to do all which may achieve and cherish*
> > > *a just and lasting peace*
> > > > *among ourselves,*
> > > > > *and*
> > > > *with all nations.*

Contrast the rhythm and clarity of the following pairs of sentences:

(Faulty)   *The President claimed that he wanted* to clean up *the environment*, improve *the public schools*, and reducing *crime in the streets*. (*infinitive, infinitive, and participle*)

(Parallel)   *The President claimed that he wanted* to clean up *the environment*, improve *the public schools*, and reduce *crime in the streets*. (*three infinitives*)

(Faulty)   *Our new fax machine is* efficient, inexpensive, *and it is easily operated*. (*two adjectives and a clause*)

(Parallel)	*Our new fax machine is efficient, inexpensive,* and *easily operated.* (*three adjectives*)
✳ (Faulty)	*Her baby has already started* walking and *to talk.* (*participle and infinitive*)
(Parallel)	*Her baby has already started* walking and *talking.* (*two participles*)

Correlative Conjunctions

You can also achieve effective parallel construction by using *correlative conjunctions.* As mentioned in Chapter 1, correlatives are connectives used in pairs, and therefore they are handy tools for linking similar grammatical patterns with ideas of similar importance. The most common correlatives are *either/or, neither/nor, not only/but also,* and *both/and.*

Here are some examples of correlative conjunctions used to achieve parallel structure:

Sheila is proficient not only *on the clarinet* but also *on the saxophone.*

Neither *the musicians* nor *the producers could have predicted the success of rock music on television.*

The President's remarks were addressed both *to Congress* and *to the American people.*

When using correlative conjunctions, be sure to place them as closely as possible to the words they join.

(Incorrect)	*She* neither *wanted our advice* nor *our help.*
(Correct)	*She wanted* neither *our advice* nor *our help.*
(Incorrect)	*Ellen will be flying* both *to Minneapolis* and *Chicago.*
(Correct)	*Ellen will be flying to* both *Minneapolis* and *Chicago.*
(Incorrect)	*Richard would* neither *apologize* nor *would he admit that he was wrong.*
(Correct)	*Richard would* neither *apologize* nor *admit that he was wrong.*

Exercise 9-6

Rewrite any of the following sentences that contain faulty parallelism. If the sentence is correct, write "C" before the number.

1. Rob's goals in life were to wear the latest clothes, drive an expensive car, and also he wanted to have a lot of money.
2. Today's buyer wants a car that is safer to drive, cheaper to maintain, and uses less gas.
3. Many people watch soap operas because they offer bizarre characters, unexpected twists in the plot, and memorable scenes.
4. Like most commencement speakers, he said that the seniors faced a future that would be both a challenge and inspiring.

5. Angelica Huston is admired as an actress because she is not only a dramatic actress but also she is good in comedy roles.
6. The ambassador from Iraq would neither apologize nor would he promise to accept the demands of the United Nations.
7. She was not only his wife but also he considered her his friend.
8. Eleanor Roosevelt was admired for her social conscience and because she visited soldiers in battlefront hospitals.
9. Winston Churchill said that victory would require blood and sweat and toil and tears.
10. Professor Adams is brilliant, patient, organized, and she is helpful as well.

Reviewing the Chapter: Writing Sentences

Illogical, inexact, or confused sentences not only irritate our reader: they also fail to make our meaning clear. This writing exercise will help you avoid such sentences.

1. Write two sentences, each containing a misplaced or dangling modifier. Using the suggestions in this chapter, revise each sentence.
2. Write two sentences, each containing an illogical comparison. Using the suggestions in this chapter, revise each sentence.
3. Write two sentences, each illustrating the correct use of adjectives after linking verbs.
4. Write two sentences, each illustrating the correct use of adverbs modifying verbs.
5. Write two sentences, each using faulty parallel structure. Using the suggestions in this chapter, revise each sentence so that it has parallel structure.

9-A

REVIEW EXERCISE

A. *Write the letter of the correct word in the space provided.*

_____ 1. After a few golf lessons Bob could hit the ball (a. real   b. really) far.

_____ 2. Consuela felt (a. bad   b. badly) because she thought she was responsible for her team's loss.

_____ 3. If Congress takes the committee's views (a. serious   b. seriously), the law will be revised.

_____ 4. As the limousine turned the corner slowly, the police tried very (a. desperate   b. desperately) to keep back the crowd.

_____ 5. Because Rodney was not wearing his eyeglasses, he read the article (a. slow   b. slowly).

B. *In the space before each sentence, write the letter corresponding to the kind of error each sentence contains.*

a. *misplaced or dangling modifier*   b. *illogical or incomplete comparison*
c. *adjective or adverb used incorrectly*   d. *faulty parallel structure*

_____ 6. The governor said that his hobbies were fly-fishing and to work on old cars.

_____ 7. Having been to Chicago three times, the city is still full of surprises and unexpected pleasures.

_____ 8. To make certain that illegal substances were not applied, the umpires examined all of the baseballs real careful.

_____ 9. The cost of a word processor is more than an electric typewriter.

_____ 10. Having forgotten to water the flowers, my petunias died.

_____ 11. She appeared real embarrassed when she could not recognize the melody.

_____ 12. The police came quick when the shooting began.

_____ 13. To be eligible for early registration, the enrollment forms must be received by September 1.

_____ 14. Despite her small size, Tina can swim faster than any girl in her class.

_____ 15. Featuring antilock brakes and an airbag, the salesman said that the new automobile was the safest car on the road.

161

_____ 16. Melba was advised to follow a diet of reduced fat, low sodium, and she was encouraged to exercise daily.

_____ 17. Although he was shy as a young boy, Rick can now sing and perform in public real confident.

_____ 18. In order to avoid bee stings, a long coat or jacket is advised.

_____ 19. Winston Churchill was admired for his leadership qualities, his personal courage, and he was an eloquent speaker.

_____ 20. Snorting and pawing at the ground, the crowd anxiously cheered for the bull.

_____ 21. Mr. Colman had to walk somewhat slow because of his injured leg.

_____ 22. Having never read any science fiction, Isaac Asimov's name was unfamiliar to me.

_____ 23. Many dry cleaners charge more for cleaning women's jackets than men.

_____ 24. Mr. Liebowitz complained that his name was often spelled incorrect.

_____ 25. Because of its emphasis on the environment, Professor Markley's speech was received very favorable by the students.

9-B

REVIEW EXERCISE

A. Write the letter of the correct word in the space provided.

_____ 1. Nanette looked (a. sad   b. sadly) at the departing train.

_____ 2. Because the refrigerator was disconnected, the meat smelled (a. bad b. badly).

_____ 3. Last Friday night we saw a (a. real   b. really) exciting movie about World War II.

_____ 4. Despite her inexperience, Helen did quite (a. good   b. well) in the semifinals.

_____ 5. Because I did not have time to reread my essay, I didn't notice that two words in its title were spelled (a. incorrect   b. incorrectly).

B. In the space before each sentence, write the letter corresponding to the kind of error each sentence contains.

a. misplaced or dangling modifier   b. illogical or incomplete comparison
c. adjective or adverb used incorrectly   d. faulty parallel structure

_____ 6. The governor was tall, slender, and seemed to be middle-aged.

_____ 7. Barking at passing cars and inspecting the shrubbery of the neighborhood, we found the dog that had escaped from its kennel.

_____ 8. Selling shoes during the summer and waiting on tables during the school year, my tuition was paid without the help of my parents.

_____ 9. Mr. Conley claimed that students of his generation worked harder than the schools today.

_____ 10. Having missed the assignment, my term paper received a low grade.

_____ 11. The supermarket manager felt happily about the sales campaign.

_____ 12. Ernie has a good sense of humor and can tell a joke really good.

_____ 13. In my opinion, staying up all night to review before an examination is more of a handicap than useful.

_____ 14. The advertisements for the computer claimed that it is real easy to operate.

_____ 15. Trying to think of a way to begin my speech, a funny story came to mind.

_____ 16. To her surprise, Roberta made higher grades in chemistry class than her brother.

_____ 17. Life in Las Vegas is not much different from any city its size.

_____ 18. Prices at a military commissary are usually lower than other retail establishments.

_____ 19. Many people join health clubs for exercise, for relaxation, and so that they can meet others of the opposite sex.

_____ 20. Featuring an electric starter and a four-stroke engine, the salesperson claimed that the lawn mower was the best on the market.

_____ 21. Waving and smiling to their friends, the television camera panned slowly across the crowd.

_____ 22. The natives of the small Pacific island are taller than any of the inhabitants of the area.

_____ 23. Despite its size, the dog barked very ferocious at the mail carrier.

_____ 24. To receive the discount, the advertisement states that we must purchase the lamp before next Monday.

_____ 25. The firefighters responded very quick when the alarm sounded at the old fireworks factory.

Chapter 10

Punctuation

When we speak, we make our meaning clear with more than just words. We pause at certain times, raise our voices for emphasis, and use various body movements. When we write, we use punctuation marks for the same purpose: to make our meaning intelligible to the reader. Every mark of punctuation carries some meaning and gives hints about how to read written English.

Careless punctuation can change meaning and confuse or even mislead the reader. Occasionally, the cost may be dramatic, as in a recently publicized Florida case in which non-profit organizations lost two million dollars because a comma changed the meaning of a sentence and thereby rendered them ineligible for sales tax exemptions. Learning to punctuate correctly is not hard. It does, however, require a little patience. In this chapter we will look at the most common situations in written English that require punctuation.

End Marks

End marks—periods, question marks, and exclamation points—are used to indicate the purpose of a sentence.

The Period

Use the period to end a statement (or declarative sentence), an indirect question, or a mild command (or imperative sentence).

Declarative sentence:	In 1831, Nat Turner led a short but bloody slave revolt in Virginia.
Indirect question:	She asked me whether I wanted to make an oral report on Turner's revolt.
Mild command:	Please make a poster for my presentation.

Use a period after most abbreviations.

Ms., Dr., A.D., a.m., oz., Nov., Conn., Assn., ft.

Periods do not usually follow acronyms and abbreviations of well-known colleges, organizations, governmental agencies, and certain other abbreviations, including two-letter state abbreviations when the ZIP code is included.

UCLA, NATO, IBM, UN, UFO, TV, IL, CA,

The Question Mark

Use a question mark after a direct question (or an interrogative sentence).

Why did the chicken cross the street?

Do not use a question mark after an indirect question.

He asked me why the chicken crossed the street.

Use a question mark to indicate uncertainty about the accuracy of a word, phrase, or date:

The Greek philosopher Plato (427?–347 B.C.) was a disciple of Socrates.

The Exclamation Point

Use an exclamation point to end an exclamation—that is, a statement that shows strong emotion—or after a strong interjection, a word that shows strong feeling.

Wow! You must be kidding!
Hurry! We'll be late!

Use an exclamation point after imperative sentences that show strong feelings or express strong commands or requests.

Please help me!
Don't run!

© 1997 Addison-Wesley Educational Publishers Inc.

Be careful not to overdo the exclamation point. When overused, it creates an almost hysterical tone in writing. Use a comma or a period instead of an exclamation point after a mild interjection.

No, I don't think I want to.

If an abbreviation comes at the end of a statement, do not use an additional period as an end mark. However, use an exclamation point or question mark if one is needed.

The Smithsonian Institution is in Washington, D.C.
Have you ever visited Washington, D.C.?

Exercise 10-1

Supply a period, question mark, or exclamation point where needed. If there is no room in the sentence, insert a caret (∧) below the line and write the appropriate punctuation above the line.

1. Your application should be mailed to D A Coleman, 19 W Bond Street, Richmond, VA 23219
2. Prof Lehane and Ms Garcia will sing duets today at 2:30 pm at the concert hall on Seventh St in Des Moines
3. Did you hear someone yell "Fire"
4. My little sister asked me whether there is a Santa Claus
5. "Do you believe in Santa Claus" I asked her
6. The newspaper columnist told our class that he types on an IBM Selectric typewriter that he purchased when he worked at the UN
7. My daughter earned her degree from UCLA but also took classes at USC and the U of Arizona
8. My alarm rings promptly at 7:00 am every day, but this morning I overslept and missed my favorite TV program and my appointment with Dr McAndrews
9. Holy cow I've just won the state lottery
10. The world's first alphabet was developed by the Sumerians around 3000 BC
11. The Rev Martin Luther King, Jr., gave a rousing speech at the Lincoln Memorial in Washington, DC
12. No I can't believe it
13. Did you remember to wind the clock and put out the cat
14. I wonder whether forces from NATO should be sent to enforce the cease-fire
15. Please take your shoes off when entering the mosque

Internal Punctuation

The Comma

The comma is the punctuation mark most frequently used inside the sentence. It also offers the widest range of individual choice. As a result, many writers are uncertain concerning its proper use, and they sprinkle commas indiscriminately through their sentences. Do not use a comma unless you have a definite reason for doing so. The rules below will help you avoid cluttering your sentences with unnecessary commas while at the same time making certain you use commas to make your meaning clear.

Use a comma to separate independent clauses joined by a coordinating conjunction (*and, but, for, nor, or, so, yet*).

> *Leo has a car, yet he prefers to ride his bicycle to college.*
>
> *Marcia and Hugo have been divorced for three years, but they continue to see each other frequently.*
>
> *Rhode Island is the smallest state, and Alaska is the largest.*

When one or both independent clauses in a compound sentence are short, you may omit the commas before the conjunction.

> *I heard the song and I liked it.*
>
> *I'm exhausted but I'm ready.*

> **Note:** Do not use a comma between two independent clauses that are not joined by a coordinating conjunction. This error creates a comma-splice (see Chapter 8). Use a semicolon, add a coordinating conjunction, or start a new sentence.

(Comma-splice)	*The chief mechanic examined the engine, his assistant checked the tires.*
(Correct)	*The chief mechanic examined the engine, and his assistant checked the tires* (or *The chief mechanic examined the engine. His assistant checked the tires.* A semicolon could also be used after *engine*).

Do not use a comma before a coordinating conjunction linking two words, phrases, or dependent clauses.

(Incorrect)	*Many sailors become proficient in navigation, but neglect the problem of anchoring.* (The conjunction *but* does not join two independent clauses.)
(Correct)	*Many sailors become proficient in navigating but neglect the problem of anchoring.*

Wesley Educational Publishers Inc.

(Incorrect)	*Shakespeare wrote plays, and acted in the London theater.*
(Correct)	*Shakespeare wrote plays and acted in the London theater.*

Exercise 10-2

Add commas in the following sentences wherever needed. If no comma is needed, place a "C" in front of it.

1. My summer job was to stock the shelves and to take weekly inventory.
2. Mark wanted a pizza with anchovies but Gracie preferred mushrooms.
3. I read and Joe slept.
4. My sister Lois is a talented pianist but she hates to practice.
5. The U.S. women's volleyball team was relatively inexperienced yet it won the silver medal at the Olympics.
6. Four cities competed for the right to host the World's Fair, but only one would be selected.
7. The committee had met in private and refused to divulge its choice.
8. The home-improvement business has become very successful in our town and many craftsmen are now extremely busy.
9. The trash collectors have been on strike for three weeks and are demanding a meeting with the mayor.
10. The plans for the new convention center were approved by the city council; construction will begin next July.

Use a comma to separate an introductory dependent clause from the main part of the sentence.

Although Luis was afraid of the water, *he learned to swim.*

When we visited Houston last summer, *we went to a baseball game at the Astrodome.*

Use a comma after a long introductory prepositional phrase.

After an arduous trek over snowcapped mountains and scorched desert floors, *the Mormons finally reached Utah.*

In preparing your annual report to the board of directors, *be sure to include predictions for next year's sales.*

Use a comma to set off an introductory participial phrase.

Pleased by the initial reaction from the voters, *the Democratic candidate stepped up his attack on his opponent.*

Remembering the promise made to his parents, *Jeff carefully kept a record of his purchases and entered each payment in his checkbook.*

Do not put a comma after participial phrases that are actually the subject of the sentence.

(Incorrect))	*Watering his lawn, was Mr. Dawson's only exercise.*
(Correct)	*Watering his lawn was Mr. Dawson's only exercise.*
(Incorrect)	*Reading about Oliver Cromwell's treatment of the Irish, made me more aware of the background behind the troubles in Ulster today.*
(Correct)	*Reading about Oliver Cromwell's treatment of the Irish made me more aware of the background behind the troubles in Ulster today.*

Use a comma to set off an introductory infinitive phrase unless the phrase is the subject of the sentence.

	To win the jackpot in Las Vegas, you must overcome tremendous odds.
But:	*To win the jackpot in Las Vegas was his dream.*
	To impress his future in-laws, Bill wore a suit and tie.
But:	*To impress his future in-laws was Bill's goal.*

Exercise 10-3

Add commas in the following sentences wherever needed. If no comma is needed in a sentence, place a "C" in front of it.

1. After the painting was given to the museum a reception was held in honor of its donor.
2. Jogging on the beach each morning was his favorite form of exercise.
3. To play professionally he practiced for years.
4. Written in 1215 the Magna Carta is the source of many of the ideas in our Constitution.
5. Singing softly to himself Reggie rang the doorbell at the home of his blind date.
6. When he is tempted to exercise Morris sits down until the temptation goes away.
7. Because of the morning traffic and the fog several of the nurses were late for work.
8. To win a medal in the baking contest was David's goal.
9. When the lead guitarist began to sing everyone joined in.
10. After eating a houseplant and destroying half the furniture in our living room the cat finally lay down for a nap.
11. Telling everyone the same joke several times Connie soon found himself ignored at the party.
12. Devastated by the news the survivors huddled together on the curb.

13. Believing that Chemistry 101 was a snap course was Harold's first mistake.
14. Because he did not live in the congressional district David was unable to vote for his brother.
15. To avoid an audit by the I.R.S. you should turn in an accurate tax form.

Use a comma after an introductory request or command.

Look, *we've been through all of this before.*

Remember, *tomorrow is the deadline for filing your tax return.*

Use a comma to separate three or more items in a series unless all of the items are joined by *and* or *or*.

The gymnasium was small, crowded, and stuffy.

But: *The gymnasium was small and crowded and stuffy.*
Rick made some sandwiches, Jo Ann brought her guitar, and I furnished the soft drinks.
John looked for the receipt in the drawer, under the bed, behind the sofa, and in his wallet.

Use a comma to separate interrupting elements (words, phrases, and clauses) when they break the flow of a sentence.

It is a fact, isn't it, *that the spleen filters the blood?*

I will hold your mail for you or, if you prefer, *forward it to your hotel.*

We could use, if possible, *six more cartons of eggs.*

Other interrupting elements (also called *parenthetical elements* or *transitional expressions*) include the following: *as a matter of fact, at any rate, for instance, nevertheless, of course, therefore, in my opinion,* and *on the other hand.* These and similar phrases are usually set off by commas when they appear in a sentence.

There are three good reasons, I believe, *for changing my major.*

The Rams and the Jets, for example, *have acquired new quarterbacks.*

Newark, on the other hand, *is an industrial city.*

Use a comma to set off direct address and words like *please, yes,* and *no.*

Will you help me, please?

Yes, *I've seen all of Kevin Costner's films.*

You should wear a helmet, Sarah, *when you ride your motorcycle.*

Exercise 10-4

Add commas in the following sentences wherever needed. If no comma is needed in a sentence, place a "C" in front of it.

1. Yes I'd love to own a convertible wouldn't you?
2. My parents on the other hand remain unconvinced of the wisdom of my plans.
3. Salsa is made with tomatoes peppers onions garlic and spices.
4. The state of Oregon for example has experimented with various forms of health insurance.
5. Her part in the play includes dancing and singing and crying hysterically.
6. Yes we have decided to stay home for the holidays.
7. Tell me please why you insist on using your good china for pizza.
8. Gerald scratched his head rubbed his nose and cracked his knuckles while filling out the application for his driver's license.
9. That speech in fact was written by his wife.
10. I would like to watch television with you Greta but I must finish my math problems.

Additional Uses of the Comma

Use a comma to set off modifiers that are not essential to the sense of the sentence. *Nonessential* (or *nonrestrictive*) modifiers are those that add information to the sentence, but they modify things or persons already clearly identified in the sentence.

Nonessential clauses are set off by commas (see Chapter 7).

> My mother, who was born in St. Louis, *is the oldest of five children. (The adjective clause* who was born in St. Louis *is not essential to the identity of the subject* mother, *nor is it required for the central meaning of the sentence. Therefore, it is nonessential and is set off by commas.)*

But: Anyone *who was born in St. Louis* is eligible to apply for the scholarship. (*The adjective clause* who was born in St. Louis *is essential to the meaning of the sentence. Not everyone is eligible to apply for the scholarship—just those born in St. Louis. The clause is therefore essential and is not set off by commas.)*

Nonessential appositives are set off by commas. Most appositives are nonessential and require commas.

> Alexander Hamilton, the first Secretary of the Treasury of the United States, *was killed in a duel. (The fact that Alexander Hamilton was the first Secretary of the Treasury gives further information about the subject, but it is not essential to the meaning of the sentence. Therefore, the appositive is set off with commas.)*

> Mr. Murphy, my physics instructor, *has won several national body-building titles. (Like the preceding appositive,* my physics teacher *gives additional but nonessential information about the subject and is therefore set off with commas.)*

© 1997 Addison-Wesley Educational Publishers Inc.

Some appositives are restrictive or essential—that is, they are needed in the sentence to identify the element they rename. In such cases they are not set off with commas.

> *The rapper Hammer once worked for the Oakland A's baseball team. (Which rapper worked for the Oakland A's baseball team? We would not know unless the appositive Hammer were included. Therefore, the appositive is essential and commas are not used.)*

Use a comma to set off coordinate adjectives. Adjectives are coordinate if *and* can be placed between them. They describe different qualities of the same noun and may be separated by a comma rather than *and*.

> *a long, boring movie (a long and boring movie)*
> *an expensive, rare gem (an expensive and rare gem)*

Some adjectives are not coordinate, and therefore no commas are used to separate them.

> *dirty blue jeans*
> *a retired staff sergeant*
> *an exciting volleyball game*

Notice that you would not write:

> *dirty and blue jeans*
> *a retired and staff sergeant*
> *an exciting and volleyball game*

Adjectives usually precede the word they describe; when they follow the word they describe, they are set off with commas.

> *(Usual order)*   *The loud and unruly crowd stormed the soccer field.*
> *(Inverted order)*   *The crowd, loud and unruly, stormed the soccer field.*

Exercise 10-5

Add commas to the following sentences wherever needed. If a sentence does not need a comma, write "C" in front of it.

1. Our guide who spoke four languages was a native of Barcelona.
2. *Homo erectus* our nearest human ancestor appeared in Africa almost two million years ago.
3. Charles Lindbergh who remains one of America's favorite heroes was a painfully shy man.

4. The rain unexpected and drenching forced us to cancel the picnic.
5. Anyone who arrives after the concert begins will not be seated.
6. Godfrey's brother who owns a fashionable restaurant brings meals to the homeless in his neighborhood every Saturday.
7. For their anniversary Earl gave his wife an expensive diamond necklace.
8. The actor Paul Newman has given millions of dollars to various charities.
9. Thomas Jefferson the third President wrote the basic draft of the Declaration of Independence.
10. At the end of the semester a long difficult examination was given.

More Uses of the Comma

Use a comma to set off contrasted elements.

> *Her birthday is in July, not August.*
> *Jeff always gets a hotel room downtown, never in the suburbs.*

Use a comma to set off quoted material.

> *Georgia announced proudly, "I've been promoted to president of the company."*
> *"My wife just gave birth to twins," Dennis said.*

Use commas to set off the year in complete dates.

> *November 22, 1963, is a day that everyone living at the time will always remember.*
> *On August 6, 1945, the first atomic bomb was dropped.*

When only the month and year are given, the comma is optional.

> **(Correct)**   *The first commercial telecast took place in April 1939.*
> **(Correct)**   *The first commercial telecast took place in April, 1939.*

Use a comma to separate the elements in an address.

> *United Nations Plaza, Riverside Drive, New York, New York*

Within a sentence, place a comma after the final element in an address.

> *Her office at the United Nations Plaza on Riverside Drive, New York, is her headquarters.*

Abbreviations standing for academic degrees are set off by commas on both sides.

James F. Dwyer, Ph.D., will address the graduating class.

A plaque recognizing her contributions to the community was given to Judith Walsh, M.D. (Notice that only one period is necessary at the end of a sentence.)

Use a comma to prevent misreading. In some sentences it is necessary to use a comma even though no rule requires one.

(Confusing)	*As you know nothing happened at the meeting.*
(Clear)	*As you know, nothing happened at the meeting.*
(Confusing)	*Shortly after he quit his job and moved to Wisconsin.*
(Clear)	*Shortly after, he quit his job and moved to Wisconsin.*
(Confusing)	*While we ate the dog continued to bark.*
(Clear)	*While we ate, the dog continued to bark.*

Exercise 10-6

Add commas where necessary in the following sentences. If a sentence does not need a comma, write "C" in front of it.

1. Mack claimed that it was her intelligence not her wealth that attracted him.
2. Although injured Beth refused to drop out of the race.
3. The creation and circulation of U. S. currency began April 2 1792 in Philadelphia Pennsylvania.
4. Charles managed to eat a banana split after a hefty dinner.
5. Rita Reeves M.D. will perform my mother's surgery next week.
6. After you've washed the dishes give the dog a bath not just a good brushing.
7. "We will now sing a hymn" said Reverend Drucker "and I want everyone to join in."
8. Alison received a degree in philosophy from Rollins College in Winter Park Florida on June 14 1995.
9. To Ralph Harold was someone special.
10. Frank Sinatra Jr. was kidnapped in Lake Tahoe California in December 1963.

Misusing Commas

When in doubt, many writers are tempted to add commas to their sentences. Too many commas, however, can slow down the thought or confuse the meaning. Here are some of the frequent situations that might tempt you to use the comma.

1. Do not use a comma after the last item in a series of adjectives preceding the noun.

(Incorrect)	*She was a dedicated, imaginative, creative, painter.*
(Correct)	*She was a dedicated, imaginative, creative painter.*

2. Do not use a comma to separate the subject from its verb.

(Incorrect)	*A good night's rest, is the best preparation for a test.*
(Correct)	*A good night's rest is the best preparation for a test.*

3. Do not use a comma between two words joined by a coordinating conjunction.

(Incorrect)	*Bruce plays piano, and tuba in the band.*
(Correct)	*Bruce plays piano and tuba in the band.*

4. Do not separate a verb from a *that* clause.

(Incorrect)	*The Surgeon General has determined, that cigarette smoking is dangerous to your health.*
(Correct)	*The Surgeon General has determined that cigarette smoking is dangerous to your health.*

5. Do not use a comma to separate independent clauses unless the comma is followed by a coordinate conjunction (see Chapter 8 for comma-splices).

(Incorrect)	*The blaze began in the arid Bull Mountains, it destroyed much of the nearby town of Roundup.*
(Correct)	*The blaze began in the arid Bull Mountains, and it destroyed much of the nearby town of Roundup.*

Exercise 10-7

Delete or add commas in the following sentences. If a sentence is punctuated correctly, write "C" in front of it.

1. The human body has 206 bones, that come in four general shapes: long, short, flat and irregular.
2. There are thirty-three, separate, spinal, vertebrae in the embryo, but only twenty-six in an adult.
3. This is due to the fact that, some vertebrae fuse together just before birth.
4. Meryl Streep is much admired for her high zygomatic bones, more commonly called cheekbones.

5. The mandible, or jawbone, is the only facial bone that moves.
6. Basketball players are able to slam dunk partly because of their extremely long femurs, tibias, and fibulas, called leg bones by most of us.
7. Each finger consists of, three bones, and the thumb consists of two.
8. Incredibly, the average human bone can tolerate a pressure of 27,000 pounds per square inch, before breaking.
9. Bones are, however, usually broken when they are twisted or when, they receive a blow from the side.
10. It is amusing that, the softer material inside human bones is called, "spongy bone."

The Semicolon

Use a semicolon to separate two related independent clauses when there is no coordinating conjunction to join them.

> *The law is clear; the question is whether it is fair.*
>
> *Competition for admittance to medical school is intense; only about one applicant in twenty is admitted.*

If you use a comma instead of a semicolon for an omitted conjunction, you will create a comma-splice (see Chapter 8 and page 168 in this chapter). There is an exception to this rule in the case of compound sentences in which the clauses are very short:

> *I came, I saw, I conquered.*

Use a semicolon to separate independent clauses joined by a *conjunctive adverb*. Conjunctive adverbs are words like the following: *however, moreover, therefore, furthermore, nevertheless, nonetheless, consequently, otherwise, besides,* and *hence* (see Chapter 8).

Conjunctive adverbs are not conjunctions, and therefore they require more than a comma before them. When they come at the beginning of an independent clause, a semicolon or period should precede them. If they are not preceded by a semicolon or period, the result is a comma-splice.

(Comma-splice)	*Puerto Rico is not a state, however, its residents are American citizens.*
(Correct)	*Puerto Rico is not a state; however, its residents are American citizens.*
(Comma-splice)	*The Rolls-Royce is an expensive automobile, moreover, its maintenance costs are also higher than for most other cars.*
(Correct)	*The Rolls-Royce is an expensive automobile; moreover, its maintenance costs are also higher than for most other cars.*

Use a semicolon to separate items in a series if the items contain commas.

Attending the sales meeting were Marino Garcia, the sales manager; Jim Gleeson, vice president; Lisa Crow, advertising manager; and John Jacobs, secretary-treasurer.

Candidates for the Most Inspiring Player of the Year Award were Bruce Stoecker, fullback; Don Cohn, tight end; Dick Farley, quarterback; and Joe Rico, fullback.

Exercise 10-8

Add a semicolon or comma where needed in the following sentences and delete any unnecessary punctuation. If a sentence is punctuated correctly, write "C" in front of it.

1. Tran speaks English at school, at home, however, he speaks Vietnamese.
2. The advertising agency selected seven cities as trial markets for the new product: Huntsville, Mobile, and Tuscaloosa, in Alabama, Yakima and Olympia, in Washington, and Carbondale and East St. Louis, in Illinois.
3. The disc jockey didn't play any of my favorite songs, I danced once.
4. Monaco has no famous colleges or universities, however, it has a ninety-nine percent literacy rate.
5. The annual number of marriages in America has increased since the 1980s, so has the death rate.
6. Jessie closed his Manhattan law practice last week, he plans to move to Cedar Rapids to take over his father's farm.
7. Charlene decided to leave before dinner because the roads were becoming icy.
8. I will have to find a job this semester or I will have to get a loan for tuition.
9. Cows will not eat hay that has a musty odor, therefore, farmers must make sure that it is dry before they bale it.
10. During our African honeymoon we visited Zanzibar, Tabora, and Linga in Tanzania, Nairobi, Nakum and Mombasa in Kenya, and Juba, Waw, and Khartoum in Sudan.

The Colon

The colon can be thought of as an equal sign; it tells the reader that what follows it is equivalent to what precedes it. The most common use of the colon is to introduce a list of items after an independent clause:

The trade minister stated that his nation offered potential investors several advantages: a good climate, a sound economy, and a reasonable wage structure.

Yiddish is made up chiefly of words from four languages: Russian, German, Polish, and Hebrew.

The colon is also used to introduce a word or phrase that renames or explains an earlier idea in the sentence:

The Hubble telescope soared into space despite a serious flaw: a distortion in one of its light-gathering mirrors.

The colon can be used between two complete thoughts when the second explains the first:

It was becoming painfully obvious to him: he was being ignored.

A less frequent use of the colon is after a list of items preceding an independent clause:

Cuba, Brazil, and Australia: these are the largest producers of cane sugar.

Do *not* place a colon between a verb and its objects or complements, or between a preposition and its objects.

(Incorrect)	*Her favorite science-fiction writers are: Robert Heinlein, Isaac Asimov, and Harlan Ellison.*
(Incorrect)	*For a good day at the beach you must bring: sunscreen, cold drinks, and a radio.*
(Incorrect)	*Charlie Chaplin was easily recognized by: his black mustache, his walk, and his black hat.*

A colon can be used to introduce a quotation that does not form part of a clause or phrase in the rest of the sentence:

As Neil Armstrong put his foot on the surface of the moon, he made a statement that has become famous: "That's one small step for a man, one giant leap for mankind."

Other uses of the colon are after salutations in business letters and between hours and minutes when referring to time:

Dear Professor Nishimura:
4:05 p.m.

Exercise 10-9

Insert a colon where needed in the following sentences, and delete any colons that are unnecessary or incorrect. If a sentence is correct, write "C" in front of it.

1. Harold faced a dilemma whether to study for his final exam or wash his car.
2. According to an authority on American slang, the most common slang terms deal with: money, sex, and drinking.

3. Only one obstacle kept Sue from a career in music lack of talent.
4. Skin is composed of three main layers the epidermis, dermis, and subcutaneous tissue.
5. The three hardest events to cope with, psychologists claim, are: the death of a spouse, divorce, and marital separation.
6. Finally, the news came that all the employees had dreaded: the factory was closing.
7. From the observation deck we could see: Golden Gate Park, the marinas in the harbor, and the lights of Marin County.
8. With her Christmas bonus check Laura bought: five compact discs, a muffler for her car, and a tie for her father.
9. Although Rita likes Los Angeles, she prefers to live in Belleville because of her job, her friends, and her family.
10. Smoking, high cholesterol, and obesity: these can lead to heart disease.

Parentheses

Use parentheses to enclose unimportant information or comments that are not an essential part of the passage. In this respect parentheses are like commas; the difference is that they evoke the reader's attention more than commas.

Mapmakers use a system of meridians of longitude (from the Latin longus, "long") and parallels of latitude (from latus, "wide").

Zane Grey (who started out as a dentist) is one of the most popular novelists of the American West.

Whitman's Leaves of Grass (published in 1855) was greeted with hostility.

Dates that accompany an event or a person's name are enclosed in parentheses.

The Iran–Contra scandal (1988) involved several members of President Reagan's administration.

Louis Armstrong (1900–1971) invented the popular "scat" style of jazz singing.

Note: *Never insert a comma, a semicolon, a colon, or a dash before an opening parenthesis.*

(Incorrect)   *Hal David, (Burt Bachrach's collaborator) wrote the lyrics to "Alfie."*

Dashes

The dash is a forceful punctuation mark, and it must be used carefully. It often takes the place of the comma, the semicolon, the colon, or parentheses in a sentence in order to separate emphatically words or groups of words. The difference between the dash and these other marks is that it focuses attention on the items being separated.

Use a dash to mark an abrupt change in the thought or structure of a sentence:

I wonder if we should—oh, let's take care of it later.

Use a dash to make parenthetical or explanatory matter more prominent:

George Halas—one of the founders of the National Football League—was known as "Papa Bear."

The family's belongings—their clothing, furniture, stereo set, and other possessions—were stolen during their weekend absence.

Use a dash to set off single words that require emphasis:

Sandra thinks about only one thing—money.

Use a dash to set off an appositive or an introductory series:

Only one northern industrial state—Illinois—has not ratified the Equal Rights Amendment.

Note: *The use of dashes in this sentence emphasizes the appositive* Illinois; *parentheses would also be correct, but they would not present the same emphasis.*

Leonardo da Vinci, William the Conqueror, Alexander Hamilton, and Richard Wagner—they were all illegitimate children.

Note: *A colon could also be correct in this sentence after* Richard Wagner.

Exercise 10-10

Depending on the desired emphasis, insert parentheses or dashes in the following sentences.

1. My oldest brother the actor who lives in Hollywood is unable to attend our cousin's wedding.
2. Excellent students usually have one trait in common self-discipline.
3. Our dinner two steaks and a bottle of champagne cost only twenty dollars with a special coupon.
4. Law, navigation, politics, medicine, war Shakespeare wrote about all of these topics in his plays.
5. I read an article in the *Times* or maybe it was the *Post-Dispatch* describing the tornado in Kansas last week.

6. The sociology class an elective required for my bachelor's degree was more inter-esting than I had expected.
7. Charley my pet dog that I told you about is prohibited from entering the house.
8. I intend to lose I really mean it ten pounds in the next month.
9. The surprise dessert strawberries soaked in brandy and dipped in chocolate cli-maxed our feast.
10. I really should go jogging this morning oh, let's go out for waffles instead.

Quotation Marks

Quotation marks have three main functions: to indicate the exact words of a speaker, to call attention to words used in an unusual sense or in definitions, and to enclose the title of certain kinds of literary and artistic works. In every case, be sure that you use them in pairs; a common mistake is to omit the last set of quotation marks.

FOR DIRECT QUOTATIONS   Use quotation marks around the exact words of a speaker.

Grandpa announced, "It's time to take my nap."
"I guess I do," the nervous bridegroom whispered.

Notice that a comma precedes quotation marks in a direct quotation and that the first word of the quotation is capitalized. Do not use quotation marks for indirect quotations.

Grandpa announced that it was time to take his nap.

Always place commas and periods *inside* the end quotation marks.

"If you wait a few minutes," she said, "we will walk to the corner with you."

When the quotation is a question or exclamation, place the question mark or exclama-tion point *inside* the quotation marks.

She asked with a smile, "Who left this on my desk?"
"That music is too loud!" my father shouted.

When the question mark or exclamation point applies to the entire sentence and not just to the quotation, it should be placed *outside* the end quotation marks.

Did she say, "I have to go to the store"?
I'm tired of being told that my writing is "adequate"!

Always place semicolons *outside* the end quotation mark.

O. Henry's most famous short story is "The Gift of the Magi"; like his others, it has a surprise ending.
The Russian delegate's vote was a loud "Nyet!"; as a result, the resolution was vetoed.

Use single quotation marks around quoted material within a direct quotation.

"We object to 'In God We Trust' on our currency," the lawyer stated.
"My favorite poem is 'Chicago,'" said Marvin.

FOR WORDS AND DEFINITIONS Use quotation marks to call attention to words used in an unusual sense and in definitions.

I like the music of Guns N' Roses; my brother calls it "cacophony."
The origin of the word "bedlam" is interesting.
The Spanish expression "Adios" comes from another expression meaning "Go with God."

Note: *Many writers prefer to italicize (underline) words when used in this sense.*

FOR TITLES OF LITERARY AND ARTISTIC WORKS Use quotation marks to enclose titles of short poems, paintings, magazine articles, television programs, short stories, songs, and any selections from a longer work.

Poems:	"Crossing Brooklyn Ferry"
	"Chicago"
Paintings:	"The Last Supper"
	"Whistler's Mother"
Articles:	"How to Be a Better Husband"
	"Princess Diana: Is She Happy?"
Television Programs:	"Sixty Minutes"
	"NBC Evening News"
Short Stories:	"The Dead"
	"The Legend of Sleepy Hollow"
Songs:	"Stardust"
	"Caminos Verdes"

Italics

When words that would be italicized when printed are typed or handwritten, they should be underlined.

Underline (italicize) the titles of books, plays, magazines, newspapers, movies, long poems, and the names of ships, airplanes, and trains.

Books:	*Writing for College: A Practical Approach*
	The Grapes of Wrath
Plays:	*Romeo and Juliet*
	Sunset Boulevard
Magazines:	*Newsweek*
	Surfer
Newspapers:	*Los Angeles Times*
	St. Louis Post-Dispatch
Movies:	*Dances With Wolves*
	Gone With the Wind
Long Poems:	*The Iliad*
	Paradise Lost
Ships:	*Old Ironsides*
	Queen Mary
Airplanes:	*Spirit of St. Louis*
	Enola Gay
Trains:	*Silver Bullet*
	Wabash Cannonball

Underline (italicize) foreign words and phrases that have not yet been adopted as English expressions. If you are not certain about the current status of a particular word or phrase, use a good modern dictionary.

caveat emptor

mea culpa

pro bono publico

Underline (italicize) when referring to letters, numbers, and words.

Carlos received two *B*'s and two *A*'s this semester.

Several American entrants were awarded *10*'s in the gymnastics competition.

© 1997 Addison-Wesley Educational Publishers Inc.

The word *mischievous* is frequently mispronounced by speakers. (As noted earlier, some writers prefer to enclose words used like this in quotation marks.)

Underline (italicize) words that receive special emphasis.

He lives in Manhattan, *Kansas*, not Manhattan, *New York*.

Exercise 10-11

Supply missing commas and quotation marks, and underline (italicize) where appropriate in the following sentences.

1. Would you please translate the French phrase noblesse oblige for me?
2. Professor Cardenas complained that too many students confuse the words to, too, and two.
3. Who said For people who like this sort of thing this is the sort of thing they would like?
4. Beverly is next in line to be editor-in-chief of the Times-Courier.
5. The Greek letter rho looks like the Roman letter p.
6. My favorite love song said Darnell is Just the Way You Are by Billy Joel.
7. I ordered garlic pizza not garlic pasta.
8. Did you read the Louisville Herald's review of the movie Singin' in the Rain?
9. Although the movie Field of Dreams was not believable the references to baseball history were interesting.
10. The expression to love, honor, and obey has been dropped from some marriage ceremonies.

The Hyphen

The most common use of the hyphen is to break a word at the end of a line when there is not enough room for the entire word. The hyphen has several other important uses, however.

The hyphen is used to set off certain prefixes.

1. After *ex-*, *self-*, and *all-* when they are used as prefixes.

    ex-husband
    self-destructive
    all-purpose

2. After prefixes that precede a proper noun or adjective.

    anti-Semitic
    pro-French

un-American

pre-Christian

trans-Atlantic

3. Between compound descriptions serving as a single adjective before a noun.

wine-red sea

soft-spoken cop

slow-moving train

4. Between fractions and compound numbers from twenty-one through ninety-nine.

three-fourths

five-eighths

fifty-four

ninety-eight

The hyphen is used between syllables at the end of a line. Never divide a one-syllable word. When you are uncertain about the use of the hyphen in the syllabication of a word or in compound words, consult a collegiate-level dictionary.

The Apostrophe

The use of the apostrophe can be somewhat tricky at times, but by following the suggestions below, you will avoid the confusion that many writers have with this punctuation mark. The apostrophe is used for the possessive case (except for personal pronouns), to indicate an omitted letter or number, and to form the plural of numbers, specific words, and letters. In the following pages we will examine each of these uses.

1. Use the apostrophe to form the possessive case.

   a. To form the possessive case of a *singular* person, thing, or indefinite pronoun, add *'s:*

   the razor's edge

   the dog's bark

   everybody's obligation

   George's motorcycle

If a proper name already ends in s in its singular form and the adding of *'s* would make the pronunciation difficult, it is best to use the apostrophe only:

Ulysses' return (Ulysses's would be difficult to pronounce but is acceptable)

Moses' teachings

Jesus' mother

b. To form the possessive case of a plural noun ending in *s*, add an apostrophe only:

the cities' population
the soldiers' wives and husbands
the cats' tails

c. To form the possessive case of a plural noun not ending in *s*, add *'s*:

women's rights
children's television programs
mice's tails
alumni's representative

d. To form the possessive of compound words, use the apostrophe according to the meaning of the construction:

Laurel and Hardy's movies (the devices that Laurel and Hardy made together)

But: *Chaplin's and Woody Allen's movies* (the movies of Chapl.n and Allen, respectively)

Her mother and father's home (the home of her mother and father)

But: *Her brother's and sister's homes* (the separate homes of her brother and sister)

e. Most indefinite pronouns form the possessive case by adding *'s*:

someone's hat
everybody's choice
anyone's guess

The following indefinite pronouns can be made possessive only with *of*:

all, any, both, each, few, many, most, much, several, some, such

Not: *Although I hadn't seen my two friends since grade school, I could remember each's name.*

But: *Although I hadn't seen my two friends since grade school, I could remember the name of each.*

f. Do not use an apostrophe with the possessive forms of personal and relative pronouns.

Incorrect	*Correct*
his'	*his*
her's, hers'	*hers*

Incorrect	Correct
our's, ours'	*ours*
your's, yours'	*yours*
their's, theirs'	*theirs*
who'se	*whose*
it's	*its*

Remember that *its* indicates ownership, and *it's* is a contraction for *it is* or *it has*. Similarly, *who's* means *who is* or *who has*.

TIPS FOR FORMING POSSESSIVES OF NOUNS

1. Make the noun singular or plural, according to your meaning.
2. If the noun is singular, add 's. If adding the 's makes the pronunciation difficult, add an apostrophe only.
3. If the noun is plural and ends in s, just add an apostrophe. If the noun is plural and ends in some other letter, add 's.

Exercise 10-12

Insert apostrophes in the following sentences where appropriate, and delete apostrophes that are incorrect. If a sentence uses apostrophes correctly, place "C" before it. Reword any sentence as needed.

1. The swimming pool schedule has been changed while its being painted.
2. Karls' grandparents came to this country from Sweden.
3. In recent years the mens rights movement has attracted many followers.
4. Over one hundred guests attended the couples wedding.
5. Is this wallet your's?
6. The mayor continued to ignore the veterans demands when they marched on City Hall.
7. The dog seems to have lost its way home.
8. I suppose it was just somebodys attempt at humor.
9. It was obvious from boths' appearance that they had been in the water.
10. Helen and Eddie's grades in Spanish began to improve after the midterm examination.
11. "Who's on First?" is one of Abbott and Costellos funniest routines.
12. The salesmens' bonus was less than they had expected.
13. The poison could be identified by its deadly smell.
14. The policeman wanted to know who's car was parked illegally in front of the firehouse.

15. Mr. and Mrs. Kellys children surprised their parents with an anniversary party.

2. Use an apostrophe to indicate an omitted letter in contracted words or an omitted number:

  class of '95
  'tis a pity
  won't
  the '76ers

3. Use an apostrophe to form the plurals of letters, specific words, and numbers.

  Watch your p's and q's.
  The yes's outnumbered the no's.
  Marlene's lowest grade was in the 80's.

Note: An apostrophe is not necessary for the plural of a year.

  Our history prof discussed student activism of the 1960s.
  Some writers prefer to form the plural of a number by merely adding *-s*, omitting the apostrophe:

  The temperature yesterday was in the 90s.

  Do not use an apostrophe when writing out a number in the plural:

(Incorrect)   *several seven's and eight's*
(Correct)   *several sevens and eights*

Numbers

1. If a number requires no more than two words, it should be spelled out.

  nine months later (not *9 months later*)
  forty-one dollars (not *41 dollars*)
  eighteen billion light years (not *18,000,000,000 light years*)

  If a number requires more than two words, use figures.

  694 tons (not *six-hundred ninety-four tons*)
  $4\frac{1}{2}$ *pounds* (not *four and one-half pounds*)
  1372 pages (not *one-thousand three-hundred seventy-two pages*)

2. Write out a number beginning a sentence.
  (Awkward) *14 patients at Broadway Hospital were treated for food poisoning.*
  (Revised)   *Fourteen patients at Broadway Hospital were treated for food poisoning.*

Exercise 10-13

Insert any omitted hyphens or apostrophes in the following sentences, and make any necessary corrections in the use of numbers, quotation marks, underlining, hyphens, or apostrophes. If a sentence is correct, write "C" before the number.

1. Approximately 50 yeas and 100 nos were recorded at last weeks vote.
2. Clarissa said that she was thirty nine and holding.
3. Many Europeans call the letter z zed or zeta.
4. Dr. Marissa Holdener prescribed an anti inflammatory drug for the foot problem Ive had for the past 3 weeks.
5. Every morning Mr. Mather walks two and a half miles.
6. The President elect was briefed by the C.I.A. prior to her inauguration.
7. Its been difficult to make the dog sleep in it's house.
8. Youre out of your mind if you think Ill babysit your little brother.
9. Margaret offered her husband 150 dollars if he would lose twenty-five pounds, but I doubt he'll accept the offer.
10. I cant meet you any earlier than 12 o'clock, although its probably too late for you.

Reviewing the Chapter: Writing Sentences

Careless punctuation can irritate our readers and often distort the meaning of our writing. In this exercise you are asked to write original sentences illustrating the correct use of punctuation.

1. Write an original sentence in which commas are used to separate interrupting elements.
2. Write a compound sentence in which a comma may be omitted before the conjunction joining the independent clauses.
3. Write a sentence using a comma after a long introductory prepositional phrase.
4. Write a sentence using a comma to set off an introductory participial phrase.
5. Write a sentence in which you correctly use the dash.
6. Write a brief dialogue (five or six sentences) between two speakers, using quotation marks correctly.

10-A

REVIEW EXERCISE

On the line preceding each number write the letter of the sentence that is punctuated correctly.

_____ 1.   a. Charles Dickens received little formal education; nevertheless, he became one of England's greatest novelists.
            b. Charles Dickens received little formal education, nevertheless, he became one of England's greatest novelists.

_____ 2.   a. The car needed new tires, a paint job, and a tuneup.
            b. The car needed: new tires, a paint job, and a tuneup.

_____ 3.   a. It was obvious to everyone, that he was embarrassed about his remark.
            b. It was obvious to everyone that he was embarrassed about his remark.

_____ 4.   a. Do you believe in that old expression, "It was love at first sight"?
            b. Do you believe in that old expression, "It was love at first sight?"

_____ 5.   a. On the same day that President Kennedy was assassinated, (November 22, 1963) the English writer C. S. Lewis died.
            b. On the same day that President Kennedy was assassinated (November 22, 1963), the English writer C. S. Lewis died.

_____ 6.   a. "Ladies and gentlemen," the announcer began, "there will be a slight delay in our program."
            b. "Ladies and gentlemen," the announcer began, "There will be a slight delay in our program."

_____ 7.   a. Barbra Streisand's appearance at the charity concert assured a sellout.
            b. Barbra Streisands' appearance at the charity concert assured a sellout.

_____ 8.   a. Students, who major in hotel management, are offered employment at hotels throughout the country.
            b. Students who major in hotel management are offered employment at hotels throughout the country.

_____ 9.   a. A thick blanket of snow, and the icicles hanging from the trees suggested the Christmas cards of my youth.
            b. A thick blanket of snow and the icicles hanging from the trees suggested the Christmas cards of my youth.

_____ 10.   a. She complained that his favorite topics were: his appearance, his intelligence, and his wealth.

           b. She complained that his favorite topics were his appearance, his intelligence, and his wealth.

_____ 11. a. The American inventor Thomas A. Edison had a home and laboratory in New Jersey.

           b. The American inventor, Thomas A. Edison, had a home and laboratory in New Jersey.

_____ 12. a. Although angered, Louis accepted the judge's decision without emotion.

           b. Although angered Louis accepted the judge's decision without emotion.

_____ 13. a. "On behalf of my colleagues" said the mathematician, "I am happy to accept this award."

           b. "On behalf of my colleagues," said the mathematician, "I am happy to accept this award."

_____ 14. a. The moon is not really made of cheese, is it?

           b. The moon is not really made of cheese is it?

_____ 15. a. Dr. Jonas Salk who discovered the Salk vaccine, lived in San Diego.

           b. Dr. Jonas Salk, who discovered the Salk vaccine, lived in San Diego.

_____ 16. a. Because many of the students are from Mexico, the school prepared registration materials in both Spanish and English.

           b. Because many of the students are from Mexico the school prepared registration materials in both Spanish and English.

_____ 17. a. "Many politicians love to use the word 'paradigm,'" said Mr. Harper.

           b. "Many politicians love to use the word "paradigm,"" said Mr. Harper.

_____ 18. a. Miss Grimaldi suffers from arthritis in her hands; consequently, she has had to give up her career as an organist.

           b. Miss Grimaldi suffers from arthritis in her hands, consequently, she has had to give up her career as an organist.

_____ 19. a. The NAFTA agreement affects: Canada, the United States, and Mexico.

           b. The NAFTA agreement affects Canada, the United States, and Mexico.

_____ 20. a. The tour guide told us that we were standing in front of the birthplace of Thomas Jefferson.

           b. The tour guide told us, "that we were standing in front of the birthplace of Thomas Jefferson."

_____ 21. a. Based on the projected ticket sales, our club will make a profit.

           b. Based on the projected ticket sales our club will make a profit.

_____ 22. a. Larry said that he preferred being handsome; rather than rich.

           b. Larry said that he preferred being handsome rather than rich.

_____ 23. a. Are you certain that it's going to rain tomorrow?

           b. Are you certain that its going to rain tomorrow?

_____ 24. a. The article that Carl wanted to read for his philosophy class was "Madonna's View of Existential Deconstructionism" in _Teenage Secrets_.

b. The article that Carl wanted to read for his philosophy class was *Madonna's View of Existential Deconstructionism* in "Teenage Secrets."

_____ 25. a. Many of those, who felt the earthquake, were afraid to return to their homes.

b. Many of those who felt the earthquake were afraid to return to their homes.

10-B

REVIEW EXERCISE

On the line preceding each number write the letter of the sentence that is punctuated correctly.

_____   1.   a. Some of the medical experts who gave testimony stated that Agent Orange was responsible for the veterans' ailments.
                b. Some of the medical experts, who gave testimony, stated that Agent Orange was responsible for the veterans' ailments.

_____   2.   a. The article that I read for my research paper was Clifford Orwin's "Democracy and Distrust" in *The American Scholar*.
                b. The article that I read for my research paper was Clifford Orwin's *Democracy and Distrust* in "The American Scholar."

_____   3.   a. I realize that its a foolish question, but is our final tomorrow?
                b. I realize that it's a foolish question, but is our final tomorrow?

_____   4.   a. Many of the components are manufactured in Japan; instead of in the United States.
                b. Many of the components are manufactured in Japan instead of in the United States.

_____   5.   a. According to one economist, a change in the way workers are paid, can end unemployment and inflation.
                b. According to one economist, a change in the way workers are paid can end unemployment and inflation.

_____   6.   a. The conductor stopped the orchestra and asked the string section to repeat the last five measures.
                b. The conductor stopped the orchestra, and asked the string section "to repeat the last five measures."

_____   7.   a. The three countries that I want to visit are: Greece, France, and England.
                b. The three countries that I want to visit are Greece, France, and England.

_____   8.   a. Polly had joined the Communist party in 1951, consequently she was fired from her job at the bank.
                b. Polly had joined the Communist party in 1951; consequently, she was fired from her job at the bank.

_____   9.   a. "Many people do not use the word 'hopefully' correctly," said Mr. Frye.

195

b. "Many people do not use the word hopefully correctly" said Mr. Frye.

_____ 10. a. As the sun sank slowly in the west the birds calls to each other began to echo across the desert.

b. As the sun sank slowly in the west, the birds' calls to each other began to echo across the desert.

_____ 11. a. My oldest brother who is a senior in college wants to become a doctor.

b. My oldest brother, who is a senior in college, wants to become a doctor.

_____ 12. a. You had a good time at the party didn't you?

b. You had a good time at the party, didn't you?

_____ 13. a. "Once again," said the mayor, "I am happy to accept your decision."

b. "Once again" said the mayor, "I am happy, to accept your decision."

_____ 14. a. Although irritated Wendell announced that, he would continue to play.

b. Although irritated, Wendell announced that he would continue to play.

_____ 15. a. The English explorer Francis Drake sailed into San Francisco Bay.

b. The English explorer, Francis Drake, sailed into San Francisco Bay.

_____ 16. a. The three ingredients necessary for success, according to my teacher, are: practice, practice, practice.

b. The three ingredients necessary for success, according to my teacher, are practice, practice, practice.

_____ 17. a. The threats of the terrorists and the civil war in the capital discouraged many tourists from visiting the country.

b. The threats of the terrorists, and the civil war in the capital discouraged many tourists from visiting the country.

_____ 18. a. Many of the animals, that are in our local zoo, are nearly extinct in the wilderness.

b. Many of the animals that are in our local zoo are nearly extinct in the wilderness.

_____ 19. a. Mark Twains novel _Life on the Mississippi,_ is an accurate description of one of the most remarkable rivers in North America.

b. Mark Twain's novel _Life on the Mississippi_ is an accurate description of one of the most remarkable rivers in North America.

_____ 20. a. "I am certain, said Vernon, "that you will not be disappointed."

b. "I am certain," said Vernon, "that you will not be disappointed."

_____ 21. a. On Sunday, December 7, 1941 (I was twelve years old), the United States was attacked by Japan.

b. On Sunday, December 7, 1941, (I was twelve years old), the United States was attacked, by Japan.

_____ 22. a. Did you see the sign that said "No one admitted beyond this point?"

b. Did you see the sign that said, "No one admitted beyond this point"?

_____ 23. a. The crew on deck are responsible for making certain, that the divers have enough oxygen, that is their main duty.
b. The crew on deck are responsible for making certain that the divers have enough oxygen; that is their main duty.

_____ 24. a. Much of American slang deals with: drinking, gambling, and sex.
b. Much of American slang deals with drinking, gambling, and sex.

_____ 25. a. The quarterback sprained his wrist in the first quarter, nevertheless, he stayed in the game.
b. The quarterback sprained his wrist in the first quarter; nevertheless, he stayed in the game.

Chapter 11

Capitalization

The capitalization of words helps the reader and serves as a guide to their meaning. The rules for capitalization are based, in general, on the following principle: the names of *specific* persons, places, and things (in other words, *proper* nouns) are capitalized; the names of *general* persons, places, and things (*common* nouns) are not capitalized.

1. Capitalize the first word in every sentence, including direct quotations that are complete sentences.

   It has snowed for six days and five nights.
   Have you washed the dishes?
   I can't believe it!
   Mr. Obata said, "My soup has too much salt in it."

2. Capitalize the first and last words in a title and all other words except *a, an, the,* and unimportant words with fewer than five letters.

   Phantom of the Opera
   Catcher in the Rye
   Last Tango in Paris

3.   Capitalize the titles of relatives and professions when they precede the person's name, or when they are used to address the person.

> *Happy anniversary, Mother and Dad.*
> *My Uncle Patrick was a mail carrier for thirty years.*
> *My advisor is Professor Valdez.*
> *I have an appointment with Doctor Shelby tomorrow.*

Do *not* capitalize titles of relatives and professions when they are preceded by possessives (such as *my, your, his, our,* and *their*) and when they are used alone in place of the full name.

> *My mother and father have been married forty years.*
> *My uncle is a retired mail carrier.*
> *My advisor is a professor of Asian studies.*
> *My doctor has an office in her farmhouse.*

4.   Capitalize official titles of honor and respect when they precede personal names.

> *General Colin Powell*
> *President George Washington*
> *Mayor Giuliani*
> *Justice Sandra Day O'Connor*
> *Ambassador Rodgers*
> *Senator Jackson*
> *Mayor Williams*

Do *not* capitalize titles of honor and respect when they follow personal names.

> *a general in the United States Army*
> *the governor of the state*
> *an ambassador from Canada*
> *the mayor of San Antonio*

An exception to this rule is made for certain *national officials* (the President, Vice President, and Chief Justice) and *international figures* (the Pope, the Secretary General of the United Nations).

> *The President and the Vice President, with their wives, arrived in Rome last night*
>   *and were greeted by the Pope and the Secretary General of the United Nations.*

5.   Capitalize the names of people, political, religious, and ethnic groups, languages, nationalities, and adjectives derived from them.

Japanese

Protestantism

Latinos

Democrats

Communists

Afro-American

Victorian

Elizabethan

Canadians

Puritans

6. Capitalize the names of particular streets, buildings, bridges, rivers, cities, states, nations, specific geographical features, schools, and other institutions.

Broadway

Wall Street

Empire State Building

Santa Monica Pier

Fox River

Passaic, New Jersey

Wheeling, West Virginia

Miami-Dade College

Sing Sing Prison

Uganda

Switzerland

Coney Island

Tellico Plains

Blue Ridge Mountains

University of North Carolina

Howard University

the United States House of Representatives

the United Nations

7. Capitalize directions only when they refer to specific regions or are part of a proper name.

out West

West Virginia

the Middle West

the West Coast

back East

the Near East

in the North

North Dakota

Do *not* capitalize these words when they merely indicate a direction or general location.

the western slope of the mountain

the south of Italy

facing north

northern Montana

on the east side of town

8. Capitalize the days of the week, months of the year, and names of holidays and religious seasons.

Friday

Good Friday

September

the Fourth of July

Father's Day

Ramadan

Passover

Veterans Day

9. Capitalize the names of particular historical events, eras, and special events.

the Civil War

World War I

the Great Depression

the Middle Ages

the Roaring Twenties

World Series

Cannes International Film Festival

Super Bowl

10. Capitalize the names of school subjects only if they are proper nouns or if they are followed by a course number.

© 1997 Addison-Wesley Educational Publishers Inc.

anthropology
Anthropology 101
Portuguese
political science
Political Science 240a
Asian studies
Asian Studies 152
psychology
Psychology 190

11. Capitalize all references to a supreme being.

God
the Almighty
the Holy Spirit
the Holy Ghost
the Lord
the Savior
Allah

12. Capitalize personal pronouns referring to a supreme being.

Ask God for His blessing.
Pray for His forgiveness.

Exercise 11-1

Circle every letter or word that should be capitalized.

1. My favorite course at portland community college was archaeology 105, taught by professor myra bernstein, ph.d.
2. I especially enjoyed learning about the works of art and architecture called the seven wonders of the world, which were admired by the ancient greeks and romans.
3. Khufu, khafra, and menkaura make up the group of pyramids of egypt; built between 3000 and 1800 b.c., they are the only surviving wonder which can still be seen.
4. The hanging gardens of babylon, built by king nebuchadnezzar in 600 b.c., lie on a terrace seventy-five feet in the air and are irrigated by the euphrates river.
5. My friend diana, who lives in southeastern greece, told me about the fourth wonder, which was a gold and ivory statue of the god zeus at olympia.
6. The sculptor chares spent twelve years building a statue of the sun god helios that was 120 feet high and overlooked the harbor near rhodes.

7. The largest temple of ancient times was the temple of artemis, near ephesus, greece.
8. The mausoleum at halicarnassus was a giant marble tomb built for mausolus, a statesman of the persian empire—hence the word "mausoleum."
9. When sailing on labor day, I always think of the seventh wonder: the pharos light-house of alexandria, which was sculpted by the greek architect sostratos, and stood an amazing two hundred to six hundred feet high.
10. More than 100,000 laborers worked for twenty years to build the great pyramid of khufu, which contains almost three million slabs of limestone.

11-A

REVIEW EXERCISE

Put an "X" next to the number of any word that should be capitalized.

1. Before serving as a (1) general in the United States (2) army, Colin Powell had been assigned to the (3) pentagon.

   (1) _____ (2) _____ (3) _____

2. While driving through the (4) southern part of Illinois, we stopped at Carbondale to visit my (5) brother Elvis, who is majoring in (6) chemistry at Southern Illinois (7) university.

   (5) _____ (6) _____ (7) _____

3. He told us that (8) chemistry 201 is the most difficult course in the curriculum, except for his course in (9) composition.

   (8) _____ (9) _____

4. A (10) preacher from the (11) state of Washington gave the invocation at the dinner for (12) mayor Golding.

   (10) _____ (11) _____ (12) _____

5. Letters by a (13) canadian (14) explorer were read to our class by (15) professor Bennett and a (16) professor from a (17) history class.

   (13) _____ (14) _____ (15) _____ (16) _____ (17) _____

6. My (18) doctor received his degree from the University of Michigan, which is in the (19) city of Ann Arbor.

   (18) _____ (19) _____

7. Innsbruck is in the (20) western part of Austria and is the home of a (21) medieval castle as well as the site of the 1976 (22) olympic ski competition.

   (20) _____ (21) _____ (22) _____

8. We invited Jorge and his family to celebrate the (23) fourth of July with us at a picnic in a (24) park in (25) downtown Indianapolis.

(23) _____ (24) _____ (25) _____

11-B

REVIEW EXERCISE

Put an "X" next to the number of any word that should be capitalized.

1. In the opening lines of John Milton's poem (1) *paradise* (2) *lost*, the poet prays to the muses and to the (3) holy (4) spirit for inspiration.

   (1) _____ (2) _____ (3) _____ (4) _____

2. Candidates for a position with the oil company must speak the French (5) language as well as (6) arabic.

   (5) _____ (6) _____

3. Students enrolled in (7) psychology classes are often surprised at the amount of knowledge they are expected to have in such areas as (8) physiology and sociology.

   (7) _____ (8) _____

4. One of the most important (9) moslem (10) religious holidays is (11) ramadan, which is the ninth month of the (12) muhammadan (13) year and celebrated throughout the (14) middle (15) east.

   (9) _____ (10) _____ (11) _____ (12) _____ (13) _____
   (14) _____ (15) _____

5. My subscription to (16) *reader's* (17) *digest* expired while I was vacationing in the (18) mountains of Kentucky last (19) summer.

   (16) _____ (17) _____ (18) _____ (19) _____

6. Walt did a term paper in (20) political (21) science 201; his subject was the (22) supreme (23) court.

   (20) _____ (21) _____ (22) _____ (23) _____

7. The pastor of the (24) church is (25) father Murphy.

   (24) _____ (25) _____

Chapter 12

Spelling

Some people seem to be born good spellers just as some people are apparently born with perfect musical pitch. Others—and perhaps they are the majority—continue to be plagued by mistakes in spelling all of their lives, to their own embarrassment and the irritation of others. To be sure, mistakes in spelling are not as serious as errors in grammar, word choice, organization, or punctuation, but they are usually more noticeable, and therefore more annoying. Like errors in punctuation, they distract the readers and make them wonder about the writer's credibility and the accuracy of his or her ideas. Whether right or wrong, most people in our society—particularly employers, instructors, and others in positions of authority—regard misspelled words as symbols of carelessness and irresponsibility.

   Poor spellers are not necessarily lacking in intelligence or linguistic skill. The poets William Butler Yeats and John Keats were both notoriously bad spellers. But that is no excuse for careless or indifferent attempts to spell a word correctly. Granted, the English language is full of irregularities and inconsistencies; many of the letters in our alphabet have more than one sound, many words have letters that are silent, and others have sounds for which there seem to be no letters. From all of this, one might think that the English spelling system is all chaos and that it is impossible to determine and apply any rules with consistency. The fact is, however, that there *are* some rules and study techniques that will help to improve the spelling skills of even the least confident speller.

Some Suggestions

If you are a weak speller, the first and probably most important suggestion for reducing the number of misspellings in your writing is to proofread your papers at least once, looking closely and carefully for words whose spelling you are uncertain of. Too often, students will guess at the spelling of a word or settle for an approximate version, hoping that the instructor will appreciate their creativity and imagination. But a series of misspelled words in an otherwise excellent paper is like spinach in your sweetheart's teeth: it does not enhance the subject. By looking over your papers carefully, you will detect some misspelled words. You may even find it helpful to have a friend read over your work, since writers are often blind to their own mistakes.

Keeping a list of troublesome words is another way of pinpointing and reducing the number of misspelled words that can occur in writing. Such a list would have not only the correctly spelled form of the word, but also its meaning. By training your eye and exercising your curiosity, you will notice the individual quirks and characteristics of words, including their spelling. Of course, having a good college-level dictionary at hand when writing is important, and using it is even more helpful. If your instructor permits, bring your dictionary to class when writing your themes and compositions.

Four Spelling Rules that Usually Work

1. *ie* and *ei*

    When *ie* and *ei* have the long *e* sound (as in *meet*), use *i* before *e* except after *c*. The old jingle will help:

    > *Put* i *before* e
    > *Except after* c
    > *or when sounded like* a
    > *As* neighbor *and* weigh.

IE	EI (After C)	EI (The Sound of Ay)
believe	ceiling	freight
cashier	conceit	neighbor
grief	perceive	sleigh
niece	receive	veil
shriek		vein
thief		weigh

Some exceptions: ancient, conscience, either, fiery, foreign, leisure, neither, seize, species, weird

2. the silent final *e*

   If a word ends in a silent *e* (as in *hope*), drop the *e* before adding any ending that begins with a vowel. Keep the final *e* before endings that begin with a consonant.

Before a Vowel

value + able = valuable

hope + ed = hoped

give + ing = giving

assure + ance = assurance

extreme + ity = extremity

fate + al = fatal

Before a Consonant

hope + ful = hopeful

sincere + ly = sincerely

nine + teen = nineteen

state + ment = statement

love + ly = lovely

Some exceptions: dyeing, hoeing, duly (due + ly), truly (true + ly), noticeable, peaceable, courageous

3. doubling the final consonant

   If a word of one syllable ends with a single consonant preceded by a single vowel (as in *hit*), double the final consonant before adding a suffix beginning with a vowel. If the word has more than one syllable, the emphasis should be on the final syllable.

Single Syllable

hit + ing = hitting

slam + ed = slammed

shop + ed = shopped

fat + est = fattest

fun + y = funny

Multisyllable

admit + ed = admitted

permit + ing = permitting

repel + ing = repelling

begin + er = beginner

prefer + ed = preferred

Some exceptions: preference, conference, benefited, signaled (also spelled signalled)

4. final *y*

   When a word ends with -*y* preceded by a consonant, change the *y* to an *i* when adding a suffix, except those suffixes beginning with an *i*:

   baby + es = babies

   twenty + eth = twentieth

   likely + hood = likelihood

   marry + age = marriage (*but* marry + ing = marrying)

   weary + ness = weariness

   When a word ends with -*y* preceded by a vowel, do not change the *y*:

```
toy + s = toys
monkey + s = monkeys
attorney + s = attorneys
display + ed = displayed
```

Some exceptions: paid, daily, said, laid

Forming the Plurals of Words

Most words form their plurals by adding *s* to the singular:

chocolates

dogs

movies

Words ending in *s*, *ch*, *sh*, or *x* form their plurals by adding *es* to the singular:

classes

crutches

wishes

taxes

The plural of hyphenated nouns is formed by adding *s* to the main noun:

mother-in-law = mothers-in-law   father-in-law = fathers-in-law
court-martial = courts-martial

Nouns ending with *ful* form their plural by adding *s* to the end of the word:

spoonful = spoonfuls   mouthful = mouthfuls
cupful = cupfuls

Some words ending in *f* change to *v* in the plural:

elf = elves   half = halves
wife = wives   life = lives
leaf = leaves   self = selves

Some exceptions: roofs, chiefs

© 1997 Addison-Wesley Educational Publishers Inc.

The plural of many nouns that end with *o* is formed by adding *s* if the *o* is preceded by another vowel:

radio = radios   ratio = ratios

studio = studios   zoo = zoos

The plural of many nouns that end with *o* is formed by adding *es* if the *o* is preceded by a consonant:

cargo = cargoes   motto = mottoes

echo = echoes   potato = potatoes

hero = heroes   zero = zeroes

The singular and the plural of some nouns are the same:

fish   series

deer   means

sheep

The plural of some nouns is formed by a change in spelling:

woman = women   foot = feet

child = children   tooth = teeth

Plurals of nouns borrowed from other languages are usually formed according to the rules of those languages. You must memorize their plural forms or use a modern dictionary to check their current status. Here are some examples:

alumna = alumnae

alumnus = alumni

analysis = analyses

basis = bases

medium = media

crisis = crises

criterion = criteria

datum = data

dictum = dicta

memorandum = memoranda

parenthesis = parentheses

Twenty-Five Sets of Homonyms: Words Often Confused

Many words in the English language are often confused because they sound the same (or almost the same) as other words. Such words are *homonyms,* and the list that follows contains some of those that are most frequently misused by writers.

Look the list over carefully, noting the differences in meaning. For additional words that are often confused, see "A Glossary of Usage" on page 245.

All ready and already	*All ready* is an adjective meaning "entirely ready." We are packed and *all ready* to go. *Already* is an adverb meaning "previously." Jack pretended to be surprised, but he had *already* heard about the party.
All together and altogether	*All together* means "in a group." The families of the bride and groom were *all together* in the reception area. *Altogether* means "completely" or "entirely." We were *altogether* exhausted after the trek through the desert.
Bare and bear	*Bare* is an adjective meaning "naked" or "undisguised." The baby wiggled out of its diaper and was completely *bare.* *Bear* as a verb means "to carry or support." As a noun it refers to "a large omnivorous animal." The bridge was too weak to *bear* the weight of the trucks. While we were in Yosemite, we saw several large *bears* foraging for food in a nearby campground.
Buy and by	*Buy* is a verb meaning "to purchase." When you *buy* a home, you are probably making the largest purchase of your life. *By* is a preposition meaning "close to or next to." I saw his Hyundai parked *by* the barn.
Capital and capitol	*Capital* is the leading city of a state, or wealth, or chief in importance. The *capital* of Nicaragua is Managua. Lorena lives on the interest from her accumulated *capital.* The low interest rate was of *capital* importance in holding down inflation.

Capitol is the building in which lawmakers sit.
> The flag of surrender flew over the *capitol*.

Coarse and course

Coarse is an adjective meaning "rough" or "inferior."
> The sandpaper was too *coarse* to use on the table.

Course is a noun meaning "direction" or "academic studies."
> By using a compass, we were able to follow the right *course*.
> The *course* in statistics was helpful in my job later.

Complement and
compliment

To complement is "to balance or complete."
> Kareem's new tie *complemented* his suit.

To compliment is "to flatter." As a noun it means "an expression of praise."
> When anyone *complimented* Bernice, she blushed, because she was unaccustomed to *compliments*.

Consul, council,
and counsel

A *consul* is a government official stationed in another country.
> The American *consul* in Paris helped the stranded New Yorkers locate their family.

A *council* is a body of people acting in an official capacity.
> The city *council* passed a zoning regulation.

Counsel as a noun means "an advisor" or "advice"; as a verb it means "to advise."
> The defendant's *counsel* objected to the question.
> The *counsel* that he gave her was based on his many years of experience.
> Saul *counseled* me on my decision.

Forth and fourth

Forth is an adverb meaning "forward in time or place."
> When the doors opened, the mob rushed *forth*.

Fourth is an adjective form of "four," the number.
> On my *fourth* attempt, the car finally started.

Hear and here

Hear is a verb meaning "to listen to."
> From our room we could *hear* the roar of the crowd.

Here is an adverb meaning "in this place."
> A new restaurant will be opened *here* next week.

Hole and whole

Hole is a noun meaning "a cavity."
> The acid etched a *hole* in the coin.

Whole as an adjective means "complete or healthy"; as a noun it means "all of the components or parts of a thing."
> I ate the *whole* cake.
> Her performance as a *whole* was rated superior.

It's and its

It's is a contraction for "it is" or "it has."
> *It's* quite an accomplishment, but I received a "C" in math.

It's been a hectic semester.

Its is the possessive form of *It*.

Every tool was in *its* proper place.

Knew and new
: *Knew* is the past tense of *know*.

Hamid thought he *knew* the combination, but he had forgotten it.

New means "recent."

New evidence was discovered linking smoking with cancer.

No and know
: *No* as an adverb means "not so"; as an adjective, it means "not any, not one."

No, I did not receive my mail yet.

We had *no* opportunity to tell Greg goodbye.

Know is a verb that means "to be aware of."

I *know* that the "No Smoking" sign is on.

Peace and piece
: *Peace* is a noun meaning "tranquility" or "the absence of war."

The Prime Minister promised *peace* in our time.

Piece as a noun means "a part or portion of something."

Virginia preferred to get paid by the hour rather than by the *piece*.

Principal and principle
: *Principal* as an adjective means "main," "chief"; as a noun it means "a sum of money" or "the head of a school."

The *principal* reason she stayed was loyalty to her family.

Scott repaid the *principal* of the loan and the interest within a month.

The *principal* of my high school encouraged me to go to college.

Principle is a noun meaning "a truth, rule, or code of conduct."

I could never learn the *principles* of the slide rule.

Gambling is based on the *principle* of greed.

Right and write
: *Right* as a noun means "a just claim or title" or "the right-hand side."

The *right* to speak freely is every American's legacy.

In Ireland we could not drive on the *right*.

Write means "to draw or communicate."

Ben was able to *write* at the age of four.

Role and roll
: *Role* is a noun meaning "a part or function."

The navy's *role* in the revolution was unclear.

Roll as a verb means "to move forward, as on wheels"; as a noun, it means "bread" or "a list of names."

The tanks *rolled* down the main street of the town.

Professor Samuels often forgets to take *roll*.

Scene and seen	*Scene* is a noun meaning "a view or setting."

Scene and seen — *Scene* is a noun meaning "a view or setting."
  The *scene* from my hotel room was unforgettable.
Seen is the past participle of *see*.
  Have you ever *seen* a falling star?

Stationary and stationery — *Stationary* is an adjective meaning "permanent" or "not moving."
  The wheels of the car were locked in a *stationary* position.
Stationery is a noun meaning "writing paper and envelopes."
  Lois gave me a box of monogrammed *stationery*.

There, their, and they're — *There* is an adverb meaning "in that place."
  Place the packages *there* on the table.
Their is the possessive form of *they*.
  They were shocked to find *their* house on fire.
They're is a contraction of *they are*.
  They're usually late for every party.

To, too, and two — *To* is a preposition; *too* is an adverb; *two* is an adjective.
  He ran *to* the door.
  I'm *too* excited to eat.
  It snowed heavily *two* days ago.

Weather and whether — *Weather* is a noun referring to climatic conditions.
  If we have warm *weather* tomorrow, let's eat outdoors.
Whether is a conjunction that introduces alternatives.
  It may rain tomorrow *whether* we like it or not.

Whose and who's — *Whose* is the possessive form of *who*.
  Whose car is in my parking space?
Who's is a contraction for *who is* or *who has*.
  Who's he dating now?
  Who's been eating my porridge?

Your and you're — *Your* is the possessive form of *you*.
  Are these *your* books?
You're is a contraction for *you are*.
  You're in big trouble.

Spelling List

Here is a list of words commonly misspelled in college students' writing. Study these words carefully and memorize the spelling of any you are not sure of.

ably   abundance   accept
absence   academic   accidentally

accommodate

accommodation

accompanied

accuracy

achieve

achievement

acknowledge

acquaintance

acquired

across

address

adequate

admittance

advice

affect

aggravate

aging

all right

allowed

almost

altar

alter

altogether

amateur

analysis

analyze

anonymous

anxiety

apparatus

apparent

appearance

arguing

argument

athletic

audience

awkward

bachelor

basically

beautiful

becoming

beginning

believed

benefited

boundary

breath

breathe

bureau

business

cafeteria

calendar

campaign

candidate

capital

capitol

career

carrying

ceiling

cemetery

certain

chief

chosen

column

coming

committee

competent

competition

condemn

conscientious

conscious

continuous

criticism

criticize

deceive

decision

definitely

definition

dependent

desirable

desperate

devastating

development

difference

dining

disappear

disappoint

disastrous

disease

dissatisfied

divide

doesn't

echoes

effect

efficient

eighth

eligible

eliminate

embarrass

emphasize

enthusiastic

environment

equipped

exaggerate

excellent
exercise
exhaust
existence
explanation
familiar
fantasy
fascinate
February
fictitious
fiery
finally
financially
forehead
foreign
foremost
forth
forty
fourth
fulfill
gases
gauge
glamorous
government
grammar
grievance
grievous
guarantee
guard
guidance
happily
happiness
harass
height

heroes
humorous
hurriedly
hygiene
hypocrisy
imitation
immense
incidentally
incredible
indefinite
independence
innocence
inquiry
insistence
intelligence
intercede
interfere
irrelevant
irresistible
its
it's
jealous
judgment
(*also* judgement)
knowledge
laboratory
legitimate
leisure
lessen
lesson
library
license
lightning
likely

literature
loneliness
loose
lose
losing
maintenance
maneuver
marriage
mathematics
medicine
mileage
mischievous
moral
morale
mountain
muscle
musician
mysterious
naturally
necessary
ninety
noticeable
obstacle
occasion
occasionally
occurred
occurrence
omission
omitted
opposed
optimistic
parallel
pastime
permissible

personnel
physician
pneumonia
possess
preceding
prejudice
presence
prevalent
privilege
probably
procedure
prominent
pronunciation
psychology
pursue
quantity
questionnaire
realize
recede
recommend
rehearsal
religious
reminiscence
repetition
restaurant
rhythm
ridiculous
sacrifice

safety
salary
Saturday
scarcely
schedule
science
secretary
seize
separate
sergeant
severely
similar
skeptical
sophomore
specimen
studying
succeed
surprise
susceptible
technique
temperament
tendency
theory
therefore
thorough
throughout
truly
Tuesday

twelfth
unanimous
unnecessary
unusual
unusually
usage
using
vacuum
valuable
village
villain
visible
warring
weather
Wednesday
whether
whisper
whole
wholly
who's
whose
women
writing
written
yield
your
you're

12-A

REVIEW EXERCISE

A. *On the line preceding each sentence, write the letter corresponding to the correct word.*

_____ 1. Player representatives and owners of the ball clubs were (a. all together b. altogether) for the last meeting before the strike deadline.

_____ 2. Because her views on abortion contradicted the (a. principals b. principles) of the majority of her constituents, she was defeated in her bid for reelection.

_____ 3. By getting up at five in the morning and arriving at the box office promptly, I managed to be (a. forth b. fourth) in line.

_____ 4. Martin claims that he rides a (a. stationary b. stationery) bicycle one hour a day.

_____ 5. Opponents of gun control claim that the Constitution grants citizens the right to (a. bare b. bear) arms.

B. *On the line preceding each number, write the letter of the correctly spelled word.*

	a.	**b.**	**c.**
_____ 6.	absense	absence	absance
_____ 7.	accidentally	accidentaly	acidentally
_____ 8.	begining	beginning	begginning
_____ 9.	candidate	canidate	cannidate
_____ 10.	cemetary	cematery	cemetery
_____ 11.	desireable	desirible	desirable
_____ 12.	eligible	elligible	eligable
_____ 13.	embarass	embarress	embarrass
_____ 14.	garauntee	guarantee	gaurentee
_____ 15.	incidentally	incidintally	incidentaly
_____ 16.	maintainance	maintanance	maintenance
_____ 17.	mathematics	mathamatics	mathemetics
_____ 18.	ocasionally	occasionally	occassionally
_____ 19.	preceding	preceeding	preceading

_____	20.	recomend	recommend	reccomend
_____	21.	religious	relegious	religous
_____	22.	shedule	schedual	schedule
_____	23.	seperate	separate	separat
_____	24.	unneccessary	uneccesary	unnecessary
_____	25.	Wenesday	Wednesday	Wensday

12-B

REVIEW EXERCISE

A. On the line preceding each sentence, write the letter corresponding to the correct word.

____ 1. A man (a. who's b. whose) voice was vaguely familiar answered the telephone.

____ 2. Because I had been away several years, I did not recognize (a. their b. there) home as we pulled into the driveway.

____ 3. The (a. peace b. piece) treaty was ratified by all seven nations.

____ 4. The clerk refused to believe that the (a. hole b. whole) was already in the bicycle tire when we bought it.

____ 5. On the advice of her (a. council b. counsel), Mrs. Rand refused to testify.

B. On the line preceding each number, write the letter of the correctly spelled word.

		a.	b.	c.
____	6.	acurracy	accuracy	accurracy
____	7.	aggravate	aggrravate	aggrevate
____	8.	athaletic	athletic	atheletic
____	9.	becoming	becomming	becomeing
____	10.	ceiling	cieling	cieleing
____	11.	comeing	coming	comming
____	12.	defenition	definetion	definition
____	13.	dissapoint	dissappoint	disappoint
____	14.	environment	enviroment	envirement
____	15.	foremost	formost	forrmost
____	16.	guideance	guidance	guidence
____	17.	indefenite	indifenite	indefinite
____	18.	iressistible	irresistible	iressistable
____	19.	acheivment	achievment	achievement
____	20.	mileage	milage	milaege
____	21.	occured	occurred	ocurred
____	22.	pastime	pasttime	pasetime

_____ 23. pernunciation   pranunciation   pronunciation
_____ 24. restraunt   restaurant   restaurent
_____ 25. wholely   wholly   wholy

Chapter 13

Writing Paragraphs

Most of the writing that you will be asked to do in college will be in the form of paragraphs. A *paragraph* consists of several related sentences that deal with a single topic or an aspect of a topic. Paragraphs frequently stand alone, as in the case of responses to questions on examinations. Usually, however, paragraphs are parts of longer pieces of writing, such as essays, reports, and term papers. In such cases paragraphs help your reader by breaking down complicated ideas into manageable parts and relating each part to the main idea or thesis of your composition.

Writing with Computers

Regardless of whether it is freestanding or part of a larger unit, a well-organized paragraph has three characteristics:

- A good paragraph is *unified:* all of its sentences relate to one main idea.
- A good paragraph is *coherent:* the thought proceeds logically from sentence to sentence.
- A good paragraph is *developed:* it contains enough information to convey the idea of the paragraph in a reasonably thorough way.

Until recent years, writing a composition of any length meant taking notes, writing one or more drafts while revising and correcting at each stage, and typing or writing a final copy. Improvements in content, mistakes in grammar, and even typographical errors were sometimes ignored because the author did not want to type another copy. In recent times, however, the act of writing has changed because of the introduction of computers. Increasing numbers of writers believe that composing on a computer makes the revising and editing process much easier and more efficient. A computer becomes a word processor when a word-processing program is loaded into it. Although computers and word-processing programs may vary in the features they offer, all word processing offers certain benefits for the writer.

The chief advantage of a word processor is that it allows you to rewrite, correct, change, and revise selected portions of your paper without retyping the whole manuscript. The parts that you do not change remain in their original form and do not have to be retyped. As you can imagine, word processors allow and encourage writers to revise their manuscripts more easily and quickly than the traditional way.

Just as there are different writing styles for those who use a pen or typewriter, so there are differing practices for users of word processors. Some writers work directly at the keyboard and compose after they have completed their first draft. They then revise and edit until they have made all of their modifications and changes. Others first write their draft by hand and then use the word processor for preparing their final copy. Still others write on the screen, print a copy, and then revise with pen or pencil, going back to the word processor for further alterations.

Regardless of the composing style that you adopt, you should not become discouraged at your first attempts to use a computer. For your initial effort, try typing your first draft on the word processor. As you master its keyboard, you will learn that you can move around or delete words, sentences, paragraphs, or entire pages; change words, phrases, or sentences; correct punctuation, mechanics, and mispelled words; and copy part or all of the manuscript to use for other purposes.

In addition to revising and editing, the word processor has other uses. In the preparation and formatting of a manuscript it can change spacing and margins, incorporate boldface, italicize words and titles, center material on a page, and close any spaces left by deletions and substitutions.

The effect of using a word processor will be obvious as you become familiar with its features. The most obvious is that revision is easier: by merely pressing a few keys, you can shift words, sentences, and entire paragraphs around. By putting down ideas as they come, you will be less worried about making mistakes and more likely to draft quickly. You can incorporate additional material and insert it in earlier copy, and because you can get a clean copy whenever you make extensive changes, you will probably revise and edit more than if you had to retype continually.

Using the word processor will not make you a good writer. You will still need to develop and plan your paragraphs carefully, arrange your ideas in the most effective and logical order, and use the most appropriate word choice and sentence structure. But for the last, important stage of the writing process—revising and editing—the word processor can be an invaluable tool.

The Unified Paragraph

Every good paragraph deals with a single topic or an aspect of a topic. The sentence that states the paragraph's subject is the *topic sentence*. It is the sentence that alerts the reader to the central idea. It also reminds the writer of that central idea in the paragraph so that he or she does not include sentences that wander off the topic. For this reason, the topic sentence is frequently placed at the beginning of the paragraph, although it can appear in other parts of the paragraph. Regardless of its location, the topic sentence is usually the most general sentence in the paragraph, and it is developed and supported by the specifics in the sentences that follow or precede it.

In your reading you will occasionally notice paragraphs by experienced writers that do not include a topic sentence. In such instances the topic sentence is implicit—that is, the controlling or central idea is implied because the details in the paragraph are clear and well organized. But until you become an adept writer and are certain that your paragraphs stick to one idea, you should provide each paragraph with a topic sentence.

The first sentence in the following paragraph is the topic sentence, and it announces the main idea of the paragraph in a general way: "There are all kinds of art in the animal kingdom." The sentences that follow present several examples that illustrate and support the topic sentence's idea. Like most well-written paragraphs, this one begins with a general point and then supports it with several specific details.

> *There are all kinds of art in the animal kingdom. This fact can be demonstrated strikingly by studying the painting, sculpture, and mosaic work among the bower birds of Australia. They decorate their bowers with shells, colored glass, shining objects. Some paint their walls with fruit pulp, wet powdered charcoal, or paste of chewed-up grass mixed with saliva. One species, the satin bower bird, makes a tool from a wad of bark to apply the paint. Others garden for a hobby. Members of one species decorate their nine-foot-high bowers with living orchids. Others build huts before which they plant lawns of moss, and on these, most painstakingly, they arrange colored fruits, flowers, fungi, and other objects. When the flowers are wilted, they throw them away and replace them with fresh ones.*

The topic sentence in the above paragraph is clear. It tells the reader what to expect in the sentences that follow, and it reminds the writer of the central idea of the paragraph so that he or she is unlikely to stray from the topic.

Exercise 13-1

Underline the topic sentence in each of the following paragraphs.

a. *The offices of most doctors today are overloaded with people who are convinced that something dreadful is about to happen to them. At the first sign of pain they run to a doctor, failing to realize that pain is rarely an indication of poor health. We are becoming a* nation of pill-grabbers and hypochondriacs who regard the slightest ache as a searing ordeal. *Instead of attacking the most common causes of pain such as tension, worry, boredom, frustration, overeating, poor diets, smoking, or excessive drinking, too many people reach almost instinctively for the painkillers—aspirins, barbiturates, codeine, tranquilizers, sleeping pills, and dozens of other desensitizing drugs.*

b. *Reasons for the popularity of fast-food chains appear obvious enough. For one thing, the food is generally cheap as restaurant food goes. A hamburger, french fries, and a shake at McDonald's, for example, cost about one-half as much as a similar meal at a regular "sit-down" restaurant. Another advantage of the chains is their convenience. For busy working couples who don't want to spend the time or effort cooking, the fast-food restaurants offer an attractive alternative. And, judging by the fact that customers return in increasing numbers, many Americans like the taste of the food.*

c. *The dolphin's brain generally exceeds the human brain in weight and has a convoluted cortex that weighs about 1,100 grams. Research indicates that, in humans, 600 to 700 grams of cortex is necessary for a vocabulary. Absolute weight of the cortex, rather than the ratio of brain weight to total body weight, is thought to be indicative of intelligence potential. The dolphin's forehead is oil-filled and contains complex sound-generating devices. Tests indicate that the dolphin is sensitive to sound at frequencies up to 120 kilocycles. Whereas human vocal cords pulsate at 60 to 120 cycles per second with about 50 selective harmonics, the dolphin's pulsate at about 600 cycles per second with a choice of many more harmonics. These facts provide convincing arguments for possible dolphin intelligence.*

Keep in mind that a topic sentence must be focused and limited enough to be discussed fully within a single paragraph. Notice the difference between the following pairs of topic sentences:

(Too broad) *The United States has many museums with excellent collections of art.*

(Focused) *The St. Louis Art Museum has an outstanding collection of Expressionist paintings and prints.*

(Too broad) *Cultures vary throughout the world with respect to body language.*

(Focused) *Hand gestures that are seemingly innocent in the United States are frequently obscene or insulting in certain Latin countries.*

(Too broad) *Shakespeare's plays indicate that he was familiar with many areas of knowledge.*

(Focused) *Shakespeare's* Romeo and Juliet *suggests that he was familiar with the law.*

Another requirement of the topic sentence is that it must be capable of being developed. If the main idea is merely factual, it does not permit development. Notice the differences between the following sentences:

(Factual) *St. Petersburg is a major city in Russia.*

© 1997 Addison-Wesley Educational Publishers Inc.

(Revised)	*St. Petersburg reminds its visitors of the Italian city of Venice.*
(Factual)	*California has more than one hundred community colleges.*
(Revised)	*Many California college freshmen prefer the community college for its many unique features.*
(Factual)	*Every school system in our county has a music appreciation course in its grade schools.*
(Revised)	*Students should be introduced to the pleasures of music while still in the lower grades.*

Exercise 13-2

The topic sentences below are either too broad or too factual. Revise each so that it will make an effective topic sentence.

1. The All-Star baseball game is held every July.
2. The Great Depression of the 1930s had a series of traumatic consequences for our nation.
3. The debate over the Vietnam War has raged for several years.
4. High blood pressure increases the risk of serious illness.
5. John Lennon was born in 1940.
6. The annual Cotton Bowl is held in Dallas.
7. A variety of reforms have been proposed for America's public schools.
8. The real name of "Dr. Seuss," the writer, is Theodore Geisel.
9. Admission of women to the service academies began in the fall of 1976.
10. Astronomy is a fascinating subject.

The best way to be certain that your paragraphs have unity is to construct a specific, focused topic sentence and then develop it through the entire paragraph. If the paragraph sticks to what is promised in the topic sentence, it has unity. Any sentence that does not develop the topic violates the unity of the paragraph and should be omitted.

In the following paragraph, notice how the sentence in bold type introduces another idea and violates the unity of the paragraph:

It is within the power of the citizens of this country to make their schools once more a place to develop their children's intellectual and physical talents rather than a stage for the performance of athletic heroes. First, they can compare the amount of money spent on teams, bands, uniforms, transportation, and maintenance of facilities with the amount of money spent on books and laboratory equipment. Second, they should compare the amount of time spent practicing during the week for a forthcoming athletic spectacle with the amount of time spent on homework and time in class. **Many high school athletes win scholarships that enable them to attend college.** *Third, they should ease the pressure on the coaches for* *winning. Finally, they should demand to know what the schools' athletic departments are doing for those students who are not athletically inclined, and they should insist that all boys and girls are included.*

The topic sentence in the preceding paragraph announced the main idea: the citizens of this country can make their schools a place to develop their children's intellectual and physical talents rather than a stage for the performance of athletic heroes. The fact that some high school athletes win scholarships to college is irrelevant and does not support the topic sentence. Therefore the bold type sentence should be deleted from the paragraph.

Exercise 13-3

Using one of the topic sentences you developed in Exercise 2, write a paragraph of at least five sentences. Underline your topic sentence.

Coherence in the Paragraph

Coherence means "sticking together," and in a coherent paragraph, all the ideas stick together. You have seen that when a paragraph is unified, all the other sentences support or develop the topic sentence. By placing the sentences in the right order with the right connecting words so that the reader is never confused, the writer's thought is easy to follow from sentence to sentence and from paragraph to paragraph.

Good writers make their paragraphs coherent in two ways: they arrange their ideas in a logical order, and they use linking words or phrases between their sentences to help the reader understand how the ideas are related.

Coherence Through Order

After jotting down your ideas for your paragraph, you should decide which ideas to discuss first, which second, and so on, according to a logical order. The purpose or content of the paragraph will usually suggest the best arrangement.

Most of your writing in college will be expository and persuasive—the kind that explains an idea or defends an opinion. In such cases you would probably arrange your ideas in one of the following patterns: *order of importance, general to specific* (sometimes called *deductive*), and *specific to general* (or *inductive*). Paragraphs that narrate an experience or present the steps in a process are normally arranged in *chronological order*, the sequence in which they happened. To describe a person or a scene, you will organize details in a *spatial order*.

ORDER OF IMPORTANCE   To organize the ideas in a paragraph according to their order of importance, you should first list the ideas that support your topic sentence. The most important ideas should come first, then the next most important, and so on. In writing the

© 1997 Addison-Wesley Educational Publishers Inc.

paragraph, take your ideas from the list in reverse order. The advantage of this pattern stems from the suspense involved and the tendency for readers to remember best what they read last. Not every paragraph can be constructed in this pattern, of course, but it can be an emphatic way to arrange ideas.

In the paragraph below, notice how the writer introduces the least important ideas first and then presents the most important idea in the last sentence.

> *Before the 100-inch telescope on Mount Wilson near Los Angeles was built, astronomers had difficulty in studying the stars. But in 1923 the American astronomer Edwin Hubble, using the new telescope, could pick out stars and calculate distances within our Milky Way. Through his measurements of the stars he calculated that the Andromeda nebula is approximately two million light-years away, a fact that places it far outside our Milky Way. As a result of his discoveries, we now realize that our galaxy is only one among billions of galaxies in the universe, each with billions of stars.*

GENERAL TO SPECIFIC   The most common type of paragraph order is the *general-to-specific* (or *deductive*) pattern. This arrangement begins with a topic sentence that makes a general statement, followed by a series of supporting sentences that supply specifics: details, examples, and facts. Because the reader knows what the main point is, he or she can follow the development of the thought more easily.

Notice how the following paragraph begins with a general statement (the topic sentence) and then proceeds to specifics that support the generalization.

> *Radioactive tracers can help scientists document the shift of chemicals from one place to another. Biologists commonly use tracers to follow the path of nutrients as they pass through the food chain. Physicians can watch iodine or thorium collect in the body and diagnose the presence of tumors. Geologists use radioactive tracers to follow the paths of rainwater through groundwater reservoirs to lakes, streams, and wells. Oceanographers adopt the same technique to trace the direction and speed of ocean currents.*

SPECIFIC TO GENERAL   The *specific-to-general* (or *inductive*) pattern presents a series of individual, specific facts, details, impressions, or observations, and ends with a generalization or conclusion, usually the topic sentence.

Notice the pattern of the following paragraph: the author presents a series of facts and then presents the conclusion, which serves as the topic sentence.

> *The Egyptians believed that garlic endowed its consumers with strength, and they fed it to the laborers who built the pyramids. The Romans thought that if a citizen were confused, he could clear his mind by eating lettuce. When tomatoes were first introduced into Europe they were thought to be an aphrodisiac; later they were seen as a surefire cancer cure. In this country, Americans spend millions of dollars yearly on diets, pills, potions, and "cures" for baldness, impotence, and a variety of other real and imaginary ailments. Food faddism—the belief in the necessity of eating certain "miraculous" foods—is as old as civilization itself.*

CHRONOLOGICAL ORDER   To tell a story, give directions, explain a process, summarize historical events, or report on the steps or actions taken by an individual, paragraphs are usually arranged in *chronological order*—they present their ideas in the order in which they happened.

In the following paragraph notice that all of the details are presented in the order in which they happened:

> *After his arrival in Illinois at the age of twenty-one, Abraham Lincoln tried his hand at a variety of occupations. In 1830 he worked as a flatboatman, making a voyage down the Mississippi River to New Orleans. On his return he worked as a storekeeper, postmaster, and surveyor. With the coming of the Black Hawk War in 1832, he enlisted as a volunteer. After a brief military career he was elected to the state assembly. In 1836, having passed the bar examination after private study, he began to practice law. The next year he moved to Springfield and began a successful career. By the time he started to become prominent in national politics in 1856, he had made himself one of the most distinguished lawyers in Illinois.*

When you use chronological order, it is important that you relate the events in the order in which they occurred. The paragraph above would have been confusing to readers if the writer had started with Lincoln's career in national politics, then detailed his early days as a storekeeper, then jumped ahead to his practice of law, and so on. You can avoid such confusion by including all points or incidents as they happened.

SPATIAL ORDER   If the purpose of your paragraph is to tell how something looks, the most effective organization pattern is usually *spatial*. Spatial order presents a visual effect. In order for your reader to see your subject, you have to select details that make the subject clear, and you have to present those details in a pattern that your reader can follow.

Notice how the use of specific details helps to make clear the image of the newborn baby:

> *Babies right after birth are not beautiful. The trip through the birth canal compresses the unfused bones of the skull, and many babies' heads are temporarily cone-shaped. The pressure also pastes back their ears. Newborns are covered with vernix, a white protective skin coating that looks like cheese, and are splotched with their mother's blood. Some have virtually no hair on their heads, and some are born with a coat of fine hair (lanugo) all over their bodies. Even after they're cleaned up, most have mottled red skin from their arduous passage to birth. The struggle to be born is so exhausting that most newborn babies fall asleep within a couple of hours and stay fast asleep for many hours afterward.*

Exercise 13-4

Following the directions given, write paragraphs arranged in each of the specified patterns.

1. Arranging your ideas *in the order of importance*, write a paragraph of at least one hundred words on one of the following topics. Underline your topic sentence.

The effects of exercise
Reasons for majoring in . . .
The benefits of travel
The advantages of a long engagement
The advantages of going away to school
The benefits of meditation
Preparing for a job interview

2. Arranging your ideas in either *general-to-specific* or *specific-to-general* order, write a paragraph of at least one hundred words on one of the following topics. Underline your topic sentence.

Discrimination on the job
Advantages of being short (or tall)
How to recognize a bargain-priced car
Hazards of teaching someone to ride a motorcycle
Technology and education
Advertising on television
Careers in computers

3. Arranging your ideas in *chronological order*, write a paragraph of at least one hundred words on one of the following topics. Underline your topic sentence.

Meeting my boyfriend's (or girlfriend's) parents
Breaking a habit
Organizing a party
An unexpected situation
Childhood memories
Learning to play a musical instrument
Getting lost in a strange city

4. Arranging your ideas in *spatial order*, write a paragraph of at least one hundred words on one of the following topics. Underline your topic sentence.

My roommate's closet
My favorite hideout
My grandparent
My city from the air
The ugliest building in town

A rock star

A favorite restaurant

Coherence Through Transitional Words and Phrases

In addition to arranging ideas in a logical order, the writer can make paragraphs coherent by linking one sentence to the next by using *transitional words and phrases*. They signal the curve and direction of the thought as you read through the paragraph. With them, the reader is prepared for each new idea and can relate each new statement to the last. Without them, a paragraph can sound like a list of unrelated ideas.

Below are some of the most common transition words that connect sentences, making them more coherent.

also	however	on the contrary
although	in addition	on the other hand
and	in conclusion	second
as a result	in fact	similarly
besides	later	still
but	likewise	that is
consequently	meanwhile	therefore
finally	moreover	though
for example	nevertheless	whereas
furthermore	next	yet

Transitional words and phrases are in bold type in this paragraph:

> *Speaking and writing are different in many ways.* **For example,** *speech depends on sounds; writing,* **on the other hand,** *uses written symbols. Speech was developed about 500,000 years ago,* **but** *written language is a recent development, invented only about six thousand years ago.* **Furthermore,** *speech is usually informal, while the word choice of writing,* **by contrast,** *is often relatively formal.* **Although** *pronunciation and accent often tell where the speaker is from, they are ignored in writing because a standard diction and spelling system prevails in most countries.* **Finally,** *speech relies on gesture, loudness, and the rise and fall of the voice,* **but** *writing lacks these features.*

Developing the Paragraph

The controlling idea of your paragraph, as expressed in the topic sentence, should be supported with specific material so that the reader can follow your line of reasoning. Several methods of paragraph development are available to you; the choice will depend on your topic, the purpose of your paper, and the way the paragraph fits with the overall design of the essay. The methods below are the most common.

Examples

One of the most common ways to develop a paragraph is by using examples. A paragraph developed in this manner begins with a generalization, which it then supports with specific cases or examples. The examples should be typical, to the point, and supportive of the generalization.

The immune system is being studied intensely today, primarily because of its importance in medical research and treatment. The AIDS virus, for example, destroys white blood cells that regulate the immune system, which then loses its ability to respond to new diseases or eliminate cancer. In organ transplants, the immune system may attack the new organ as "foreign" unless physicians can find ways to suppress the response. And many scientists believe that regulating and stimulating immune system molecules like interferon provides the best hope for developing cures for cancer.

Exercise 13-5

Write a paragraph of at least six sentences on one of the topics below, using examples to develop your paragraph. Begin by writing your topic sentence and listing at least three specific examples that make the topic sentence clear. Then write your paragraph.

addictions	sexism in language
comic strips	campus slang
clothing styles	heroes
hobbies for profit	foreign customs

Comparison and Contrast

A paragraph developed by comparison and contrast presents the similarities and differences between two items. Paragraphs using the block method first present all of the relevant details or aspects of one object, and then all of the corresponding qualities of the other. The following paragraph follows this pattern, describing first the skills needed for the piano and then those required for the typewriter.

Students of the piano often find that their dexterity at the keyboard aids them when learning to use the typewriter. Playing the piano requires the ability to coordinate the movements of the eyes and hands, as the pianist reads the musical score and places her fingers on the appropriate keys. And if the pianist hopes to play with any measure of success, she also needs a sense of rhythm. Typing requires these same skills. An accurate typist must read carefully the material she is typing, scarcely glancing at her hands on the keyboard. If she wishes to type rapidly, she must develop a rhythmic pattern in the movements of her fingers. It is not surprising, then, that many pianists are excellent typists.

Another way to develop the comparison and contrast paragraph is to move back and forth between the two items point by point, as in the following paragraph.

College freshmen are often surprised by the differences between their high school days and their experiences in college. In high school, attendance was taken daily and a school secretary often called the student's home to verify that a missing student was not truant. In college, many instructors never take attendance, nor do they make any effort to contact parents concerning absences or failing work. In high school, counselors and teachers gave individual help and attention to students who needed it, and after-school sessions were available for extra tutoring. In college, the student is responsible for his own academic performance, and it is up to him to seek help. In most high school classes the students are approximately the same age, but in a typical college class the students range in age from teenagers to grandmothers. Social life is important in high school, but in college it is squeezed in only when possible. Finally, students in high school are often treated as children, but they are assumed to be responsible adults in college.

Exercise 13-6

Write a paragraph of at least six sentences using either the block or point-by-point arrangement. The following pairs may serve as topics, or you may choose your own. In either case, write a topic sentence for your paragraph and underline it.

Two popular comedians or entertainers
Two friends or relatives
Two instructors
Two different sports
Two religions
Two political parties
Two views of capital punishment
Two cars

Classification

When you group information into categories to show how they differ, you use classification as your organizing pattern. The following paragraph classifies the various types of personality disorders according to the particular characteristic that is most prominent in each.

Several types of personality disorders have been identified by psychologists and psychiatrists. It must be kept in mind that in given cases the dividing lines are often unclear and that an in-

Definition

When you want to clarify a term that might have several meanings, or when you want to explain a complex concept or word, you may develop your paragraph by definition. Such paragraphs usually combine definition with other methods of development in order to make clear the meaning of the term or idea. In the following paragraph, notice that examples are used to make the meaning of "sex roles" clear.

Sex roles are the set of social standards that prescribe appropriate behavior for males and females. Sex-role definitions provide the basis for stereotypes. In Western societies, for example, men are supposed to be dominant, competitive, logical, and unemotional. Women are supposed to be warm, caring, emotionally responsive, and socially adept. The learning of sex roles begins in the preschool years, and by the end of that period, the behavior of boys and girls has become different in many ways. Some of the differences may be due to biological factors. But most of the sex-linked differences in children's behavior can be explained by the ways that parents' expectations and behavior with their children differ according to the child's sex. In addition, other adults who interact with children probably have the same expectations.

Exercise 13-10

Write a definition of one of the following terms or ideas in a paragraph.

romance	happiness
a good movie	fear
sin	patriotism
beauty	honesty
macho	virtue

Chapter 14

Outlining

Although this book presents a review of grammar and offers suggestions for writing paragraphs, you may occasionally have to write longer compositions for other classes this semester. A discussion of outlining will be appropriate, therefore, because outlining is a very helpful tool when writing essays and other compositions. The outline helps you avoid organizational blunders when you write your first draft. It serves to test the relevance of your ideas—to make sure that you have not strayed from your thesis statement or central idea that you want to develop in your essay.

The time to outline is before writing your first draft. Jot down all the components you can think of that might belong in your essay: examples, statistics, facts, details, evidence. Do not worry about their order; you will take care of that later. Test each idea on your list in terms of your thesis statement: does it belong in your essay, or is it off the subject? If it is irrelevant, cut it.

Look over your topic and thesis again to see if their wording suggests the best way to organize your essay. For instance, an essay that explains how to do something is best arranged *chronologically*, and a topic that implies a visual impression would normally require a *spatial order*. On the other hand, content that does not lend itself to either a time or space pattern could be arranged in a logical order: *in order of importance, from general to specific*, or *from specific to general*. The ideas on your list will often trigger a suitable arrangement.

Next, group related ideas. Make separate "stacks" or "piles" of ideas, either on the paper or in your head. In each group, select the main idea that includes all the others. Arrange the major groups according to the pattern that you have selected. Then you are ready to make your outline.

The informal outline is suitable for shorter compositions and essays. It is usually written in topic form and contains only the major ideas and divisions of the essay. The formal outline is more complicated and more thorough than the informal outline. It is usually written in sentences. The formal outline is appropriate for long compositions and term papers.

Below are examples of the informal and the formal outline, both on the same topic. You will notice the difference in detail and thoroughness between them. Notice, too, that both begin with the thesis statement.

Informal Outline

DATE RAPE

THESIS: The traditional definition of rape as a violent sexual assault by a stranger is no longer valid.

- Myths about rape
- Date rape
- Women's complaints
- The law's reaction
- A revised definition of rape
- The need to sensitize men

Formal Outline

DATE RAPE

THESIS: The traditional definition of rape as a violent sexual assault by a stranger is no longer valid.

I.   Several myths about rape are still widely held.
   A.   Most girls are raped by strangers.
   B.   Most rapes are reported.
   C.   Only a tiny minority of women are raped.
   D.   Most rapists are convicted and go to jail.
II.   Date rape has traditionally been overlooked by police.
   A.   Date rape occurs frequently on college campuses.
   B.   It is not always violent.
   C.   Alcohol is a frequent component.
   D.   The man usually claims that it was consensual.
   E.   The business world also provides scenes conducive to rape.

III.   Women have a variety of complaints about date rape.
    A.   It is not taken seriously.
    B.   Authorities believe that rape cannot occur between two people on a date.
    C.   Physical intimidation is often employed by men.
    D.   Verbal harassment and inappropriate innuendo also constitute rape, according to some women.
IV.   The reaction of the law is to side with the man.
    A.   Juries want to know the past sexual history of the woman.
    B.   Police ignore one-fourth of all reports of sexual assaults.
    C.   Judges and lawyers are less inclined to believe a woman's testimony than a man's.
    D.   Men need to be sensitized and taught that rape is not necessarily violent.

As you can see, the informal topic outline is merely a list of the ideas in the order in which they will be developed in the essay. Each topic will probably be a section or paragraph in the essay. The formal outline, on the other hand, is more detailed. In fact, the formal outline here is less detailed than many formal outlines.

A few words of advice concerning the formal outline are in order. Main items or ideas should be preceded by roman numerals; ideas supporting the main ideas should be preceded by capital letters; the next sublevel is indicated by arabic numerals; the third by lowercase letters; the fourth by arabic numerals in parentheses; and fifth-level ideas are identified by lower case letters in parentheses. All letters and numbers at the same level should be indented so that they fall directly under one another.

The arrangement of numerals and letters in a very complex and detailed formal outline might appear as follows:

I.
  A.
  B.
    1.
    2.
      a.
      b.
        (1)
        (2)

Additional Suggestions for Outlines

1.   Write your thesis at the top of your outline to remind yourself of the scope and purpose of your composition.
2.   Items (both topics and sentences) at the same level should be of equal importance if possible.

3. You should have at least two subdivisions for each category. The reason is simple: a number or letter represents a division of the topic. If you cannot think of a second point, absorb the first one into the preceding heading.

4. Your outline does not have to be symmetrical—that is, if you have two points under a heading, you don't necessarily have to have two points under the other parallel headings.

5. Remember that an outline is merely a plan—it is not written in concrete, and you can move ideas around in the essay if you find that they do not follow logically in your outline.

A Glossary of Usage

This glossary is an alphabetical guide to words that frequently cause problems for writers. Some entries are labeled "colloquial," and some "nonstandard." A colloquialism is a word or phrase more appropriate to informal speech than to writing. Although colloquialisms are not grammatically incorrect, they should be avoided in formal writing, and even in informal writing they should be used sparingly. A nonstandard word or phrase is avoided at all times by careful speakers and writers. It is the kind of error sometimes labeled "incorrect" or "illiterate."

If you want to know more about the words in this glossary, consult *Webster's Third New International Dictionary* or a modern college-level dictionary. Other troublesome words that often cause problems for writers can be found on pages 214–217 ("Twenty-five Sets of Homonyms: Words Often Confused") in Chapter 12.

accept, except *Accept* is a verb meaning "to receive," and *except* is a preposition meaning "but," or a verb meaning "to exclude or leave out." "I will *accept* your invitation." "Everyone *except* Henry went." "We voted to *except* the new members from the requirements."

advice, advise *Advice* is an opinion you offer; *advise* means to recommend. "Her *advice* was always helpful." "The counselor will *advise* you concerning the proper course to take."

affect, effect *To affect* is to change or modify; *to effect* is to bring about something; an *effect* is a result. "The drought will *affect* the crop production." "I hope the treatment will *effect* a change in his condition." "The *effect* should be noticeable."

aggravate, annoy These two are often confused. *To aggravate* is to make a condition worse: "The treatment only *aggravated* his condition." *To annoy* is to irritate: "The ticking clock *annoyed* Dean as he read."

agree to, agree with You agree *to* a thing or plan: "Mexico and the United States *agree to* the border treaty." You agree *with* a person: "Laura and Herb *agreed with* each other about the price of the computer."

ain't Although *ain't* is in the dictionary, it is a nonstandard word never used by educated or careful speakers and writers except to achieve a deliberate humorous effect. The word should be avoided.

allusion, illusion An *allusion* is an indirect reference to something: "He made an *allusion* to his parents' wealth." An *illusion* is a false image or impression: "It is an *illusion* to think that I will be a millionaire soon."

among, between Use *between* for two objects and *among* for more than two: "The humming-bird darted *among* the flowers." "I sat *between* my mother and father."

amount, number *Amount* refers to quantity or to things in the aggregate; *number* refers to countable objects: "A large *amount* of work remains to be done." "A *number* of jobs were still unfilled."

anyone, any one *Anyone* means "any person at all": "I will talk to *anyone* who answers the telephone." *Any one* means any single person: "*Any one* of those players can teach you the game in a few minutes."

anyways, anywheres These are nonstandard forms for *anyway* and *anywhere*, and they should be avoided.

bad, badly *Bad* is an adjective; *badly* is an adverb. Use *bad* before nouns and after linking verbs; use the adverb *badly* to modify verbs or adjectives. "Her pride was hurt *badly* [not *bad*]." "She feels *bad* [not *badly*]."

being as, being that These are nonstandard terms and should be avoided. Use *since* or *because*.

beside, besides *Beside* is a preposition meaning "by the side of": "The doctor sat *beside* the bed talking to his patient." *Besides* may be a preposition or adverb meaning "in addition to" or "also": "*Besides* my homework, I have some letters to write."

between, among See *among, between*.

between you and I A common mistake. Use *between you and me*.

breath, breathe *Breath* is the noun: "He tried to conceal the smell of alcohol on his *breath*." *Breathe* is the verb: "The air we *breathe* is contaminated with pollutants."

burst, bursted, bust, busted *Burst* remains the same in the past, present, and past participle forms; *bursted*, *bust*, and *busted* are incorrect or nonstandard forms.

can, may *Can* refers to ability; *may* refers to permission. "After taking only a few lessons, Tom *can* play the trumpet beautifully. Because of the neighbors, however, he *may* play only in the afternoon."

can't hardly, barely, scarcely These are double negatives and are to be avoided. Use *can hardly*, *can barely*, and *can scarcely*.

can't help but Avoid this expression. Use *can't help doing something* but not *can't help but do something*.

conscience, conscious A *conscience* is a sense of right or wrong: "His *conscience* wouldn't allow him to cheat on the exam." To be *conscious* is to be aware: "I was not *conscious* of the noise in the background."

continual, continuous *Continual* means "repeated frequently," as in "We heard a series of *continual* beeps in the background." *Continuous* means "without interruption": "I was lulled to sleep by the *continuous* hum of the motor in the deck below."

could of A nonstandard form. Use *could have*: "I could *have* gone with him if I wanted."

criterion, criteria *Criterion* is singular; *criteria* is plural.

different from, than One thing is different *from* another, not different *than.*

disinterested, uninterested To be *disinterested* is to be impartial: "The judge was a *disinterested* listener in the case." To be *uninterested* is to lack interest: "It was obvious that Jack was *uninterested* in the lecture because he dozed off several times."

double negative Unacceptable in formal writing and in most informal situations except for humorous effect. Double negatives range from such obvious errors as "I don't have no paper" to more subtle violations ("I can't scarcely" and "It isn't hardly"). Avoid them.

due to, because of In formal writing, use *due to* after any form of the verb *be* (*am, are, is, was,* and so on): "My headache is *due to* not eating breakfast or lunch." Use *because of* in other situations: "*Because of* my diet, I often have a headache."

enormity, enormousness *Enormity* means "atrociousness"; *enormousness* means "of great size." "The *enormity* of the crime shocked the hardened crime reporters." "Because of the *enormousness* of the ship, it could not be docked in the local harbor."

enthused Nonstandard. Use "enthusiastic." ("He was *enthusiastic* about our plans for next summer," *not* "He was *enthused* about our plans for next summer.")

farther, further Use *farther* for physical distance ("They live *farther* from town than we do") and *further* for degree or quantity ("Their proposal was a *further* attempt to reach an agreement").

fewer, less Use *fewer* for items that can be counted, and *less* for quantity: "*Fewer* jobs are available for young people this summer." "He paid *less* for that car than I paid for mine."

finalize Avoid this term. Use *finish.*

good, well *Good* is an adjective, never an adverb. "She perform *well* [not *good*] in that role." *Well* is an adverb and an adjective; in the latter case it means "in a state of good health": "I am *well* now, although last week I didn't feel very *good.*" See Chapter 9.

hanged, hung Criminals are *hanged*; pictures are *hung.*

hisself A nonstandard term. Use *himself.*

if, whether Use *if* to introduce a clause implying a condition: "*If* you go to summer school, you can graduate early." Use *whether* to introduce a clause implying a choice: "I'm not sure *whether* I will go to summer school."

imply, infer "To imply" is to hint strongly; "to infer" is to derive the meaning from someone's statement by deduction. You *infer* the meaning of a passage when you read or hear it; the writer or speaker *implies* it.

irregardless Nonstandard. Use *regardless.*

is when, is where Avoid these expressions to introduce definitions, as in "A sonnet is when you have fourteen lines of iambic pentameter in a prescribed rhyme scheme." Better, "A sonnet is a poem with fourteen lines of iambic pentameter in a prescribed rhyme scheme."

kind of, sort of These are colloquial expressions acceptable in informal speech but not in writing. Use "somewhat" or "rather" instead.

leave, let *Leave* means "to go away," and *let* means "to allow." Do not use *leave* for *let*. "Please *let* [not *leave*] me go."

liable, likely, apt *Liable* means "legally responsible" or "susceptible to"; *likely* means "probably"; and *apt* refers to a talent or a tendency. "He is *liable* for the damage he caused." "Those clouds indicate it's *likely* to rain this afternoon." "She is an *apt* tennis player."

like *Like* is a noun, verb, adjective, and preposition; do not use it as a conjunction: "He acted as if [not *like*] he wanted to go with us."

loose, lose "To loosen" means to untie or unfasten; "to lose" is to misplace. *Loose* as an adjective means "unfastened" or "unattached." "He *loosened* his necktie." "Did he *lose* his necktie?" "His necktie is *loose*."

maybe, may be *Maybe* means "perhaps"; *may be* is a verb phrase. "*Maybe* we'll win tomorrow." "It *may be* that we'll win tomorrow."

must of Nonstandard. Write (and say) "must have," and in similar constructions use "could have" (not "could of") or "would have" (not "would of").

myself *Myself* is correct when used as an intensive or reflexive pronoun ("I helped *myself* to the pie," and "I hurt *myself*"), but it is used incorrectly as a substitute for *I* and *me* as in the following: "My brother and *myself* were in the army together in Germany." "They spoke to George and *myself* about the matter."

precede, proceed To *precede* is "to go before or in front of"; to *proceed* is "to continue moving ahead." "Poverty and hunger often *precede* a revolution." "They *proceeded* down the aisle as if nothing had happened."

quiet, quite, quit Read the following sentences to note the differences: "I wanted to get away from the noise and find a *quiet* spot." "They are *quite* upset that their son married without their permission." "When college starts next fall, he will *quit* his summer job."

raise, rise *Raise* is a verb meaning "to lift or help to rise in a standing position." Its principal parts are *raised*, *raised*, and *raising*. *Rise* means "to assume an upright position" or "to wake up"; its principal parts are *rose*, *risen*, and *rising*.

set, sit To *sit* means "to occupy a seat"; the principal parts are *sat*, *sat*, and *sitting*. *Set* means "to place something somewhere," and its principal parts are *set*, *set*, and *sitting*. See Chapter 6.

shall, will Most authorities, writers, and speakers use these interchangeably. Follow the advice of your instructor.

somewheres Nonstandard. Use *somewhere*; similarly, avoid *nowheres*.

theirselves A nonstandard term. Use *themselves*.

try and Use *try to:* "Some men wear toupees in an effort to *try to* hide their baldness."

Wesley Educational Publishers Inc.

A Glossary of Grammatical Terms

This glossary is an alphabetical guide to the grammatical terms used in this book, as well as to other helpful words. Some entries contain references to other terms or to sections of the text in which they are discussed in detail. For further references and explanation you should consult the index.

abstract noun A noun that refers to an idea or quality that cannot be identified by one of the senses. *Examples:* shame; delight; tolerance. See also *concrete noun*.

action verb See *verb*.

adjective A word that modifies (limits or describes) a noun or pronoun. "The concert was *long,* but it was *exciting.*" (The adjective *long* modifies the noun *concert*, and the adjective *exciting* modifies the pronoun *it*.) See Chapter 1.

adjective clause A dependent clause that modifies a noun or pronoun. "The delegates *who voted for the amendment* changed their minds." (The adjective clause modifies the noun *delegates*.) See Chapter 7.

adverb A word that modifies (limits or describes) an adjective, a verb, or another adverb. "He cried *softly.*" (*Softly* modifies the verb *cried*.) "They are *extremely* wealthy." (*Extremely* modifies the adjective *wealthy*.) "He left the room *very* hurriedly." (*Very* modifies the adverb *hurriedly*.) See Chapter 1.

adverb clause A dependent clause that modifies an adjective, verb, or another adverb. "I think of her *when I hear that song.*" (The adverb clause modifies the verb *think*.) "He became angry *because he had forgotten his keys*." (The adverb clause modifies the adjective *angry*.) "The band played so loudly *that I got a headache*." (The adverb clause modifies the adverb *so*.) See Chapter 7.

agreement The correspondence of one word with another, particularly subjects with verbs and pronouns with antecedents. If the subject of a sentence is singular, the verb is singular ("My *tire is* flat"); if the subject is singular, pronouns referring to it should also be singular ("The *carpenter* forgot *his* hammer"). Plural subjects require plural verbs, and plural pronouns are used to refer to plural antecedents. ("My *tires are* flat." "The *carpenters* forgot *their* tools.") See Chapters 3 and 5.

antecedent A word or group of words a pronoun refers to. "Jimmy, *who* used to play in a rock group, decided *he* would go back to college to complete *his* degree." (*Who, he,* and *his* all refer to the antecedent *Jimmy.*) See Chapter 5.

appositive A word or phrase following a noun or pronoun which renames or explains it. "London, *the capital*, was bombed heavily." "The author *Mark Twain* lived in Connecticut." In the first example, *the capital* is a nonessential appositive because it is not needed to identify the word it follows. In the second example, *Mark Twain* is an essential appositive because it is needed to identify the general term *author.* Only nonessential appositives are set off by commas. See Chapter 10.

article *A, an,* and *the* are articles. *A* and *an* are indefinite articles; *the* is a definite article. Articles are usually regarded as adjectives because they precede nouns.

auxiliary verb A helping verb used to form verb phrases. The most common auxiliary verbs are forms of *be* ("am," "are," "is," "have been," and so on) and *have* ("had," "has," and so on); others include the various forms of *do, can, shall, will, would, could, should, may, might,* and *must.* See Chapters 1 and 2.

case The form of a pronoun or noun to show its use in a sentence. Pronouns have three cases: the *nominative* or subject case (*I, he, she, they,* and so on), the *objective* case (*me, him, her, them,* and so on), and the *possessive* (*my, his, her, their,* and so on). Nouns change their spelling only in the possessive case (*Larry's, man's,* and so on). See Chapter 4.

clause A group of words containing a subject and a verb. A clause may be either independent or dependent. Independent clauses may stand alone as simple sentences. The dependent clause must be joined to an independent clause. "The restaurant was closed by the health department [*independent clause*] because the chef had hepatitis [*dependent clause*]." See Chapters 2 and 7.

collective noun A noun that names a group of persons or things, such as *army, committee, flock.* Collective nouns usually take singular verbs ("The troop *was* ready to leave") except when the individual members are thought of ("The class *were* arguing among themselves"). See Chapter 3.

colloquialism An informal word or expression more appropriate to speech than to writing.

comma-splice The misuse of a comma between two independent clauses in a compound sentence: "Herb's sister studied architecture in college, she designed the new office building downtown." Comma-splices can be corrected by substituting a semicolon for the comma or by inserting a coordinating conjunction after the comma. See Chapter 8.

command See *imperative sentence.*

common noun A noun that names a general category or class of persons, places, or things: *city, tool, song.* Common nouns are not capitalized except when they begin a sentence. See also *proper noun* and Chapter 1.

comparative degree The *more, less,* or *-er* form of those adjectives that can be compared.

comparison The change in the spelling of adjectives and adverbs to show degree. The degrees of comparison in English are *positive* (*slowly, loud*), *comparative* (*more slowly,* *louder*), and *superlative* (*most slowly, loudest*). Some modifiers cannot be compared: *round, dead, unique, full*, and so on.

complement A word or expression that completes the sense of a verb. See *direct object, indirect object, predicate adjective, predicate noun*, and *predicate pronoun*.

complex sentence A sentence containing one independent clause and at least one dependent clause: "The grain embargo *that was announced last year* was criticized by the farmers." The dependent clause is italicized. See Chapter 7.

compound Two or more words or word groups linked to form a single unit. For instance, two nouns can form a compound subject: "*Merchants and businesspeople* were united in their opposition to the new tax"; and two verbs can function as a compound predicate: "She *danced and sang* in the leading role."

compound-complex sentence A sentence containing at least two independent clauses and one or more dependent clauses: "Although the demand for oil has declined, the price of gasoline continues to climb, and the OPEC nations threaten a new price hike." See Chapter 7.

compound sentence A sentence with two or more independent clauses but no dependent clauses: "She wanted to read the book, but someone had previously borrowed it." See Chapter 7.

concrete noun A noun naming something that can be perceived by one of the senses: butter, elevator, scream, buzz. See also *abstract noun*.

conjunction A word that connects words, phrases, and clauses. See also *coordinate conjunction, subordinate conjunction*, and Chapter 1.

conjunctive adverb An adverb that connects independent clauses after a semicolon: "I had looked forward to seeing the movie; *however*, after reading the reviews I changed my mind." See Chapter 8.

contraction A word formed from the union of two words, with an apostrophe replacing the missing letters: *hasn't* (has not), *I'm* (I am).

coordinate adjectives Two or more adjectives of equal importance that modify the same noun: "The *tall, scowling* doorman finally let us in."

coordinate conjunction A word that connects two or more words, phrases, or clauses of equal rank. The most common coordinate conjunctions are *and, but, for, or, nor, so*. See Chapter 1.

correlative conjunctions Pairs of conjunctions used to join parts of a sentence of equal rank. The most common correlative conjunctions are *either . . . or; neither . . . nor; not only . . . but also; both . . . and*. See Chapters 1 and 9.

dangling modifier A modifier that has no word in the sentence for it to modify. It is left "dangling" and consequently ends up modifying an unintended word, as in the following: "Raising his bow triumphantly, the violin concerto ended in a crescendo." See Chapter 9.

dangling participle A participle serving as a modifier that has no word in the sentence for it to modify: "Looking out the window, a car drove by." See Chapter 9.

declarative sentence: A sentence that states a fact or makes a statement: "The capital of Kentucky is Frankfort."

demonstrative pronoun: A word used as an adjective or a pronoun to point out an item referred to. The demonstrative pronouns are *this*, *that*, *these*, and *those*.

dependent clause A group of words containing a subject and verb but unable to stand alone. A dependent clause must be subordinated to an independent clause in the same sentence: "*If you are on the honor roll*, you may be eligible for reduced insurance rates." See Chapter 7.

direct object A word that receives the action of the verb: "She helped *him* with the math problem." "I pried the *lid* off the can." See Chapter 4.

elliptical construction A construction in which one or more words are omitted but understood: "He is heavier than I (*am*)."

essential modifier A word or group of words necessary for the identification of the object being identified: "The man *with the checkered vest* wants to talk to you." Essential modifiers can be words, phrases, or clauses; they are not separated from the words they modify by commas. See Chapter 10.

exclamatory sentence A sentence expressing emotion, usually followed by an exclamation point: "Stop that yelling!"

formal language Language appropriate to formal situations and occasions, as distinguished from informal language and colloquialisms.

fragment See *sentence fragment*.

fused sentences See *run-on sentence*.

gender The grammatical expression of sex, particularly in the choice of pronouns: *he* (masculine), *she* (feminine), and *it* (neuter), and their related forms.

gerund The *-ing* form of a verb when it is used as a noun: "*Jogging* is one of the most popular forms of exercise among Americans in the 1990s."

helping verb See *auxiliary verb*.

imperative sentence A sentence expressing a command: "Please turn off your motor."

indefinite pronoun A pronoun that does not refer to a specific person or thing. Some of the most common indefinite pronouns include *anyone*, *someone*, *few*, *many*, and *none*. See Chapters 4 and 5.

independent clause A group of words containing a subject and a verb and capable of standing alone. See Chapters 2 and 7.

indirect object The person or thing receiving the direct object, and usually placed in a sentence between an action verb and the direct object: "Jay's lawyer gave *him* several documents to sign."

infinitive The form of the verb preceded by *to: to hesitate, to think, to start*, and so on.

informal language Language appropriate to informal situations and occasions. Informal language often uses contractions and colloquialisms.

intensive pronouns Pronouns that end in *-self* or *-selves* and emphasize their antecedents: *myself, yourself, himself, ourselves,* and so on. See Chapter 4.

interjection A word or phrase expressing emotion but having no grammatical relationship to the other words in the sentence. Interjections include the following: *Yes, no, oh, well,* and so on. See Chapter 1.

interrogative pronoun A pronoun that is used to form a question: *who, whom, what, which, whose.* "*Who* wants to play softball?"

intransitive verb A verb that does not require an object: "They slept." See also *transitive verb.*

inverted order A sentence that is not in the usual word order of *subject-verb-object.* "Angry and dejected was he." See Chapter 2.

irregular verb A verb that forms its past tense or past participle by changing its spelling: *bring* (brought); *think* (thought); *run* (ran). See *regular verb* and Chapter 6.

linking verb A verb that connects a subject in a sentence with another word (usually a noun, pronoun, or adjective) that renames or describes the subject. "The bacon *was* crisp." "You *seem* bored." See Chapters 1 and 4.

main clause See *independent clause.*

mass noun A noun referring to something usually measured by weight, degree, or volume rather than by count. Mass nouns are words like *assistance* (we don't say *one assistance, two assistances,* and so on), *money,* and *height.*

misplaced modifier A word or group of words misplaced in the sentence and therefore modifying the wrong word: "I watched the parade *standing on the balcony.*" See Chapter 9.

modifier A word or group of words describing or modifying the meaning of another word in the sentence.

nonessential modifier A word or group of words modifying a noun or pronoun but not essential to the meaning of the sentence. Nonessential modifiers are set off by commas: "My father, *who was born in Illinois,* was a metallurgical accountant." See Chapter 10.

noun A word that names a person, place, thing, or idea. See Chapter 1.

noun clause A dependent clause functioning as a subject, direct object, predicate nominative, or indirect object in a sentence: "He told me *what I wanted to hear.*" See Chapter 7.

number The form of a word that indicates one (*singular*) or more than one (*plural*). See Chapters 3 and 11.

object A word or group of words receiving the action of or affected by an action verb or a preposition. See *direct object, indirect object,* and *object of preposition.*

object of preposition A word or group of words following a preposition and related to another part of the sentence by the preposition: "Vince drove his motorcycle across *the United States.*" See Chapter 1.

participle The *-ing* form of a verb (the *present participle*) when it is used as an adjective (a *swimming* pool), or the *-d*, *-ed*, *-t*, or *-n* form of a verb (the *past participle*) when it is used as an adjective (the *painted* house).

past participle See *participle*.

person The form of a pronoun or verb used to show the speaker (*first person:* I am), the person spoken to (*second person:* you are), or the person spoken about (*third person:* she is). See Chapter 5.

personal pronoun A pronoun that changes its form to show person: *I, you, he, she, they,* and so on.

phrase A group of words lacking both a subject and a verb.

plural More than one. See also *number*.

positive degree The form of the adjective or adverb that makes no comparison: *heavy* (positive degree); *heavier* (comparative degree); *heaviest* (superlative degree). See also *comparative degree* and *superlative degree*.

possessive pronouns Pronouns that show ownership: *my, mine, your, yours, his, her, hers, its, our,* and so on. See Chapters 1 and 4.

predicate The verb, its modifiers, and any objects in a sentence. The predicate makes a statement about the subject of the sentence.

predicate adjective An adjective that follows a linking verb and modifies the subject: "We were *happy* to get the news." See Chapter 1.

predicate noun A noun that follows a linking verb and names the subject: "Harry is the *captain* of the lacrosse team."

predicate pronoun A pronoun that follows a linking verb and identifies the subject: "My closest friend is *you*." See Chapter 4.

preposition A word that shows a relationship between its object and another word in the sentence. Common prepositions include *at, to, behind, below, for, among, with,* and so on. See Chapter 1.

prepositional phrase A preposition and its object: *on the table, above the clouds, for the evening,* and so on. See Chapter 1.

present participle See *participle*.

pronoun A word that takes the place of a noun or another pronoun. See Chapters 1, 4, and 5.

pronoun antecedent See *antecedent* and Chapter 5.

pronoun form The form of a pronoun based on its use. Pronouns change their forms when they are used as subjects or objects, or to show possession. See also *case* and Chapter 4.

pronoun reference See *antecedent* and Chapter 5.

proper adjective An adjective formed from a proper noun: *Italian* painting, *African* nations, *Irish* whiskey. Proper adjectives are usually capitalized except in phrases like "china cabinet" or "french fries."

proper noun A noun referring to a specific person, place, or thing. Proper nouns are capitalized: *Denver; Mr. McAuliffe; Taj Mahal*. See Chapter 1.

© 1997 Addison-Wesley Educational Publishers Inc.

reflexive pronoun A pronoun ending in *-self* or *-selves* and renaming the subject. Reflexive pronouns are objects of verbs and prepositions; "He perjured *himself*." "They went by *themselves*." See Chapter 4.

regular verb A verb that forms its past tense by adding *-d*, or *-ed: start, started; hope, hoped.* See also *irregular verb* and Chapter 6.

relative pronoun A pronoun that introduces an adjective clause. The relative pronouns are *who, whom, whose, which, that.* See Chapter 7.

restrictive modifier See *essential modifier.*

run-on sentence Two independent clauses run together with no punctuation to separate them: "Her uncle works as a plumber in Des Moines he used to be a professor of philosophy in Boston." The run-on sentence is corrected by placing a semicolon or a comma and coordinate conjunction between the two clauses. See Chapter 8.

sentence A group of words containing a subject and a verb and expressing some sense of completeness. See Chapter 2.

sentence fragment A group of words lacking an independent clause and therefore unable to stand alone. See Chapter 8.

sentence types Sentences classified on the basis of their structure. There are four types of sentences in English: simple, compound, complex, and compound-complex. See also *complex, compound, compound-complex, simple,* and Chapter 7.

simple sentence A sentence containing one independent clause.

slang An informal word or expression not accepted in formal writing by careful or educated users of the language. Slang is usually short-lived or temporary, and should be used sparingly.

split infinitive An infinitive with a modifier between the *to* and the verb. Split infinitives are avoided by most careful speakers and writers. Some examples: *to really want; to hardly hear.*

squinting modifier A modifier that makes the meaning of a sentence ambiguous because it modifies two words at the same time: "We stood around *nervously* waiting to be introduced"; "I asked them *politely* to leave." See Chapter 9.

standard English The English of careful and educated speakers and writers.

subject The part of the sentence about which the predicate makes a statement. See also *predicate* and Chapter 2.

subordinate clause See *dependent clause.*

subordinate conjunction A word that joins a dependent clause to an independent clause. See Chapters 1 and 7.

superlative degree The *most, least,* or *-est* form of those adjectives and adverbs that can be compared: *most beautiful; least valid; greatest.* See also *comparative degree, comparison,* and *positive degree.*

tense The form of a verb that shows the action as being in the past, present, or future times. The most common tenses are simple present, present perfect, simple past, past perfect, simple future, and future perfect. See Chapter 6.

transitive verb A verb that requires an object in order to complete its meaning: "We *saw* the accident." "They *helped* their neighbors." See also *intransitive* verb.

verb A part of speech that describes the action or state of being of a subject. See Chapters 1 and 6.

Index

© 1997 Addison-Wesley Educational Publishers Inc.

Instructor's Manual to Accompany

Reviewing Basic Grammar

Fourth Edition

Mary Laine Yarber
Robert E. Yarber
Emeritus, San Diego Mesa College

LONGMAN

An imprint of Addison Wesley Longman, Inc.

New York • Reading, Massachusetts • Menlo Park, California • Harlow, England
Don Mills, Ontario • Sydney • Mexico City • Madrid • Amsterdam

Contents

Preface

For the convenience of the instructor, this manual contains four tests—Forms A, B, C, and D—for each chapter of *Reviewing Basic Grammar*, 4th edition, as well as four final examinations. Because the chapter tests and the final examinations cover the same material and are of equal difficulty, they may be used as additional review and pretests. All tests may be duplicated without retyping. Suggested answers for all the exercises in the book are also included.

M. L. Y.

R. E. Y.

Suggested Answers
to Exercises

Chapter 1: The Parts of Speech

Exercise 1

1. *Nouns:* 1977, Elvis Presley, subject, books, documentaries, legends *Pronouns:* he, he, one, our
2. *Nouns:* Elvis, 1935, Tupelo, Mississippi, parents, Memphis, Tennessee *Pronouns:* he, his
3. *Nouns:* father, mother, friends, family, interest, music, guitar *Pronouns:* His, they, their, him
4. *Nouns:* truck driver, Elvis, church basements, school, backyards *Pronouns:* anyone, who, him
5. *Nouns:* songs, music, style, performers, South, 1950s *Pronouns:* He, who
6. *Nouns:* personality, nervousness, clothes, hair, pompadour *Pronouns:* his, his, he, his
7. *Nouns:* records, studio, show, South *Pronouns:* He
8. *Nouns:* records, value, attention, Colonel Tom Parker, manager *Pronouns:* Those, whose, who, his
9. *Nouns:* Parker, Elvis, style, musicians *Pronouns:* [none]
10. *Nouns:* 1956, hit, "Heartbreak Hotel," success, career *Pronouns:* his, its, his
11. *Nouns:* months, recordings, sellers, popularity, Europe, charts *Pronouns:* his, their, they
12. *Nouns:* appearances, concerts, mobs, teenagers, gyrations, music, symbols, decay, society *Pronouns:* His, many, his, our
13. *Nouns:* career, Elvis, movies, 1960s, critics, fans *Pronouns:* they, his

14. *Nouns:* death, 1977, millions, fans, world, reaction, idols *Pronouns:* His, his, that one

15. *Nouns:* admirers, respects, grave, Graceland, home, Tennessee *Pronouns:* his, their, his, his

Exercise 2

1. 3	6. 1	11. 2
2. 1	7. 2	12. 3
3. 1	8. 3	13. 1
4. 2	9. 3	14. 3
5. 1	10. 2	15. 2

Exercise 3

A.

1. rumor	6. clues
2. story	7. clues
3. days	8. image
4. years	9. denials
5. Beatles	10. statement

B.

1. understood	6. similar
2. able	7. critical
3. capable	8. responsible
4. active	9. important
5. different	10. vital

Exercise 4

A.

1. million	6. stems
2. crash	7. have
3. Japanese	8. famous
4. popular	9. gross
5. derives	10. popular

B.

1. well	6. very
2. wildly	7. increasingly
3. very	8. also
4. increasingly	9. financially
5. finally	10. seriously

Exercise 5

1. of Alzheimer's disease *(adj.)*; in most older people *(adj.)*; of memory *(adj.)*
2. of the problem *(adv.)*; for an appointment *(adj.)*; with a doctor *(adj.)*
3. of the areas *(adj.)*; of the brain *(adj.)*
4. in learning something initially *(adv.)*; in other areas *(adv.)*; of the brain *(adj.)*
5. For that reason *(adv.)*; with learning and remembering new things *(adj.)*; at remembering old things *(adv.)*
6. of cells *(adj.)*; like bricks *(adv.)*

7. of the cell (*adj.*)
8. to memory (*adv.*); to another (*adv.*)
9. of the theories (*adj.*); by scientists (*adv.*); in Alzheimer's patients (*adv.*)
10. As a result (*adv.*); of memory (*adj.*); of the first effects (*adj.*)

Exercise 6

1. and; but
2. and; yet
3. Neither/nor
4. and; and; either/or
5. but

Review Exercise 1-A

A. 1. d 2. a 3. c 4. b 5. a 6. a 7. c 8. d 9. b 10. c
B. 11. a 12. b 13. c 14. a 15. b
C. 16. c 17. a 18. c 19. a 20. a 21. c 22. b 23. b 24. a 25. a

Review Exercise 1-B

A. 1. d 2. c 3. c 4. b 5. a 6. a 7. a 8. b 9. a 10. d
B. 11. b 12. b 13. c 14. a 15. a
C. 16. a 17. b 18. c 19. a 20. a 21. c 22. b 23. b 24. a 25. a

Chapter 2: Finding the Subject and Verb in the Sentence

Exercise 1

1. wails/vibrate
2. describe
3. moves/bunch up/pile up
4. happens/stretch out
5. changes

6. comes/increases
7. creates
8. reaches/passes
9. declines/stretch out/reach
10. call

Exercise 2

1. was
2. became
3. felt
4. appeared
5. tastes

6. were
7. is
8. seems
9. are
10. remain

Exercise 3

1. have destroyed
2. can claim
3. should run/have been running/can cover
4. were assigned
5. will present
6. has failed
7. had warned/might provoke
8. have been offered
9. is born
10. should have been notified/have won

Exercise 4

1. look
2. are/have
3. is/has been traced
4. has inherited/has
5. carry/suffers
6. clog/cause/damage/cause/ supply/are blocked
7. die
8. contain
9. live
10. have
11. concluded/improves
12. is/remains
13. is/survives
14. kills/are
15. has/is

Exercise 5

1. b 2. a 3. c 4. a 5. b 6. a 7. a 8. a 9. c 10. b 11. a 12. c 13. a
14. b 15. c

Exercise 6

1. water
2. Oceans and atmospheres
3. worlds
4. eruptions/earthquakes
5. Politicians
6. New York/Los Angeles
7. pollens
8. stream
9. troposphere
10. "wind chill factor"

Exercise 7

Student answers will vary.

Exercise 8

1. Locating/can be
2. method/has been
3. drillers/prefer
6. device/begins
7. Those/use
8. drillers/found

4. dowsers/carry

5. They/walk

9. drillers/were

10. dowsers/can find

Exercise 9

1. Acupuncture/is; it/is used
2. word/comes; treatments/are
3. Needles/are inserted; they/are twirled
4. location/depends; part/corresponds
5. needle/is inserted; needle/is inserted
6. explanation/is; twirling/stimulates
7. nerve/is; other/is
8. impulse/reaches; it/closes
9. Acupuncture/is used; needle/is placed
10. Acupuncture/encounters; numbers/are investigating

Exercise 10

1. (Although <u>autism</u> <u>is</u> very rare); disorder/has been
2. (Because <u>it</u> <u>appears</u> in infancy); clinicians/have used
3. (although <u>they</u> <u>may respond</u> to social situations); infants/do seek
4. (when <u>they</u> <u>are</u> alone); symptom/is
5. (if there is even a slight <u>change</u> in their environment); symptom/is
6. (when <u>they</u> <u>want</u> or <u>need</u> something); characteristic/is
7. (Although some autistic <u>children</u> <u>do</u> eventually <u>use</u> language); many/do
8. (although no <u>one</u> <u>has</u> yet <u>been</u> able to identify it); Autism/is caused
9. (If an autistic <u>child</u> <u>has</u> a nonverbal I.Q. score below 50); outlook/is
10. (if <u>they</u> <u>are shown</u> appropriate social and conversational behavior); Those/have

Review Exercise 2-A

A. 1. a 2. c 3. a 4. d 5. c 6. a 7. d 8. a 9. d 10. c 11. c 12. b
B. 13. b 14. a 15. b 16. b 17. a 18. d 19. a 20. a 21. a 22. a 23. b
    24. b 25. c

Review Exercise 2-B

A. 1. a 2. d 3. a 4. a 5. c 6. c 7. d 8. d 9. c 10. a 11. c 12. b
B. 13. b 14. a 15. b 16. a 17. b 18. c 19. a 20. a 21. a 22. a 23. b
    24. b 25. a

Chapter 3: Making the Subject and Verb Agree

Exercise 1

1. smile, own
2. keep, arrive
3. stay, feel
4. eats, sleeps
5. hope, need

6. accept, touch, ask
7. knows, sings
8. goes, takes, believes
9. tell, drive
10. wants, proves

Exercise 2

1. a   2. a   3. b   4. b   5. b   6. a   7. a   8. b   9. b   10. b

Exercise 3

1. a   2. a   3. b   4. a   5. b   6. b   7. b   8. a   9. a   10. a

Exercise 4

1. a   2. b   3. b   4. a   5. a   6. a   7. a   8. b   9. a   10. b

Exercise 5

1. a   2. a   3. a   4. b   5. b   6. b   7. a   8. a   9. b   10. a

Exercise 6

1. b   2. b   3. a   4. b   5. b   6. a   7. b   8. b   9. a   10. b   11. b   12. a   13. b
14. b   15. b

Review Exercise 3-A

1. a   2. b   3. a   4. b   5. b   6. a   7. a   8. a   9. a   10. a   11. b   12. a   13. a
14. b   15. b   16. a   17. b   18. b   19. b   20. b   21. a   22. b   23. b   24. b   25. b

Review Exercise 3-B

1. b   2. b   3. a   4. b   5. a   6. b   7. a   8. b   9. a   10. b   11. b   12. b   13. a
14. b   15. b   16. b   17. a   18. b   19. a   20. b   21. b   22. b   23. a   24. b   25. a

Chapter 4: Using the Correct Form of the Pronoun

Exercise 1

1. we (A)
2. we (A); it (A); he (B)
3. They (A)
4. I (A); we (A)
5. I (C)

6. It (A); who (A); he (A)
7. it (A); you (B)
8. We (A); we (A); they (A); we (A)
9. who (A)
10. I (A)

Exercise 2

1. them (C)
2. him (B); me (A)
3. me (C)
4. us (A)
5. you (A); me (A)

6. me (C); me (A)
7. him (A)
8. us (C); us (A)
9. him (A); me (A)
10. me (C)

Exercise 3

1. a   2. b   3. b   4. b   5. a   6. b   7. b   8. b   9. b   10. b   11. b   12. a   13. b
14. b   15. b

Exercise 4

1. b   2. b   3. b   4. a   5. a   6. b   7. b   8. b   9. b   10. b   11. b   12. a   13. b
14. a   15. b

Exercise 5

1. a   2. a   3. a   4. a   5. b   6. a   7. a   8. b   9. b   10. a   11. a   12. b   13. b
14. a   15. b

Review Exercise 4-A

A.   1. a   2. c   3. b   4. a   5. c
B.   6. a   7. b   8. a   9. c   10. a
C.   11. a   12. a   13. b   14. b   15. a   16. b   17. a   18. b   19. b   20. a   21. b
       22. a   23. b   24. b   25. a

Review Exercise 4-B

A. 1. a   2. c   3. b   4. a   5. b
B. 6. a   7. b   8. a   9. c   10. a
C. 11. a   12. a   13. a   14. b   15. a   16. b   17. a   18. b   19. a   20. a   21. a
22. a   23. b   24. b   25. a

Chapter 5: Common Errors in Pronoun Agreement and Reference

Exercise 1

1. a   2. b   3. a   4. a   5. b   6. a   7. a   8. b   9. a   10. b

Exercise 2

1. a   2. a   3. a   4. b   5. b   6. b   7. a   8. a   9. a   10. a

Exercise 3 (Answers will vary. Suggested revisions are below.)

1. When you do not exercise or follow a proper diet, it is likely that you will gain weight.
2. CORRECT
3. When one first studies a foreign language, it is difficult to remember all of the rules of pronunciation.
4. When we left the hotel to go shopping, we had to turn in our key to the clerk.
5. Alberto complained that if he wanted something done right, he had to do it himself.
6. Once you have heard her distinctive voice, you will never forget it.
7. CORRECT
8. Americans driving for the first time in Ireland should remember that they have to drive on the left side of the road.
9. If a student does not do homework or attend class regularly, he cannot expect a good grade at the end of the semester.
10. Voters should vote intelligently and be informed about the issues so that they can make intelligent choices at the polls.

Exercise 4 (Answers will vary. Suggestions follow.)

1. Margaret plays the piano very well, but she keeps her talent hidden.
2. Ray's secret ambition is to be a chef, but he has never studied cooking.
3. At registration time the clerk checks your record and transcript.
4. After having been an executive of a large bank for many years, Anne has taken a job at a small company, but this change in career has created several problems.
5. Mel has been taking tap-dancing lessons, but he still can't dance very well.

6. As Burl talked to Conn, his voice began to rise in anger.
7. Because of unemployment and the recession, Maxine and Bob delayed their marriage.
8. Luciano Pavarotti is a great tenor who claims that he has practiced singing every day since he was a child.
9. Many companies use lie-detectors because they believe they are effective when interviewing job applicants.
10. Although Vince has never been to Mexico, he likes Mexican food.

Review Exercise 5-A

A. 1. c 2. c 3. b 4. c 5. b 6. b 7. a 8. b 9. b 10. b 11. c 12. d 13. a
14. b 15. d
B. 16. a 17. b 18. b 19. a 20. b 21. a 22. b 23. b 24. a 25. a

Review Exercise 5-B

A. 1. c 2. c 3. b 4. c 5. b 6. b 7. a 8. d 9. b 10. b 11. c 12. d 13. a
14. b 15. b
B. 16. a 17. b 18. b 19. a 20. b 21. a 22. a 23. a 24. a 25. a

Chapter 6: Common Errors Involving Verbs

Exercise 1

1. arose 2. struck 3. dived (or dove) 4. dug 5. burst 6. bore 7. grew
8. became 9. gave 10. began

Exercise 2

1. known 2. flown 3. begun 4. written 5. given 6. borne 7. come 8. seen
9. torn 10. become

Exercise 3

1. present
2. present perfect
3. present perfect
4. present
5. future perfect
6. past perfect
7. past
8. future
9. past perfect
10. future

Exercise 4

1. are   2. have slept   3. ate   4. have drunk   5. grew   6. have sat   7. Draw
8. left   9. have laid   10. speed

Exercise 5 (Answers will vary. Suggestions follow.)

1. Most people know that cigarettes are bad for their health . . .
2. First, the nicotine speeds up the heart beat and the blood pressure rises.
3. The tar found in cigarettes is even more harmful because it bears ingredients that cause cancer.
4. CORRECT
5. Your lungs also take . . .
6. It then becomes . . .
7. People who hang onto their smoking habits take . . .
8. But they enjoy sitting down and lighting up a cigarette.
9. People now begin . . .
10. Most smokers know they should quit, but this is easier said than done.

Exercise 6

A. 1. lay   2. lain   3. lying   4. lay   5. laid   6. lying   7. laid   8. lie   9. laying
    10. lay   11. lay   12. laid   13. lay   14. lying   15. lay
B. 16. set   17. sat   18. sit   19. set   20. sit   21. set   22. set   23. sat   24. sitting
    25. set   26. sat   27. sat   28. set   29. sitting   30. sat

Review Exercise 6-A

A. 1. c   2. b   3. d   4. a   5. d   6. d   7. a   8. d   9. b   10. c
B. 11. b   12. a   13. b   14. b   15. b   16. a   17. a   18. b   19. a   20. b   21. b
    22. a   23. b   24. a   25. a

Review Exercise 6-B

A. 1. c   2. d   3. d   4. b   5. d   6. a   7. a   8. d   9. b   10. c
B. 11. a   12. b   13. a   14. a   15. b   16. b   17. a   18. b   19. a   20. a   21. a
    22. b   23. b   24. a   25. a

Chapter 7: Compound and Complex Sentences

Exercise 1

Student responses

Exercise 2

1. in Sportsmen's Park, but now
2. CORRECT
3. from Italy, or she has
4. CORRECT
5. from college, yet she was
6. CORRECT
7. CORRECT
8. CORRECT
9. first two games, but they
10. CORRECT

Exercise 3

1. dep   2. ind   3. dep   4. ind   5. dep   6. dep   7. ind   8. dep   9. ind   10. ind

Exercise 4

Student responses

Exercise 5

1. Although interest rates on credit cards are high,
2. Because credit cards are a profitable business for banks,
3. when AT&T introduced its Universal card.
4. Because more than six thousand financial institutions issue cards,
5. when cardholders use their cards to charge anything from meals to vacations.
6. because it is not necessary to have cash at hand.
7. when they use a credit card.
8. Although most U.S. consumer spending is by cash and checks,
9. Though economists talk about the cashless society,/before such a phenomenon occurs.
10. If the card companies have their way,

Exercise 6

1. orange crate (that served as a bookcase)
2. an award (whose recipients have often been the subjects of controversy)
3. an ex-President (who has become more admired since leaving office)
4. clause (which was not clearly stated)
5. conditions (that have caused starvation and poverty in that country)
6. Margaret Thatcher (who was the first woman Prime Minister of England)
7. driver (whom I argued with)

8. game (that had been rained out)
9. lab (which had inadequate ventilation)
10. Letters (that do not have ZIP codes)

Exercise 7

1. Dickens, who wrote the novel *Bleak House*,
2. which are worthless during the painter's lifetime
3. who have fair skin
4. that erupted in the Philippines
5. that can be observed only by astronomers
6. who conduct major symphony orchestras
7. Bernstein, who conducted the New York Philharmonic Orchestra,
8. baseball fans, who are long-suffering,
9. whose parents graduated from a prestigious college
10. Eliot, who was born in St. Louis,
11. who hopes to be a chess grandmaster
12. Redford, who is known by most people as an actor and a director,
13. that are criticized by the critics
14. who embark on a vigorous exercise program
15. California, which has a state income tax,/that is similar to the federal form

Exercise 8

1. that the algebra test was canceled
2. Whatever he does
3. that the problem of the homeless requires the cooperation of all segments of society
4. that Mozart liked to play billiards
5. when I heard/that President Kennedy had been assassinated
6. how to make Irish soda bread
7. how others act/what they are told
8. What Lincoln said that afternoon at Gettysburg
9. that Reno is farther west than San Diego
10. by what the speaker said.

Exercise 9

1. c   2. d   3. a   4. b   5. b   6. c   7. a   8. b   9. b   10. a

Review Exercise 7-A

A.   1. b   2. a   3. a   4. b   5. c
B.   6. c   7. a   8. b   9. c   10. a
C.   11. a   12. b   13. a   14. b   15. b   16. b   17. a   18. a   19. b   20. b   21. b
        22. a   23. b   24. a   25. a

Review Exercise 7-B

A. 1. a   2. a   3. b   4. b   5. c
B. 6. b   7. c   8. a   9. c   10. c
C. 11. a   12. b   13. a   14. a   15. b   16. b   17. b   18. b   19. a   20. a   21. b
    22. b   23. a   24. a   25. a

Chapter 8: Correcting Sentence Fragments, Run-on Sentences, and Comma-Splices

Exercise 1 (Methods of correcting the sentence fragments will vary.)

1. Throughout much of human history. (*prepositional phrase*)
2. CORRECT
3. Consisting of silk sails stretched across bamboo frames. (*participle phrase*)
4. To perform a variety of tasks. (*infinitive phrase*)
5. Measuring weather, delivering love notes, and carrying signals. (*participle phrase*)
6. CORRECT
7. To fly in stunt formations or even hover. (*infinitive phrase*)
8. To make parachutes for American soldiers in World War II. (*infinitive phrase*)
9. Throughout the fabric after the kite is accidentally punctured. (*prepositional phrase*)
10. Coming in a variety of complex styles and costing as much as a hundred dollars or more. (*participle phrase*)

Exercise 2

Number 4 is correct; student responses for the other sentences will vary.

Exercise 3

Number 3 is correct; student responses for the other sentences will vary.

Exercise 4

Numbers 2, 3, 4, 6, and 10 are correct; student responses for the other sentences will vary.

Exercise 5

Numbers 2 and 5 are correct; student responses for the other sentences will vary.

Review Exercise 8-A

1. b   2. c   3. b   4. d   5. a   6. c   7. b   8. d   9. c   10. a   11. d   12. a   13. b   14. c
15. d   16. c   17. d   18. c   19. a   20. d   21. d   22. c   23. a   24. d   25. a

Review Exercise 8-B

1. d   2. b   3. c   4. d   5. d   6. c   7. c   8. c   9. c   10. a   11. a   12. a   13. b   14. b
15. a   16. b   17. b   18. d   19. c   20. c   21. a   22. a   23. b   24. b   25. c

Chapter 9: Confused Sentences

Exercise 1

Number 9 is correct; student responses for the other sentences will vary.

Exercise 2

Numbers 7 and 10 are correct; student responses for the other sentences will vary.

Exercise 3

Number 4 is correct; student responses for the other sentences will vary.

Exercise 4

Number 8 is correct; student responses for the other sentences will vary.

Exercise 5

1. a   2. b   3. b   4. a   5. b   6. b   7. b   8. b   9. b   10. b

Exercise 6

Numbers 3 and 9 are correct; student responses for the other sentences will vary.

Review Exercise 9-A

A.   1. b   2. a   3. b   4. b   5. b
B.   6. d   7. a   8. c   9. b   10. a   11. c   12. c   13. a   14. b   15. a   16. d   17. c
     18. a   19. d   20. a   21. c   22. a   23. b   24. c   25. c

Review Exercise 9-B

A.   1. b   2. a   3. b   4. b   5. b
B.   6. d   7. a   8. a   9. b   10. a   11. c   12. c   13. d   14. c   15. a   16. b   17. b
     18. b   19. d   20. a   21. a   22. b   23. c   24. a   25. c

Chapter 10: Punctuation

Exercise 1

1. Your application should be mailed to D. A. Coleman, 19 W. Bond Street, Richmond, VA 23219.
2. Prof. Lehane and Ms. Garcia will sing duets today at 2:30 p.m. at the concert hall on Seventh St. in Des Moines.
3. Did you hear someone yell "Fire!"?
4. My little sister asked me whether there is a Santa Claus.
5. "Do you believe in Santa Claus?" I asked her.
6. The newspaper columnist told our class that he types on an IBM Selectric typewriter that he purchased when he worked at the UN.
7. My daughter earned her degree from UCLA but also took classes at USC and the U. of Arizona.
8. My alarm rings promptly at 7:00 a.m. every day, but this morning I overslept and missed my favorite TV program and my appointment with Dr. McAndrews.
9. Holy cow! I've just won the state lottery!
10. The world's first alphabet was developed by the Sumerians around 3000 B.C.
11. The Rev. Martin Luther King, Jr., gave a rousing speech at the Lincoln Memorial in Washington, D.C.
12. No! I can't believe it! (also: I can't believe it.)
13. Did you remember to wind the clock and put out the cat?
14. I wonder whether forces from NATO should be sent to enforce the cease-fire.
15. Please take your shoes off when entering the mosque.

Exercise 2

1. CORRECT
2. anchovies,
3. CORRECT
4. pianist,
5. inexperienced,
6. CORRECT
7. CORRECT
8. town,
9. CORRECT
10. CORRECT

Exercise 3

1. museum,
2. CORRECT
3. professionally,
4. 1215,
5. himself,
6. exercise,
7. fog,
8. CORRECT
9. sing,
10. living room,
11. times,
12. news,
13. CORRECT
14. district,
15. I.R.S.,

Exercise 4

1. Yes,/convertible,
2. parents,/hand,
3. tomatoes, peppers, onions, garlic,
4. Oregon,/example,
5. CORRECT
6. Yes,
7. me, please,
8. head,/nose,
9. speech, in fact,
10. you, Greta,

Exercise 5

1. guide,/languages,
2. *erectus*,/ancestor,
3. Lindbergh,/heroes,
4. rain,/drenching,
5. CORRECT
6. brother,/restaurant,
7. anniversary,
8. CORRECT
9. Jefferson,/President,
10. long,

© 1997 Addison-Wesley Educational Publishers Inc.

Exercise 6

1. intelligence,/wealth,
2. injured,
3. April 2, 1792,/Philadelphia,
4. CORRECT
5. Reeves, M.D.,
6. dishes,/bath,
7. hymn,"/Drucker,
8. Winter Park, Florida,/June 14,
9. Ralph,
10. Sinatra, Jr.,/Lake Tahoe, California,/December, 1963 *or* December 1963.

Exercise 7

1. The human body has 206 bones that come in four general shapes: long, short, flat, and irregular.
2. There are thirty-three separate spinal vertebrae in the embryo, but only twenty-six in an adult.
3. This is due to the fact that some vertebrae fuse together at the time of birth.
4. CORRECT
5. CORRECT
6. Basketball players are able to slam dunk partly because of their extremely long femurs, tibias, and fibulas, called leg bones by most of us.
7. Each finger consists of three bones, and the thumb consists of two.
8. Incredibly, the average human bone can tolerate a pressure of 27,000 pounds per square inch before breaking.
9. Bones are, however, usually broken when they are twisted or when they receive a blow from the side.
10. It is amusing that the softer material inside human bones is called "spongy bone."

Exercise 8

1. Tran speaks English at school; at home, however, he speaks Vietnamese.
2. The advertising agency selected seven cities as trial markets for the new product: Huntsville, Mobile, and Tuscaloosa, in Alabama; Yakima and Olympia, in Washington; and Carbondale and East St. Louis, in Illinois.
3. The disc jockey didn't play any of my favorite songs; I danced once.
4. Monaco has no famous colleges or universities; however, it has a ninety-nine percent literacy rate.
5. The annual number of marriages in America has increased since the 1980s; so has the death rate.

6. Jessie closed his Manhattan law practice last week; he plans to move to Cedar Rapids to take over his father's farm.
7. CORRECT
8. I will have to find a job this semester, or I will have to get a loan for tuition.
9. Cows will not eat hay that has a musty odor; therefore, farmers must make sure that it is dry before they bale it.
10. During our African honeymoon we visited Zanzibar, Tabora, and Linga in Tanzania; Nairobi, Nakum, and Mombassa in Kenya; and Juba, Was, and Khartoum in Sudan.

Exercise 9

1. Harold faced a dilemma: whether to study for his final exam or wash his car.
2. According to an authority on American slang, the most common slang terms deal with money, sex, and drinking.
3. Only one obstacle kept Sue from a career in music: lack of talent.
4. Skin is composed of three main layers: the epidermis, dermis, and subcutaneous tissue.
5. The three hardest events to cope with, psychologists claim, are the death of a spouse, divorce, and marital separation.
6. CORRECT
7. From the observation deck we could see Golden State Park, the marinas in the harbor, and the lights of Marin County.
8. With her Christmas bonus check Laura bought five compact discs, a muffler for her car, and a tie for her father.
9. CORRECT
10. CORRECT

Exercise 10

Depending on the desired emphasis, students should insert dashes or parenthesis where an "X" is placed in the following sentences. Sentences 2, 4, and 10 require a dash only.

1. My oldest brother X the actor who lives in Hollywood X is unable to attend our cousin's wedding.
2. Excellent students usually have one trait in common—self-discipline.
3. Our dinner X two steaks and a bottle of champagne X cost only twenty dollars with a special coupon.
4. Law, navigation, politics, medicine, war—Shakespeare wrote about all of these topics in his plays.
5. I read an article in the *Times* X or maybe it was the *Post-Dispatch* X describing the tornado in Kansas last week.

6. The sociology class X an elective required for my bachelor's degree X was more interesting than I had expected.
7. Charley X my pet dog that I told you about X is prohibited from entering the house.
8. I intend to lose X I really mean it X ten pounds in the next month.
9. The surprise dessert X strawberries soaked in brandy and dipped in chocolate X climaxed our feast.
10. I really should go jogging this morning—oh, let's go out for waffles instead.

Exercise 11

1. Would you please translate the French phrase *noblesse oblige* for me?
2. Professor Cardenas complained that too many students confuse the words "to," "too," and "two."
3. Who said, "For people who like this sort of thing, this is the sort of thing they would like"?
4. Beverly is next in line to be editor-in-chief of the *Times-Courier.*
5. The Greek letter *rho* looks like the Roman letter *p.*
6. "My favorite love song," said Darnell, "is 'Just the Way You Are' by Billy Joel."
7. I ordered garlic pizza, not garlic pasta.
8. Did you read the *Louisville Herald's* review of the movie *Singin' in the Rain?*
9. Although the movie *Field of Dreams* was not believable, the references to baseball history were interesting.
10. The expression "to love, honor, and obey" has been dropped from some marriage ceremonies.

Exercise 12

1. The swimming pool schedule has been changed while it's being painted.
2. Karl's grandparents came to this country from Sweden.
3. In recent years the men's rights movement has attracted many followers.
4. Over one hundred guests attended the couple's wedding.
5. Is this wallet yours?
6. The mayor continued to ignore the veterans' demands when they marched on City Hall.
7. CORRECT
8. I suppose it was just somebody's attempt at humor.
9. It was obvious from the appearance of both that they had been in the water.
10. Helen's and Eddie's grades in Spanish began to improve after the midterm examination.
11. "Who's on First?" is one of Abbott and Costello's funniest routines.
12. The salesmen's bonus was less than they had expected.
13. CORRECT

14. The policeman wanted to know whose car was parked illegally in front of the firehouse.
15. Mr. and Mrs. Kelly's children surprised their parents with an anniversary party.

Exercise 13

1. Approximately fifty yea's and one hundred no's were recorded at last week's vote.
2. Clarissa said that she was thirty-nine and holding.
3. Many Europeans call the letter *z* *zed* or *zeta*.
4. Dr. Marissa Holdener prescribed an anti-inflammatory drug for the foot problem I've had for the past three weeks.
5. Every morning Mr. Mather walks $2\frac{1}{2}$ miles.
6. The President-elect was briefed by the C.I.A. prior to her inauguration.
7. It's been difficult to make the dog sleep in its house.
8. You're out of your mind if you think I'll babysit your little brother.
9. Margaret offered her husband 150 dollars if he would lose twenty-five pounds, but I doubt he'll accept the offer.
10. I can't meet you any earlier than 12 o'clock, although it's probably too late for you.

Review Exercise 10-A

1. a 2. a 3. b 4. a 5. b 6. a 7. a 8. b 9. b 10. b 11. a 12. a 13. b 14. b
15. a 16. a 17. a 18. a 19. b 20. a 21. a 22. b 23. a 24. a 25. b

Review Exercise 10-B

1. a 2. a 3. b 4. b 5. b 6. a 7. b 8. b 9. a 10. b 11. b 12. b 13. a 14. b
15. a 16. b 17. a 18. b 19. b 20. b 21. a 22. b 23. b 24. b 25. b

Chapter 11: Capitalization

Exercise 1

1. My favorite course at Portland Community College was Archaeology 105, taught by Professor Myra Bernstein, Ph.D.
2. I especially enjoyed learning about the works of art and architecture called the Seven Wonders of the World, which were admired by the ancient Greeks and Romans.
3. Khufu, Khafra, and Menkaura make up the group of pyramids of Egypt; built between 3000 and 1800 B.C., they are the only surviving wonder which can still be seen.

© 1997 Addison-Wesley Educational Publishers Inc.

4. The Hanging Gardens of Babylon, built by King Nebuchadnezzar in 600 B.C., lie on a terrace seventy-five feet in the air and are irrigated by the Euphrates River.
5. My friend Diana, who lives in southeastern Greece, told me about the fourth wonder, which was a gold and ivory statue of the god Zeus at Olympia.
6. The sculptor Chares spent twelve years building a statue of the sun god Helios, which was 120 feet high and overlooked the harbor near Rhodes.
7. The largest temple of ancient times was the temple of Artemis, near Ephesus, Greece.
8. The mausoleum at Halicarnassus was a giant marble tomb built for Mausolus, a statesman of the Persian empire—hence the word "mausoleum."
9. When sailing on Labor Day, I always think of the seventh wonder: the Pharos Lighthouse of Alexandria, which was sculpted by the Greek architect Sostratos, and stood an amazing two-hundred to six-hundred feet high.
10. More than 100,000 laborers worked for twenty years to build the great pyramid of Khufu, which contains almost three million slabs of limestone.

Review Exercise 11-A

1.	10.	19.
2. X	11.	20.
3. X	12. X	21.
4.	13. X	22. X
5.	14.	23. X
6.	15. X	24.
7. X	16.	25.
8. X	17.	
9.	18.	

Review Exercise 11-B

1. X	10.	19.
2. X	11. X	20. X
3. X	12. X	21. X
4. X	13.	22. X
5.	14. X	23. X
6. X	15. X	24.
7.	16. X	25. X
8.	17. X	
9. X	18.	

Chapter 12: Spelling

Review Exercise 12-A

A. 1. a   2. b   3. b   4. a   5. b
B. 6. b   7. a   8. b   9. a   10. c   11. c   12. a   13. c   14. b   15. a   16. c   17. a
    18. b   19. a   20. b   21. a   22. c   23. b   24. c   25. b

Review Exercise 12-B

A. 1. b   2. a   3. a   4. a   5. b
B. 6. b   7. a   8. b   9. a   10. a   11. b   12. c   13. c   14. a   15. a   16. b   17. c
    18. b   19. c   20. a   21. b   22. a   23. c   24. b   25. b

Chapter 13: Writing Paragraphs

Exercise 1

a. We are becoming a nation of pill-grabbers and hypochondriacs who regard the slight-
    est ache as a searing ordeal.
b. Reasons for the popularity of fast-food chains appear obvious enough.
c. These facts provide convincing arguments for possible dolphin intelligence.

Exercise 2-10

Student responses.

1-A

CHAPTER TEST

A. *Identify the parts of speech of the italicized words by using the appropriate letter.*

a. noun   b. pronoun   c. adjective   d. adverb

_____ 1. Health care is the career *field* expected to create the most new jobs by the year 2000.

_____ 2. I dream of owning an *original* painting by my favorite American impressionist, Mary Cassatt.

_____ 3. I can tell *she* is an Army colonel by the silver eagle on her uniform.

_____ 4. Because Los Angeles is famous for its love of cars, many people are surprised to learn that *four* railroads criss-cross the city.

_____ 5. The sun is about 92,900,000 miles from the *earth*.

_____ 6. The Declaration of Independence was signed by fifty-six men, most of *whom* were farmers, merchants, or lawyers.

_____ 7. The Mandarin dialect of Chinese is the world's most *widely* spoken language.

_____ 8. *Each* year the Lady Byng Memorial Trophy is given to professional hockey's Most Gentlemanly Player.

_____ 9. Algeria, Malaysia, Pakistan, and *Turkey* all have a crescent moon in their national flags.

_____ 10. I wonder how many residents *actually* bowl in Bowling Green, Kentucky.

B. *Identify the parts of speech of the italicized words by using the appropriate letter.*

a. preposition   b. conjunction   c. interjection

_____ 11. Phillis Wheatley was the first black woman *in* America to have her writing published.

_____ 12. *With* six sons and four daughters, William Henry Harrison had more children than any other U.S. president.

_____ 13. *Stop!* You're parking too close to my new Miata!

_____ 14. I rode my motorcycle to school today *because* my car would not start.

_____ 15. April enjoys living in New York *but* misses her family in California.

C. *Identify the italicized words by using the appropriate letters.*

a. action verb   b. linking verb   c. helping verb

_____   16.   I *hear* my favorite song being played next door.
_____   17.   Your little brother *has become* taller than both of us!
_____   18.   A skulk of foxes *was* spotted at Diana's ranch.
_____   19.   Tobacco *has always been* a valued crop in Virginia.
_____   20.   You *need* thick ear plugs to belong to the National Hot Rod Association.
_____   21.   We *could have* eaten more chowder, but wanted to save room for pie.
_____   22.   Females *outnumber* males in the United States.
_____   23.   I *might have* been an olympic swimmer if I weren't so afraid of water.
_____   24.   Julie *runs* every morning to prepare for next month's marathon.
_____   25.   Belarus, a republic formed in 1994, *is* growing in population.

1-B

CHAPTER TEST

A. *Identify the parts of speech of the italicized words by using the appropriate letter.*

a. noun   *b. pronoun*   *c. adjective*   *d. adverb*

_____ 1. A water shortage is *one* of the problems facing California.
_____ 2. The *evidence* cited by the prosecution convinced the jury of the suspect's guilt.
_____ 3. The tail of the kite was too *short* to give it much stability.
_____ 4. Mr. Khan was *very* proud of his son, a senior at the Naval Academy.
_____ 5. Knowing how to locate information is *sometimes* as important as actually knowing the information.
_____ 6. Paying one's income taxes after the *deadline* can often lead to a penalty and additional interest.
_____ 7. *Everyone* would probably agree that practice makes perfect.
_____ 8. Calvin was urged by his doctor to drink at least eight glasses of water *daily*.
_____ 9. A smiling and *confident* waiter approached us at the door of the restaurant.
_____ 10. My neighbors' insurance premiums were increased because *they* have had several automobile accidents within the last year.

B. *Identify the parts of speech of the italicized words by using the appropriate letter.*

a. preposition   *b. conjunction*   *c. interjection*

_____ 11. *Help!* An alligator is in my bed!
_____ 12. Clarice studied the violin for six years, *but* she can play only two selections.
_____ 13. *During* the last act of the play a member of the audience began to cry uncontrollably.
_____ 14. Ray wanted a Dixieland band to play *for* his birthday party.
_____ 15. Corrections to the manuscript were written in red ink *and* inquiries to the editor were in blue pencil.

C. *Identify the italicized words by using the appropriate letter.*

a. action verb   b. linking verb   c. helping verb

_____   16.   Dozens of balls *are used* during an average professional baseball game.
_____   17.   Many prisons *have become* training schools for crime.
_____   18.   The candidate *prepared* for the debate by studying videotapes of previous debates.
_____   19.   Millions of Americans *are* suffering from inadequate diets.
_____   20.   You *had* a good time at the barbecue, didn't you?
_____   21.   Scientists *do* not completely understand the causes of diabetes.
_____   22.   Several members of the church *resigned* as a protest against the dismissal of the pastor.
_____   23.   Do you know how many books *are* published annually in the United States?
_____   24.   *Are* you active in any musical or athletic groups on campus?
_____   25.   Companies in Taiwan *print* many of the art books that are sold in this country.

© 1997 Addison-Wesley Educational Publishers Inc.

1-C

CHAPTER TEST

A. *Identify the parts of speech of the italicized words by using the appropriate letter.*

a. noun   b. pronoun   c. adjective   d. adverb

_____   1. Lewis Carroll was the *author* of Alice's Adventures in Wonderland.
_____   2. Do you know the name of the *last* emperor of Japan?
_____   3. The Mississippi River runs through the *middle* of the country.
_____   4. Because the office was *extremely* cold, I had to wear gloves to type.
_____   5. Pete is proud of his cooking ability, but *he* prefers to eat at restaurants.
_____   6. The organization was regarded as *dangerous* and subversive during the 1950s.
_____   7. *Who* prefers to stay home tonight instead of going to the movie?
_____   8. The threat of a civil war discouraged *many* travelers from going to the country last summer.
_____   9. Although I was *somewhat* surprised by her decision, I decided to accept it without protest.
_____ 10. Jonathan told *me* that he bought a new table for his computer.

B. *Identify the parts of speech of the italicized words by using the appropriate letter.*

a. preposition   b. conjunction   c. interjection

_____ 11. The judge ruled that conditions at the jail constituted cruel *and* unusual punishment.
_____ 12. Several of the events listed *in* the brochure were canceled at the last minute.
_____ 13. *Wow?* Did you see that?
_____ 14. Hank received job offers in Portland *and* in Bangor.
_____ 15. The witness was hypnotized *by* a police psychologist.

C. *Identify the italicized words by using the appropriate letter.*

a. action verb   b. linking verb   c. helping verb

_____ 16. The Mets *were* easy winners in the Eastern Division.

_____ 17. Harold *advertised* his car for sale in the newspaper.

_____ 18. Sam *signs* his name with a flourish and an exaggerated style.

_____ 19. Many babies experience traumas at birth which *are* cited as the cause of later problems they experience.

_____ 20. Do you believe that the combination of pink and purple *is* attractive on me?

_____ 21. The sirens of the police cars *wailed* all night.

_____ 22. Hilda *was* happy to receive the results of her bar examination.

_____ 23. Meteorites *can be seen* more often in August than at any other time.

_____ 24. It *would* help to know what kind of financing is available to you when you set out to buy a car.

_____ 25. Mrs. Kelly *explained* to our history class the origins of the calendar.

1-D

CHAPTER TEST

A. *Identify the parts of speech of the italicized words by using the appropriate letter.*

a. noun   *b. pronoun*   *c. adjective*   *d. adverb*

_____   1.   *Many* grocery stores now accept credit cards as payment for their purchases.

_____   2.   Although Kitty had to drop out of college for a while, she was *eventually* to return and complete her degree requirements.

_____   3.   The chlorine level of the water in the pool is tested *daily*.

_____   4.   The mail carrier told *us* that dogs present a serious obstacle to the delivery of mail on our route.

_____   5.   *Those* are the flowers that I picked yesterday.

_____   6.   Many soldiers who retire after long *careers* in the service often seek employment rather than do nothing.

_____   7.   *Parking* spaces for the handicapped are provided at our university.

_____   8.   If all goes well, Sheila will receive her letter of acceptance *tomorrow*.

_____   9.   The *final* examination at barber college was to shave a balloon without bursting it.

_____   10.   Boris used to speak Russian *fluently*, but he has forgotten most of it now.

B. *Identify the parts of speech of the italicized words by using the appropriate letter.*

a. preposition   *b. conjunction*   *c. interjection*

_____   11.   *Well*, I wish you wouldn't do that.

_____   12.   The era of the big bands has passed, *but* some musicians are trying to revive it.

_____   13.   It was obvious *by* his remarks that Jordan was against the resolution.

_____   14.   The filter in the air conditioner was clogged *with* dirt.

_____   15.   Despite the false alarm, Lillie *and* her mother were afraid that the large tent would catch fire.

C. *Identify the italicized words by using the appropriate letter.*

a. action verb   *b. linking verb*   *c. helping verb*

_____ 16. The receptionist *notified* the sales manager that a customer was waiting in the outer office.

_____ 17. The bridge across the channel *is painted* by county employees.

_____ 18. The bridegroom *appeared* confused as he answered for the bride during the wedding ceremony.

_____ 19. *Was* Christopher Columbus the first European to land in the New World?

_____ 20. Motorists who park in the fire lane *will* receive citations from the police.

_____ 21. A young clarinetist from Canada *performed* my concerto.

_____ 22. Witnesses to the accident *have been* asked to tell what they saw.

_____ 23. My skin *feels* softer as a result of using softer water when I shave.

_____ 24. When Wanda *peels* onions, her eyes begin to fill with tears.

_____ 25. The history of the Social Security Act *is* interesting.

2-A

CHAPTER TEST

A. By *writing the appropriate letter on the line preceding each sentence, identify the italicized word or words.*

a. *action verb*   b. *linking verb*   c. *helping verb*   d. *none of the above*

_____ 1. Margo's home-cooked pasta *tastes* as good as the dishes many expensive restaurants serve.

_____ 2. Most back pain *can be* treated at home with exercises and nonprescription pain relievers.

_____ 3. All passengers who drank orange juice *felt* ill before the flight's end.

_____ 4. Julius Caesar and his fellow Romans *conquered* France in about 53 B.C.

_____ 5. About seven percent of the gold *used* in the United States is utilized in dentistry.

_____ 6. New York *hosts* the highest number of immigrants to America.

_____ 7. After a parade of hit films, Steven Spielberg finally *won* an Oscar in 1994.

_____ 8. Judy *has* become a close friend since moving to our neighborhood last year.

_____ 9. "Stand by your man," Loretta Lynn *advised* in her famous country western song.

_____ 10. Doug won the foot race only because my Rottweiler escaped and *chased* him.

_____ 11. Louisiana *has been* dubbed the Pelican State, although I think of it as the Zydeco State.

_____ 12. Kelly and Shana *have cooked* many delicious meals for me.

_____ 13. Julio *may have paid* for the concert tickets already.

B. On the blank before each sentence, write the letter that corresponds to the simple subject of the sentence.

_____ 14. Corporate bonds are generally safer to own than corporate stock.

  a. bonds   b. corporate   c. stock

_____ 15. Covering more than 650,000 square miles, Alaska is the largest U.S. state.

a. miles   b. Alaska   c. state

_____ 16.   In 1967, the first Super Bowl featured the victorious Green Bay Packers over the Kansas City Chiefs.

a. 1967   b. Super Bowl   c. Green Bay Packers

_____ 17.   Leticia's brother has produced three popular TV shows.

a. brother   b. three   c. shows

_____ 18.   Tired from too much volleyball, Shereen lay down for a long nap.

a. Tired   b. volleyball   c. Shereen

_____ 19.   Disappointed by huge amounts of paperwork and little glamour, many lawyers are switching to other careers.

a. amounts   b. paperwork   c. lawyers

_____ 20.   The distance run by race horses is measured in units called furlongs.

a. distance   b. horses   c. furlongs

_____ 21.   Everyone was surprised to hear of Luis and Susan's elopement.

a. Everyone   b. Luis   c. Susan

_____ 22.   Not wishing to insult my host, I hid the burnt vegetables in a planter.

a. host   b. I   c. vegetables

_____ 23.   After eating a pizza with extra garlic, do you really expect a goodnight kiss?

a. pizza   b. you   c. kiss

_____ 24.   Only a small percentage of household cats are pedigreed.

a. percentage   b. cats   c. pedigreed

_____ 25.   Especially at the end of a tough school day, Junior Mints are a delightful treat.

a. end   b. day   c. Junior Mints

2-B

CHAPTER TEST

A. By *writing the appropriate letter on the line preceding each sentence, identify the italicized word or words.*

a. action verb   b. linking verb   c. helping verb   d. none of the above

_____ 1. We *should have planned* our vacation more carefully.
_____ 2. Our senator *voted* against the income tax reduction.
_____ 3. The 1970s *were* known for disco dancing, among other things.
_____ 4. Communism as a political force *has been* virtually eliminated in this decade.
_____ 5. Chips from the plaster *had* covered the dining table.
_____ 6. A. J. Foyt *retired* from auto racing.
_____ 7. Thousands of Russian citizens wanted *to leave* their country.
_____ 8. The Social Security office *files* the records of all applicants in the area.
_____ 9. Computer literacy *has become* a requirement among most high school and college students in this country.
_____ 10. While in Virginia, we *visited* Monticello, the home of Thomas Jefferson.
_____ 11. Elvis Presley *was* inspired by the music of Buddy Holly.
_____ 12. Anyone *taking* up skiing should first take a few lessons.
_____ 13. We decided *to leave* Salt Lake City before the snow storm approached the area.

B. *On the blank before each sentence, write the letter that corresponds to the simple subject of the sentence. Some sentences have more than one subject.*

_____ 14. The prohibition against gambling was enacted by the city council.

    a. prohibition   b. gambling   c. city council

_____ 15. Bicycles, as well as skateboards, were barred from the boardwalk.

    a. Bicycles   b. skateboards   c. boardwalk

_____ 16. As a form of entertainment, the piano is incomparable.

    a. form   b. entertainment   c. piano

_____ 17. Of the various types of irritations, loud music is particularly annoying.

a. types   b. irritations   c. music

_____ 18. In addition to bottles carrying liquor, cans of beer were prohibited at the stadium.

a. bottles   b. liquor   c. cans

_____ 19. There are many paths to the White House, according to the political columnist.

a. There   b. paths   c. columnist

_____ 20. Refusing to admit his mistake, Rodney left the room in anger.

a. mistake   b. Rodney   c. room

_____ 21. At the age of thirty-eight, Ken decided to apply to medical school.

a. age   b. Ken   c. medical school

_____ 22. Didn't you watch the game on television last night?

a. you   b. game   c. television

_____ 23. Where are the books that I lent you last week?

a. Where   b. books/I   c. week

_____ 24. Unwilling to leave, Mr. Ramsey sat at the table.

a. Unwilling   b. Mr. Ramsey   c. table

_____ 25. Too many Americans ignore the opportunity to vote.

a. Americans   b. opportunity   c. vote

2-C

CHAPTER TEST

A. By *writing the appropriate letter on the line preceding each sentence, identify the italicized word or words.*

a. *action verb*   b. *linking verb*   c. *helping verb*   d. *none of the above*

_____ 1. Instead of *playing* jazz, the band decided to feature modern show tunes.
_____ 2. Many of the statements about him *were* false, claimed the candidate.
_____ 3. *Is* there anything to be gained by leaving now?
_____ 4. The dark clouds *obscured* the sun and suggested the approaching storm.
_____ 5. After Raymond *joined* the Boy Scouts, he learned to swim.
_____ 6. Learning *to play* the piano has helped Clarence learn to type.
_____ 7. By purchasing a reliable car, you *will* avoid repair bills later.
_____ 8. The *ringing* of the doorbell told us that Jo Ann had finally arrived.
_____ 9. Many Americans who *remember* Pearl Harbor believe that Japan actually won the war because of that nation's economic recovery.
_____ 10. What *is* the difference between longitude and latitude?
_____ 11. Mitchell keeps a pitcher of iced tea near his desk while *working*.
_____ 12. Many of the immigrants who *have* come to this country from Viet Nam are now successful professionals and businesspeople.

B. *On the blank before each sentence, write the letter that corresponds to the simple subject of the sentence. Some sentences have more than one subject.*

_____ 13. Declaring his love for Muriel, Don asked her to marry him.

a. love   b. Muriel   c. Don

_____ 14. Doesn't your new car have a CD player?

a. car   b. have   c. CD player

_____ 15. The walls of the cave are painted red, and the floor is clay.

a. walls/cave   b. cave/clay   c. walls/floor

_____   16.   Despite his tendency to exaggerate, Roy's story about the fish was true.

a. Despite   b. story   c. fish

_____   17.   Here are some of the reasons for my decision.

a. Here   b. some   c. reasons

_____   18.   There was an oak tree on this spot many years ago.

a. There   b. oak tree   c. spot

_____   19.   The convertible, not the van, was fully insured by its owner.

a. convertible   b. van   c. owner

_____   20.   Because of his high blood pressure, Dave was no longer able to ski.

a. blood pressure   b. Dave   c. ski

_____   21.   The insurance company, not the car dealer, will furnish the policy.

a. insurance company   b. car dealer   c. policy

_____   22.   One of the most popular restaurants in town has gone out of business.

a. One   b. restaurants   c. business

_____   23.   Beyond the bright facade of the building was hidden its decay.

a. facade   b. building   c. decay

_____   24.   For her birthday Maxine was given a subscription to *National Geographic*.

a. birthday   b. Maxine   c. subscription

_____   25.   Ben, as well as his brother, was born in Wisconsin.

a. Ben   b. brother   c. Wisconsin

2-D

CHAPTER TEST

A. By writing the appropriate letter on the line preceding each sentence, identify the italicized word or words.

a. action verb   b. linking verb   c. helping verb   d. none of the above

_____ 1. The reporter *refused* to identify his sources for the story.

_____ 2. A woman with a large hat sat in front of me, *obscuring* my view.

_____ 3. The umpire *threw* the manager out of the game.

_____ 4. After the curtain *was* lowered, the conductor joined the cast to receive the applause of the audience.

_____ 5. By *adding* some garlic to the stew, Hal improved its flavor.

_____ 6. Some companies *were* adding water to their product in order to save money.

_____ 7. Some of the stories about his wealth *were* untrue, according to his son.

_____ 8. *To save* money for his vacation, Rick opened a separate bank account.

_____ 9. Clem pretended that the party *was* a complete surprise to him.

_____ 10. Spring floods *destroyed* thousands of acres of farmland in the southern part of the nation.

_____ 11. Robert *was* certain that his door key had been stolen from his locker.

_____ 12. Because of her generosity, several students *have* traveled to conferences and conventions representing the college.

B. On the blank before each sentence, write the letter that corresponds to the simple subject of the sentence. Some sentences have more than one subject.

_____ 13. Last summer the heat wave discouraged many tourists from visiting our city.

a. summer   b. heat wave   c. tourists

_____ 14. Here is the book that contains the story of the discovery of DNA.

a. Here   b. book/that   c. story

_____ 15. Where should we buy a stereo set, Mark?

a. Where   b. we   c. stereo set

_____   16.   Because of her allergies, Tina does not like to go on picnics in the country.

a. allergies   b. Tina   c. picnics

_____   17.   Unable to get a passport in time to leave with his family, Steve joined them a week later.

a. passport   b. family   c. Steve

_____   18.   The pool table is made of marble and mahogany.

a. pool table   b. marble   c. mahogany

_____   19.   Beyond the view of the naked eye lie other universes, according to Mr. Powell, our astronomy instructor.

a. universes   b. Mr. Powell   c. instructor

_____   20.   The quarterback, not the center, fumbled the football.

a. quarterback   b. center   c. football

_____   21.   The language of the immigrants and their customs identified them as being "different" to some people.

a. language/customs   b. immigrants/people   c. language/people

_____   22.   Of the many professors in the mathematics department, I recommend Mr. Robinson.

a. professors   b. department   c. I

_____   23.   When shopping for a car, there are several things you should remember.

a. car   b. things   c. you

_____   24.   There are several native American dialects that are spoken by only a few small tribes.

a. native   b. dialects/that   c. tribes

_____   25.   The tuba is an awkward instrument to carry in a parade.

a. tuba   b. instrument   c. parade

3-A

CHAPTER TEST

Identify the correct verb by using the appropriate letter.

_____ 1. Stephanie and Julie (a. makes   b. make) sure that every volunteer receives a Certificate of Appreciation.

_____ 2. Whether viewing violence on television (a. encourage   b. encourages) real-life violence is still hotly debated.

_____ 3. Sergio always (a. surfs   b. surf) when he visits Hawaii.

_____ 4. Most waiters (a. rely   b. relies) on tips, so they are often forced to tolerate rude customers.

_____ 5. The faculty (a. is   b. are) arguing among themselves.

_____ 6. Fish (a. breathes   b. breathe) through gills, not nostrils.

_____ 7. Carol frequently (a. hosts   b. host) lavish and memorable parties for her fellow English instructors.

_____ 8. Mary Winzerling (a. find   b. finds) it is relaxing to jog along the beach after school.

_____ 9. Diana Garcia and Mark Berger (a. was   b. were) married on the cliffs of Malibu.

_____ 10. Each of my favorite TV shows (a. feature   b. features) fictional teachers.

_____ 11. Two tracks of train rail (a. carries   b. carry) as many passengers in an hour as sixteen lanes of freeway.

_____ 12. A number of team members (a. has   b. have) asked me to stop coaching so they can end their losing streak.

_____ 13. A sport such as polo or skiing (a. is   b. are) expensive.

_____ 14. Rob Thais is one of those lucky musicians who (a. has   b. have) perfect tonal pitch.

_____ 15. Your chihuahua (a. have   b. has) eaten another pair of my socks.

_____ 16. That's the man who (a. mow   b. mows) our lawn.

_____ 17. Anyone who avoids fats and sweets (a. eats   b. eat) a fairly healthy diet.

_____ 18. The cost of movie tickets (a. continue   b. continues) to rise, but library books are still free.

_____ 19. Coach Talsky and her friends (a. plan   b. plans) to watch the Raiders football game tonight.

_____ 20. Two rolls of film (a. is   b. are) adequate for Rose's birthday party.

_____ 21. A cup of blueberries (a. do not   b. does not) fill the pie shell sufficiently.

_____ 22. The pictures from your prom (a. shows   b. show) what a splendid evening you had.

_____ 23. My brothers, not my parents, (a. cook   b. cooks) all family meals.

_____ 24. There (a. exist   b. exists) an endless stream of statistics for baseball fans to master.

_____ 25. Connecticut and Massachusetts, along with California, (a. rank   b. ranks) as my favorite states.

3-B

CHAPTER TEST

Identify the correct verb by using the appropriate letter.

_____ 1. A number of bomb threats (a. has   b. have) caused panic and fear among the populace.

_____ 2. The frequency of his absences from meetings of the city council (a. has b. have) triggered rumors that he will resign.

_____ 3. Members of the band (a. travel   b. travels) together in a large bus.

_____ 4. Politics often (a. attract   b. attracts) those who merely seek fame.

_____ 5. Rita is one of those drivers who (a. take   b. takes) unnecessary chances.

_____ 6. Across the river (a. was   b. were) three hunting dogs that were stranded.

_____ 7. Soccer, rather than football and other sports, (a. appeal   b. appeals) to many European athletes.

_____ 8. Every tile and shingle (a. was   b. were) blown loose by the storm.

_____ 9. On the last page of the manuscript (a. was   b. were) the signature of the author.

_____ 10. Everyone who volunteered (a. has   b. have) experience at the job.

_____ 11. Mrs. Saunders is one of those instructors who (a. are   b. is) easy to speak to outside of the classroom.

_____ 12. One of the ladders (a. has   b. have) a broken rung.

_____ 13. Mel is the only one of the players who consistently (a. practice   b. practices) every day.

_____ 14. The chief disadvantage of her new job (a. are   b. is) the long hours.

_____ 15. The President, not the cabinet officers, (a. believe   b. believes) that the treaty should be signed.

_____ 16. Emil insisted that it was Barbara's personality, not her riches, that (a. fascinate   b. fascinates) him.

_____ 17. Michael Jackson, along with his brothers and sisters, (a. has   b. have) become wealthy as a result of musical fame.

_____ 18. There (a. remain   b. remains) two additional problems to solve.

_____ 19. Here (a. was   b. were) the site of the first home built in this area.

_____ 20. When practicing golf, there (a. are   b. is) several things that you must consider besides merely hitting the ball.

_____ 21. A hobby such as chess or checkers sometimes (a. take b. takes) hours of one's time.

_____ 22. Dr. McCormick is one of those people who (a. possess b. possesses) a photographic memory.

_____ 23. One of the benefits of the new models (a. are b. is) their reduced price.

_____ 24. Here is a photograph of the only survivor of the tragedy who (a. reside b. resides) in Chicago.

_____ 25. Anyone who studies bees and wasps soon (a. learn b. learns) how to handle them without fear.

3-C

CHAPTER TEST

Identify the correct verb by using the appropriate letter.

_____ 1. The president and the chairman of the board (a. plan   b. plans) to meet with the directors tomorrow morning.

_____ 2. Neither Lithuania nor Latvia (a. maintain   b. maintains) a consulate in my hometown.

_____ 3. Interest in the birds of Canada (a. has   b. have) stimulated George to take several ornithological expeditions to Calgary.

_____ 4. The show, which features flamenco dancers and guitar music played by Spanish musicians, (a. sell   b. sells) out in every city.

_____ 5. Most of the Americans who travel to Europe (a. prepare   b. prepares) for their trips by studying the culture and the language of the countries.

_____ 6. Everyone on the committee (a. expect   b. expects) to be renamed for another term.

_____ 7. The number of applicants for scholarships (a. has   b. have) increased over the last year.

_____ 8. Forty dollars (a. was   b. were) reported stolen from the locker.

_____ 9. Gwen, not her sisters, (a. play   b. plays) the cello and sings.

_____ 10. There (a. remain   b. remains) doubts about his innocence.

_____ 11. Neither Fred nor his sisters (a. visit   b. visits) the family home any more.

_____ 12. An angry reception, not hugs and kisses, (a. was   b. were) what I expected when I got home.

_____ 13. There (a. has   b. have) been a number of problems with the plumbing in our new condominium.

_____ 14. Alaska is one of those exotic places that (a. attract   b. attracts) adventurous tourists.

_____ 15. A marriage characterized by arguments often (a. end   b. ends) in divorce.

_____ 16. Most Christmas presents, according to one study, (a. are   b. is) bought within the week preceding Christmas.

_____ 17. Both butter and cream (a. contain   b. contains) large amounts of fat.

_____ 18. Here (a. begin   b. begins) the concluding scene of the opera.

_____ 19. There (a. remain   b. remains) only a few details to take care of before we leave.

_____ 20. Interest in Salvador Dali's paintings (a. are   b. is) reflected in the high prices they bring in auctions.

_____ 21. Neither corn nor beans (a. grow   b. grows) in the Sahara desert.

_____ 22. A number of expensive homes on our block (a. was   b. were) vandalized over the weekend.

_____ 23. Fifteen minutes (a. was   b. were) long enough to wait, I decided.

_____ 24. Of the many speakers before this convention who (a. has   b. have) addressed us, Dr. Foley was the most interesting.

_____ 25. Parked at the curb in a black limousine (a. was   b. were) my best man and the ushers.

3-D

CHAPTER TEST

Identify the correct verb by using the appropriate letter

_____ 1. On the deck of the ship next to the barrels (a. are   b. is) the winch for the anchor.

_____ 2. There (a. are   b. is) without doubt several good reasons to delay driving to Toledo next week.

_____ 3. Not one of the movie stars who were featured in the film (a. plan   b. plans) to attend its premiere tonight.

_____ 4. Neither the waves nor the tide (a. affect   b. affects) the compass of the ship.

_____ 5. The decision to change the tires and adjust the sparkplugs (a. mean   b. means) that I will have to borrow Mike's tools.

_____ 6. Not one dollar from the proceeds of the sales (a. remain   b. remains) in her bank account today.

_____ 7. A long story about unexpected coincidences and delayed arrivals (a. serve   b. serves) as the opening of the third act.

_____ 8. Both Ireland and England (a. has   b. have) had a glorious literary history.

_____ 9. Most of the acreage now (a. produce   b. produces) corn and soybeans.

_____ 10. All of the contraband (a. was   b. were) recovered by the police.

_____ 11. Some of the rumors about the former President (a. continue   b. continues) to be repeated by his detractors.

_____ 12. Every tip, rumor, and lead (a. was   b. were) followed up by the police.

_____ 13. Most of the paper that was given to the students (a. contain   b. contains) drafts of their essays.

_____ 14. My conversation with the neighbors and my friends on the next block (a. was   b. were) about the collection of trash on the corner.

_____ 15. One of the benefits of long vacations (a. are   b. is) that they offer a chance to unwind and relax away from the job.

_____ 16. (a. Has   b. Have) either of you decided where you want to eat?

_____ 17. Either the zipper or the buttons (a. keep   b. keeps) the pants from falling down.

_____ 18. There (a. seem   b. seems) to be a leak coming from the radiator.

_____ 19. In his toolbox there (a. was   b. were) several wrenches and a hammer.

_____ 20. Every participant and spectator (a. receive   b. receives) two free tickets to the party that follows.

_____ 21. All of the fruit trees in the orchard (a. suffer   b. suffers) from the parasites.

_____ 22. Neither the cows nor the horse (a. are   b. is) owned by my uncle.

_____ 23. A piece of toast loaded with berries and preserves (a. serve   b. serves) as her daily breakfast.

_____ 24. Some of the material in the skits (a. was   b. were) written by Simon.

_____ 25. The family members, as well as his fiancee, (a. intend   b. intends) to visit him in the hospital tonight.

4-A

CHAPTER TEST

A. *Write the appropriate letter corresponding to the use of the italicized pronoun in each sentence.*

a. object of a preposition   *b. direct object*   *c. indirect object*

_____ 1. Give *me* a phone call when you're ready to meet for dinner.
_____ 2. The teacher asked both of *us* why we had arrived so late to class.
_____ 3. Please leave room so Mary Kay can sit beside *you*
_____ 4. Uncle Jack took *me* boating at Cape Cod last summer.
_____ 5. You'd better send *them* your financial aid forms before the deadline.

B. *Write the appropriate letter corresponding to the use of the italicized pronoun in each sentence.*

a. subject of a verb   *b. predicate pronoun*   *c. appositive identifying the subject*

_____ 6. Only two guests remained at the end of the party: Sherry and *I*.
_____ 7. It was *he* who accidentally phoned you late last night.
_____ 8. They received their college admission letters much later than *we*.
_____ 9. Mother said it was they *who* ate all the cookies.
_____ 10. We should go now, you and *I*, before the roads become to icy.

C. *Write the appropriate letter corresponding to the correct pronoun.*

_____ 11. Amy is the woman (a. who   b. whom) I intend to marry.
_____ 12. Look at the shirt that April bought for (a. me   b. myself).
_____ 13. I must remind (a. me   b. myself) to turn out the light before leaving.
_____ 14. Sam drank a strong cup of coffee (a. who   b. which) will keep him awake for hours.
_____ 15. We plan to give our old furniture to (a. whoever   b. whomever) has none.
_____ 16. Selma was distracted by (a. my   b. me) humming.
_____ 17. Anita has asked Bob and (a. us   b. we) to help paint her house.
_____ 18. Davis has finally grown taller than (a. I   b. me).

_____   19.   (a. He   b. Him) and you play the piano very well together.

_____   20.   Three drivers, including Tim and (a. she   b. her), were cited for speeding on Merritt Parkway.

_____   21.   When Mexico's economy changes dramatically, (a. our's   b. ours) is affected too.

_____   22.   (a. Who's   b. Whose) skateboard did I just trip over?

_____   23.   They've gotten (a. theirselves   b. themselves) into quite a bit of mischief.

_____   24.   The city is selling bonds to fund (a. it's   b. its) new public parking lot.

_____   25.   St. Louis has a sprawling airport (a. who   b. that) I have used many
times.

4-B

CHAPTER TEST

A. *Write the appropriate letter corresponding to the use of the italicized pronoun in each sentence.*

a. object of a preposition   b. direct object   c. indirect object

_____ 1. Mel prefers to play badminton with Jean rather than with *me*.
_____ 2. Leon sent *us* some postcards while he was in Mexico City.
_____ 3. The security guard caught Anne, Kenny, and *me* as we were trying to get into the concert.
_____ 4. As they passed us, the passengers in the red car made an obscene gesture at Marcia and *me*.
_____ 5. After the food drive, Mrs. Tillotson thanked *us* volunteers for our help.

B. *Write the appropriate letter corresponding to the use of the italicized pronoun in each sentence.*

a. subject of a verb   b. subject complement   c. appositive identifying the subject

_____ 6. For months Edgar and *I* have been jogging together every morning.
_____ 7. The most awkward couple on the dance floor was Helen and *he*.
_____ 8. *Whoever* answered the door accepted the telegram.
_____ 9. Three finalists—Hilda, Earl, and *you*—have been selected to represent the club.
_____ 10. Rickie can throw the shot put much farther than *I*.

C. *Write the appropriate letter corresponding to the correct pronoun.*

_____ 11. I soon realized that (a. its   b. it's) difficult to fake the answers on a chemistry final.
_____ 12. The first ones to enter the room—Mr. Lynch and (a. I   b. me)—were almost overcome by the smoke.
_____ 13. Ron and (a. I   b. myself) have been offered jobs at the bowling alley.
_____ 14. The boys were able by (a. themselves   b. theirselves) to decode the message from the spy.
_____ 15. What are (a. your   b. you're) views concerning the abortion issue?

_____ 16. Conn offered Emil and (a. I   b. me) a piece of his birthday cake.

_____ 17. A man (a. whose   b. who's) name I can't remember called you this afternoon.

_____ 18. Although he has a broken arm, Dave changed the tire on the car by (a. himself   b. hisself).

_____ 19. (a. Its   b. It's) not always easy to pick a winner in the Rose Bowl.

_____ 20. It was difficult to hear the music because of (a. their   b. them) talking throughout the concert.

_____ 21. Although Emil is older than (a. I   b. me), he can run the mile faster.

_____ 22. While skiing in Austria last year, Sigrid and (a. he   b. him) visited her parents in Innsbruck.

_____ 23. James offered my brother and (a. I   b. me) a chance to invest in his company.

_____ 24. The only club members who had not voted were Louise and (a. I   b. me).

_____ 25. Summer vacations offer (a. us   b. we) students an opportunity to rest from our rigorous studies and to save some money.

4-C

CHAPTER TEST

A. *Write the appropriate letter corresponding to the use of the italicized pronoun in each sentence.*

a. object of a preposition   *b. direct object*   *c. indirect object*

_____ 1. The audience admired *her* because of her excellent voice and talent.

_____ 2. Paul's supervisor gave *him* permission to bring his child to work on days when the babysitter was ill.

_____ 3. Weldon gave his ticket to *me* in exchange for my helping him prepare for his botany test.

_____ 4. Many of *us* are reluctant to jump into the surf when the weather is freezing.

_____ 5. The parking attendant brought Dustin and *her* the wrong car.

B. *Write the appropriate letter corresponding to the correct pronoun in each sentence.*

_____ 6. The receptionist greeted Lillian and (a. I   b. me) at the elevator.

_____ 7. We realized that it would be (a. he   b. him) who answered the telephone.

_____ 8. Fortunately, the officer gave Martin and (a. I   b. me) a warning instead of a ticket.

_____ 9. Abe Lincoln taught (a. himself   b. hisself) enough law to pass the bar examination.

_____ 10. No one applauded louder than (a. her   b. she) when her dog won the show prize.

_____ 11. After telling Rachel and (a. I   b. me) about his fortune, Al asked us to lend him five dollars.

_____ 12. Some music concerts have featured singers (a. whose   b. who's) voices are dubbed.

_____ 13. His father did not approve of (a. him   b. his) dropping out of school to join the army.

_____ 14. Some of (a. us   b. we) older members decided to initiate the new members into the club.

_____ 15. Because Antonio was raised in Brazil, he speaks Portuguese much better than (a. I   b. me).

_____ 16. Four skiiers injured (a. theirselves   b. themselves) because they did not properly adjust their ski boots.

_____ 17. Two members of the racing crew—Don and (a. I   b. me)—cannot swim.

_____ 18. Which of the two—Jackie or (a. he   b. him)—would make a better lead vocalist?

_____ 19. The coach was fed up with (a. him   b. his) quarreling with his team-mates.

_____ 20. Why didn't you give (a. us   b. we) contestants a better hint at the answer?

C. *Write the appropriate letter corresponding to the use of the italicized pronoun in each sentence.*

a. *subject of a verb*   b. *subject complement*   c. *an appositive identifying the subject*

_____ 21. To no one's surprise, the last to arrive at the party were Max and *I*.

_____ 22. The police decided that it was *she* who made the anonymous telephone call.

_____ 23. Your wife and *you*, according to our records, have a reservation for dinner at seven o'clock.

_____ 24. Only two members of my family—my father and *I*—are left-handed.

_____ 25. Sharon, who is older than *I*, can remember when our grandfather died.

© 1997 Addison-Wesley Educational Publishers Inc.

4-D

CHAPTER TEST

A. *Write the appropriate letter corresponding to the use of the italicized pronoun in each sentence.*

a. object of a preposition   *b. direct object*   *c. indirect object*

_____ 1. The stereo salesman sold *me* a VCR but did not explain how to use it.
_____ 2. All of *us* were happy when Hugh's story finally came to an end.
_____ 3. The painter asked Mario and *me* about our choice of colors for the house.
_____ 4. The strong gust of wind blew *me* off the top of the ladder.
_____ 5. I was amazed that a total stranger could know so much about *me*.

B. *Write the appropriate letter corresponding to the use of the italicized pronoun in each sentence.*

a. subject of a verb   *b. subject complement*   *c. an appositive identifying the subject*

_____ 6. Your brother and *you* are totally different in appearance.
_____ 7. It was Jim, not *I*, who ordered the lobster.
_____ 8. We three—Patrick, Sheila, and *I*—bought roundtrip tickets to Ireland.
_____ 9. *They* invested their retirement funds in a small company.
_____ 10. I'm afraid that it will be *we* who are responsible for cleaning up this mess.

C. *Write the appropriate letter corresponding to the correct pronoun.*

_____ 11. Sharon asked my sister and (a. I   b. me) to help her tune her engine.
_____ 12. The officers of the Helmut Dantine Fan Club are Reginald, Maurice, and (a. I   b. me).
_____ 13. That loud racket is probably (a. them   b. they) at the door now.
_____ 14. The burglars fell through the skylight and injured (a. theirselves b. themselves).
_____ 15. Please notify Clarence or (a. I   b. me) before you mail the package.
_____ 16. Bernie and (a. I   b. me) received severe sunburns after spending the day at the beach.
_____ 17. If you were (a. he   b. him), what would you do?
_____ 18. I tried to explain the ideas of Aristotle to Josie and (a. her   b. she), but they preferred to watch television.

I-53

_____   19.   Ruth admitted that it was (a. her   b. she) who called you after midnight last Sunday.

_____   20.   (a. Us   b. We) Americans have more telephones than Mexicans have.

_____   21.   The animal trainer was afraid that the monkeys would bite (a. us b. we) visitors to the zoo if we tried to feed them.

_____   22.   The driver of the passing car made a face at Sara and (a. I   b. me) as he passed us on the freeway.

_____   23.   Three members of our band—Rick, Page, and (a. I   b. me)—often sing as a trio.

_____   24.   Between you and (a. I   b. me), this test is easy.

_____   25.   Although Victor is younger than Louis, he is as tall as (a. he   b. him).

5-A

CHAPTER TEST

A. *On the line in front of each number write the letter corresponding to the kind of error in pronoun usage each sentence contains. If the sentence is correct, write "d."*

a. shift in person   *b. unclear pronoun reference*   *c. failure to agree in number*   *d. correct*

_____ 1. If people in Illinois are called Illini, what do people in Connecticut call themselves?

_____ 2. Alicia is very superstitious, and one of them is never walking under a ladder.

_____ 3. Sheila said that she has stopped buying records because she prefers its more convenient competitor, the compact disc.

_____ 4. Neither Cathy nor Anne has paid their dues to me yet.

_____ 5. When college students live on campus, you can be much more easily distracted from studying than when you live at home.

_____ 6. After I eat pasta topped with extra onions and anchovies, you have to brush your teeth thoroughly.

_____ 7. Every time that Ron attended a rock concert, he wanted to be one.

_____ 8. All of the voters were confused by the language on their ballots.

_____ 9. Each of the students admitted that they had not studied for the test.

_____ 10. These kind of clams are found on the East Coast.

_____ 11. My English professor praised the poet when he gave his lecture.

_____ 12. The players in the trio were praised for their performances.

_____ 13. Drivers of expensive cars often find that you get the best valet parking spaces at restaurants.

_____ 14. Cheryl and Maria agreed never to let her boyfriend interfere in their friendship.

_____ 15. I complained to Vince about his dog today, explaining that I want him to stop licking my face whenever I visit.

B. *On the line in front of each number write the letter corresponding to the correct pronoun.*

_____ 16. All college applicants must take the Scholastic Aptitude Test to complete (a. their b. your) applications.

_____ 17. Mary and Amy have moved into (a. her   b. their) new home.

_____ 18. Those (a. kind   b. kinds) of movies make me laugh so much that I embarrass my companions.

_____ 19. Every team member tried (a. her   b. their) hardest but still lost the game.

_____ 20. The Fifteenth Amendment guarantees that citizens cannot be barred from voting because of (a. your   b. their) race.

_____ 21. You have three new cavities and (a. its   b. their) cause is clearly the amount of candy you eat.

_____ 22. Finding and keeping jobs has become a growing concern for many voters, and our governor is now paying more attention to (a. your   b. their) concern.

_____ 23. China has the world's largest army and (a. it's   b. they're) very well-trained.

_____ 24. Santa Monica High School has existed for more than a hundred years, surviving many (a. kind   b. kinds) of budget crises, natural disasters, and mischievous students.

_____ 25. A sure way for a student to impress her teacher is to do (a. your   b. her) homework.

5-B

CHAPTER TEST

A. *On the line in front of each number write the letter corresponding to the kind of error in pronoun usage each sentence contains. If the sentence is correct, write "d."*

A. shift in person   b. unclear pronoun reference   c. failure to agree in number   d. correct

_____ 1. When an Englishman drives an automobile in downtown Manhattan for the first time, they are probably confused by the traffic.

_____ 2. Neither of the two workers has remembered to bring their lunch.

_____ 3. Oliver practiced long hours and rehearsed with the band, which surprised his friends.

_____ 4. Everyone is entitled to their own viewpoint concerning the best candidate.

_____ 5. Many older people in this country do not have health insurance, which is unfortunate.

_____ 6. Both Valerie and Jeannette were disappointed in her chemistry grade.

_____ 7. Reggie was told that he must take a course in composition in order to be eligible for a teaching certificate.

_____ 8. Some immigrants from Eastern Europe told us about their experiences living in Communist nations after World War Two.

_____ 9. The reason that Mac is such an expert at cooking is that he had once been one.

_____ 10. John has been transferred to a job out of town, which pleases his friends very much.

_____ 11. A beginning chef is assigned to making sauces and salads after they are first taught the principles of cooking.

_____ 12. Maxine bought a sweater and a tennis racquet and then returned it.

_____ 13. Harriet was too nervous to ask Mark for a date, and she was teased about it.

_____ 14. Native speakers of English often have trouble when you try to pronounce certain sounds in other languages that have no equivalent in English.

_____ 15. Visitors to Mexico from the United States must tell the customs agents what you have purchased during your stay in Mexico.

B. *On the line in front of each number write the letter corresponding to the correct pronoun.*

_____   16. Every applicant for a job with the police department must pass a background check before (a. he   b. they) can be hired.

_____   17. (a. That b. Those) kinds of flowers do not grow in Minnesota.

_____   18. Many a gambler has lost (a. his   b. their) entire fortune on a single bet.

_____   19. Clearing your throat or wiping your brow is often a sign that (a. a person b. you) are nervous.

_____   20. (a. That   b. Those) kind of entertainment appeals primarily to children.

_____   21. Each of the climbers was responsible for furnishing (a. his   b. their) own equipment.

_____   22. Each sheriff and his deputy (a. was   b. were) given training in first aid.

_____   23. Both Pauline and Moira have completed (a. her   b. their) undergraduate requirements.

_____   24. An applicant for a job should try to learn something about the company before (a. he   b. they) meets the prospective employer.

_____   25. Everyone should remember that (a. he   b. they) will be evaluated on neatness, punctuality, and poise.

5-C

CHAPTER TEST

A. On the line in front of each number write the letter corresponding to the kind of error in pronoun usage each sentence contains. If the sentence is correct, write "d."

a. shift in person   *b. unclear pronoun reference*   *c. failure to agree in number*   *d. correct*

_____ 1. Owners of bicycles were advised by the campus police that you cannot ride them on the campus.

_____ 2. The Murphy family has had their own box at the stadium for many years.

_____ 3. A reporter who had wanted to attend the conference was stopped by the Secret Service because he had forgotten his identification tag.

_____ 4. Vitamin C assists your body's capacity to resist illness and helps to keep one's tissues healthy.

_____ 5. Serious auto accidents often occur on our city's freeways; they should be studied.

_____ 6. Visitors were allowed to enter the mosque if you took off your shoes.

_____ 7. The pianist stated that as a student he had practiced four hours a day and it had helped him.

_____ 8. Earl's SAT scores were higher than Ralph's, which surprised him.

_____ 9. The stories of the Argentine writer Jorge Borges are known for its complexity.

_____ 10. Mrs. Walsh's purse was returned to her, which proves that people are honest.

_____ 11. My uncle claims that everybody gets what they deserve in life.

_____ 12. When a skier is just learning to ski, it is important that you learn to bend your knees and relax.

_____ 13. Grace's father is an architect, but she is not interested in it.

_____ 14. Customers who purchased a 1990 model were told that they should return their cars to the dealer to correct a defect in the clutch.

_____ 15. Subscribers who are planning to move should notify the publisher so that you will receive your magazines at your new address.

B. On the line in front of each number write the letter corresponding to the correct pronoun.

_____   16.   All students are required to bring (a. her   b. their) identification cards when they register.

_____   17.   Every purchaser of a new car was given (a. his   b. their) choice of an air conditioner or automatic transmission.

_____   18.   Neither the police chief nor the officers like (a. his   b. their) new uniforms.

_____   19.   The doctor said that scoliosis is a disease more common among girls than among boys, although (a. she   b. they) could not explain why.

_____   20.   The field hockey team elected Marlene as (a. its   b. their) captain for next year.

_____   21.   Visitors from the United States to Russia are no longer treated with suspicion as (a. they   b. you) once had been.

_____   22.   Every applicant should keep an updated record of (a. his   b. their) experience and previous employment.

_____   23.   Neither diamonds nor a precious gem should be bought by (a. its   b. their) weight or size alone.

_____   24.   The manufacturer claims that (a. these   b. this) kind of roof shingle will last for at least twenty-five years.

_____   25.   Each delegate and alternate to the convention was given (a. his   b. their) registration card.

5-D

CHAPTER TEST

A. On the line in front of each number write the letter corresponding to the kind of error in pronoun usage each sentence contains. If the sentence is correct, write "d."

a. shift in person   b. unclear pronoun reference   c. failure to agree in number   d. correct

_____ 1. Owners of dogs were notified by the city that you must have them inoculated every two years.

_____ 2. Last September the faculty received their first raise in salary in three years.

_____ 3. An astronaut from the United States made history when he stepped on the surface of the moon in 1969.

_____ 4. Your daily diet should include the four basic food groups so that one's body is supplied with the proper nutrients.

_____ 5. Several mysterious fires have occurred at the nuclear power plants; they should be analyzed.

_____ 6. Visitors to Lincoln's home in Springfield are admitted free if you are a student.

_____ 7. The translator said that as a young man he had lived in several foreign countries and it had helped him learn several languages.

_____ 8. Mel's starting salary was less than Bob's, which surprised him.

_____ 9. The vineyards of Italy are particularly known for its red wine.

_____ 10. George blurted out the answer, which shows that boys can't keep secrets.

_____ 11. It seems to me that no one likes their middle name.

_____ 12. Students who intend to register will receive your enrollment materials in your mail.

_____ 13. Ticket-holders were told that they should apply to the box office for a refund in case of a cancellation of the game.

_____ 14. Marilyn's major is biology, but she does not intend to become one.

_____ 15. When you cross the street in heavy traffic in our city, a pedestrian runs the risk of being hit by a car.

B. On the line in front of each number write the letter corresponding to the correct pronoun.

_____ 16. Left-handed persons who have been forced to write with the right hand often claim that (a. one's b. their) handwriting suffered as a result.

_____ 17. Everyone over the age of forty can remember when (a. he b. they) heard the news of John F. Kennedy's assassination.

_____ 18. Neither the Prime Minister nor the cabinet officers would reveal (a. his b. their) source of information.

_____ 19. My mechanic says that the new cars from Detroit use less gas than (a. it b. they) did last year.

_____ 20. (a. That b. Those) kind of tree grows only in Central America.

_____ 21. Each playwright and poet was paid royalties for (a. his b. their) contribution to the anthology.

_____ 22. Neither the books nor the encyclopedia was returned to (a. its b. their) place on the shelf.

_____ 23. Every chef has experienced the dilemma of not knowing how many people (a. he or she b. they) must prepare meals for.

_____ 24. The jury selected a retired mail carrier as (a. its b. their) foreman.

_____ 25. When a prisoner is released from our county jail, (a. he b. they) must report to a probation officer.

6-A

CHAPTER TEST

A. Identify the tense of the italicized verb in each sentence by using the appropriate letter.

a. *present perfect tense*   b. *past tense*   c. *past perfect tense*   d. *present tense*

_____ 1. Willie *misbehaves* when he eats too much sugar.
_____ 2. Connecticut *has boasted* the highest public school teacher pay for years.
_____ 3. The Eighteenth Amendment *outlawed* alcohol consumption in 1919, but it was repealed in 1933.
_____ 4. Most of Los Angeles' residents *were* asleep when the early morning earthquake hit.
_____ 5. I *had told* Tamika to expect us by six o'clock.
_____ 6. Charles *has been studying* diligently for his exams.
_____ 7. She *had been taking* acting lessons for years before appearing on stage.
_____ 8. Julie *trained* for several months before running her first marathon.
_____ 9. We *hope* to be first in line for tickets to Woodstock Three.
_____ 10. They are the best friends I *have ever had*.

B. Using the appropriate letter, select the correct form of the verb in the following sentences.

_____ 11. I noticed on the national news tonight that it has finally (a. begun b. begin) to snow in Chicago.
_____ 12. The balloon would not have (a. burst b. bursted) if you had kept it away from the candle.
_____ 13. Buck (a. choosed b. chose) to become a teacher despite the hard work.
_____ 14. Sheryl makes her passengers nervous when she (a. speeds b. sped) through yellow traffic lights.
_____ 15. The sun was (a. raising b. rising) as the fishermen tugged their boat into the water.
_____ 16. When our portable swimming pool (a. sprung b. sprang) a leak, our guests leapt out screaming.
_____ 17. Tania's phone had (a. rang b. rung) twice before she answered eagerly.
_____ 18. Don't tell Mom that I have (a. torn b. tored) a hole in her new lace tablecloth.

_____   19.   Kelly had (a. gone   b. went) to Allegheny College before studying law at USC.

_____   20.   I was proud of how my new loafers (a. shine   b. shone) after I polished them.

_____   21.   Sam has lost so much weight that I think even his ears have (a. shrunk b. shrank).

_____   22.   Stuart (a. swam   b. swum) his way to three gold medals.

_____   23.   Kadijah (a. sneaked   b. snuck) her own popcorn into the movie theatre and we were both thrown out.

_____   24.   He had only (a. sung   b. sang) a few lyrics before his friends begged him to stop.

_____   25.   We (a. laid   b. lay) in the sun for hours and now our noses are crimson.

6-B

CHAPTER TEST

A. *Identify the tense of the italicized verb in each sentence by using the appropriate letter.*

a. *present perfect tense*   b. *past tense*   c. *past perfect tense*   d. *present tense*

_____ 1. After the race, Lino *drank* nearly a gallon of water.
_____ 2. We shouldn't make a toast until the guest of honor *has arrived*.
_____ 3. Lois *shops* at the mall every Friday after cashing her paycheck.
_____ 4. Phil *screamed* when the bug hopped into his oatmeal.
_____ 5. Thanks to some handy glue, no one noticed that I *had broken* the antique wine glass.
_____ 6. Although Mary Roberta is usually softspoken, she *has been known* to misbehave now and then.
_____ 7. Several prisoners *dug* their way out of their cells.
_____ 8. Although I *have eaten* lunch already, the pasta Pomodoro looks too good to resist.
_____ 9. My loyal dog *lay* at my feet while I was sick in bed.
_____ 10. Please *set* the new dictionary on the shelf.

B. *Using the appropriate letter, select the correct form of the verb in the following sentences.*

_____ 11. I have (a. ran   b. run) into three garage doors while learning to drive with a stick-shift.
_____ 12. Alicia has (a. began   b. begun) to make friends at her new school.
_____ 13. Ray (a. did   b. done) a great job of decorating his apartment.
_____ 14. You haven't really seen Los Angeles until you have (a. gone   b. went) to Venice Beach.
_____ 15. We couldn't believe that Tran had (a. brang   b. brought) his mother to his bachelor party.
_____ 16. Jackie filled the balloon with water until it (a. burst   b. bursted).
_____ 17. Harley-Davidson was (a. chose   b. chosen) as the favored motorcycle of the Weekend Rebels.
_____ 18. Our principal has (a. sat   b. set) a limit on our use of the copying machine.

_____ 19. Although James drank plenty of orange juice, he (a. catched   b. caught) a cold.

_____ 20. Larry (a. dived   b. doved) into the pool, although he cannot swim.

_____ 21. Who (a. laid   b. layed) my new jacket on the floor?

_____ 22. Mary (a. sat   b. set) patiently while Dr. Eide explained the results of her x-rays.

_____ 23. He has not yet (a. written   b. wrote) thank-you notes for the birthday gifts he received.

_____ 24. We managed to find our seats just as the concert (a. began   b. begun).

_____ 25. Eric and Sheila had (a. chose   b. chosen) Aspen as their honeymoon destination.

6-C

CHAPTER TEST

A. *Identify the tense of the italicized verb in each sentence by using the appropriate letter.*

a. *present perfect tense*   b. *past tense*   c. *past perfect tense*   d. *present tense*

_____ 1. I *have drawn* the conclusion that most people would rather inherit money than earn it.
_____ 2. Matt usually *drags* his girl friend along to help him shop for clothes.
_____ 3. Mom hid the cookies after she *caught* me eating them again.
_____ 4. We *had begun* to eat when the cook left angrily.
_____ 5. My cousins *have come* from Illinois to visit San Diego.
_____ 6. If we *had known* it was your birthday, we would have taken you to a movie.
_____ 7. The birds *flew* in all directions when they saw Kip's German shepherd dog.
_____ 8. Frank *bears* quite a burden as a single father.
_____ 9. My dog *hides* under the bed when she realizes it's time for her bath.
_____ 10. Beth *has come* to my birthday parties since our college days.

B. *Using the appropriate letter, select the correct form of the verb in the following sentences.*

_____ 11. The news of the rock star's death has (a. shaken   b. shook) her hometown friends.
_____ 12. Angela had (a. taken   b. took) the driver's exam twice before she finally passed it.
_____ 13. The blast of the horn (a. waken   b. woke) Lyle from his nap.
_____ 14. Laura has (a. began   b. begun) to design clothes for fashion shows and plays.
_____ 15. Buck (a. sings   b. sung) beautifully in the shower, but nowhere else.
_____ 16. Within a few years the small sprout had (a. grew   b. grown) into an imposing tree.
_____ 17. Let's hope that George (a. seen   b. sees) the error of his ways.
_____ 18. You (a. have swam   b. have swum) much faster in your recent races.

_____   19. We left before the fire had (a. ran   b. run) its course down the valley.
_____   20. I know where my father (a. has hid   b. has hidden) my Chanukah presents.
_____   21. The hunter (a. lay   b. laid) the gun down when he realized that the wolf was friendly.
_____   22. Sacramento (a. lies   b. lays) north of San Francisco.
_____   23. The telephone had (a. rang   b. rung) a dozen times before the message machine clicked on.
_____   24. Sandor (a. hanged   b. hung) the mistletoe over every door in the house.
_____   25. Have you (a. ridden   b. rode) in Tom's new Pontiac yet?

6-D

CHAPTER TEST

A. *Identify the tense of the italicized verb in each sentence by using the appropriate letter.*

a. present perfect tense   b. past tense   c. past perfect tense   d. present tense

_____   1.   Most people *speed* from time to time while driving, but seldom receive speeding tickets.
_____   2.   Troy *left* Santa Monica to attend college in Colorado.
_____   3.   The Hispanic population in the United States *has grown* significantly within the last decade.
_____   4.   Beth *had told* me that learning cart-wheels was easy.
_____   5.   Francisco *had seen* the car accident occur, but forgot the license plate numbers of the car.
_____   6.   Telephones in automobiles *have become* relatively common in most large cities.
_____   7.   My jeans *shrank* after their first washing, even though the manufacturer claimed they would not.
_____   8.   Some people don't realize that breast cancer *strikes* men as well.
_____   9.   I *knew* that it was Robert who sent me the roses.
_____   10.   All of the boats that Sarah has skippered *have sunk*.

B. *Using the appropriate letter, select the correct form of the verb in the following sentences.*

_____   11.   The building inspector has (a. came   b. come) to examine the smoke detectors.
_____   12.   Sally (a. arise   b. arose) early to make waffles for her daughter's house guests.
_____   13.   Moira has (a. broke   b. broken) several school track records without any effects on her excellent academic record.
_____   14.   The school year (a. begins   b. begun) in September throughout most of the United States.
_____   15.   Have you (a. froze   b. frozen) enough meals to eat while we're away on vacation?
_____   16.   Yesterday's strong winds (a. blew   b. blown) the Sawayas' tree into our front yard.

_____ 17. Because David had (a. chose   b. chosen) the movie for us, we teased him about how bad it was.

_____ 18. Mrs. Orozco (a. has gone   b. has went) to church every Sunday for forty years.

_____ 19. I have (a. burst   b. busted) out laughing at his jokes during class, but sometimes he is not humorous when he tries.

_____ 20. Professor Huang (a. drank   b. drunk) coffee to stay awake while reading the class essays.

_____ 21. It was no secret that José had (a. gone   b. went) to Princeton on a full academic scholarship because of his grades.

_____ 22. Despite his age, Paul (a. awake   b. awoke) early every morning and jogged four miles while on his vacation.

_____ 23. No one has (a. driven   b. drove) Vince's new Mercedes-Benz except him.

_____ 24. Showanda (a. came   b. come) with her family to receive her prize in the poetry contest.

_____ 25. I had never (a. flew   b. flown) in a helicopter before today.

7-A

CHAPTER TEST

A. *If the italicized group of words in each of the following sentences is an independent clause, write "a" on the line in front of the sentence; if it is a dependent clause, write "b"; if it is not a clause, write "c."*

_____ 1. *After visiting the Grand Canyon,* let's tour the Dollhouse Museum in Dallas, Texas.

_____ 2. *The right bait makes all the difference in fishing,* my father always told me.

_____ 3. Once you've finished eating, *please wash your dishes* and put them away.

_____ 4. Chip saw a strange orange streak in the sky last night, but he doubts *that it was a UFO.*

_____ 5. Haiti has suffered political turmoil *in recent years.*

B. *Using the appropriate letter, identify the structure of the following sentences.*

a. simple sentence   b. compound sentence   c. complex sentence

_____ 6. Oh, I see a bug!

_____ 7. Unless you are still hungry, I'd like to have that remaining pork chop.

_____ 8. U. S. President William McKinley was welcoming guests to the Pan-American Exposition when he was assassinated in 1901.

_____ 9. Whichever suit you choose to wear, you will be the most striking man at the party.

_____ 10. Leontyne Price is my favorite opera singer, and I wish I could have seen her perform before her recent retirement.

C. *Each of the following sentences contains one or two blanks. If a comma should be inserted in one or both blanks, write "a" on the line in front of the sentence; if no commas should be inserted, write "b."*

_____ 11. The Mach _____ a unit used to measure sound _____ is named for Austrian physicist Ernst Mach.

_____ 12. Mercury _____ is the smallest planet in our solar system.

_____ 13. It was my neighbor _____ Dan Vogel _____ who taught me how to be a good conversationalist at parties.

_____ 14. Hurry and finish your homework _____ so you can come to the movies with us.

_____ 15. Does Bobby really plan to change his name _____ to Herman?

_____ 16. You know _____ of course _____ that your new plant requires daily watering.

_____ 17. Please help us carry this box _____ into the shed.

_____ 18. Diana wants to know _____ whether you plan to join her for lunch.

_____ 19. Although John Kennedy was President for a short time _____ he is one of the most admired leaders in our nation's history.

_____ 20. While Sarah was taking a nap _____ Alfredo and I saw a movie, planted two rose bushes, and cooked a four course meal.

_____ 21. We must rewind the videotape _____ before we return it _____ to the video store.

_____ 22. Allen is playing soccer every day _____ in order to lose weight.

_____ 23. That's the dog _____ that stars in my favorite potato chip commercial!

_____ 24. My oldest daughter _____ whom you met yesterday _____ will attend Smith College in the fall.

_____ 25. Shopping bores Felix _____ but Stan enjoys it.

7-B

CHAPTER TEST

A. *If the italicized group of words in each of the following sentences is an independent clause,*
write "a" on the line in front of the sentence; if it is a dependent clause, write "b"; if it is not a
clause, write "c."

_____ 1. *Overcoming the disadvantage of not learning English* until he was an adult,
Vladimir Nabokov wrote several novels in the English language.

_____ 2. *Bob Hope relies on his writers,* but Jay Leno depends on his quick wit.

_____ 3. Cricket is a game *that I have never understood.*

_____ 4. Last week I received a telephone call from a friend *who has been living in*
England for the past two years.

_____ 5. *To everyone's surprise, including the owner's,* the horse came in first.

B. *Using the appropriate letter, identify the structure of the following sentences.*

a. *simple sentence*   b. *compound sentence*   c. *complex sentence*

_____ 6. Janice carefully packed up her camera and film, but she forgot them
while leaving for the airport the next morning.

_____ 7. Ms. Sheehy claims that it is unwise to cram at the last minute for an
examination.

_____ 8. Boasting of his ability to hit the ball out of the park Chris strode to the
plate and promptly struck out.

_____ 9. Mr. Wiggins watered the cabbage while Mrs. Wiggins slept.

_____ 10. Interviewed on television last night, the ambassador announced the date
for the opening of the conference.

C. *Each of the following sentences contains one or two blanks. If a comma should be inserted in*
one or both blanks, write "a" on the line in front of the sentence; if no commas should be inserted,
write "b."

_____ 11. Carlos angrily quit his job; _____ he regretted his decision later.

_____ 12. The news _____ that he brought me _____ was very discouraging.

_____ 13. Anyone _____ who wants to lose weight _____ must exercise as well as
eat properly.

_____ 14. Although they angrily denied it _____ the boys had forgotten their father's birthday.

_____ 15. The driver claimed that he had not been drinking _____ but he could not pass the sobriety test.

_____ 16. The legislators raised the minimum age for drinking to twenty-one _____ because they were concerned about the increase in teenage alcoholism.

_____ 17. We tend to forget that Babe Ruth _____ who is remembered for his hitting _____ was an excellent pitcher before he played the outfield.

_____ 18. Our English class was given eight weeks in which to write our term papers _____ but several students were unable to complete it in time.

_____ 19. A group of Scouts _____ who had bicycled across the state _____ discussed their trip at our meeting last night.

_____ 20. The old hotel was torn down _____ and replaced by a parking lot.

_____ 21. Willa Cather _____ who was from Nebraska _____ wrote several novels about first-generation Americans.

_____ 22. The mayor fired his press secretary _____ and refused to be interviewed by the television reporters.

_____ 23. When Clive visited Italy last summer _____ he took a gondola trip in Venice.

_____ 24. I had studied for several days _____ but failed the test.

_____ 25. Your offer of help is appreciated; however _____ I have solved the problem.

7-C

CHAPTER TEST

A. *If the italicized group of words in each of the following sentences is an independent clause, write "a" on the line in front of the sentence; if it is a dependent clause, write "b"; if it is not a clause, write "c."*

_____ 1. *Hydroelectric power is making a comeback* in several New England states.
_____ 2. When George Washington was elected president, *some of his supporters wanted to make him king of the United States.*
_____ 3. *There is always something to do and see in Manhattan.*
_____ 4. I bought several paperback novels at a rummage sale *sponsored by our church every spring.*
_____ 5. *Until videotape was perfected in the 1960s,* everything that the viewer saw on television was happening live.

B. *Using the appropriate letter, identify the structure of the following sentences.*

a. simple sentence   b. compound sentence   c. complex sentence

_____ 6. She was referring to me while looking in another direction.
_____ 7. Weight lifting is becoming increasingly popular among women, according to a recent magazine article.
_____ 8. Jacqueline complained that I don't do the tango.
_____ 9. Many Americans spend their whole lives watching television, and they often have trouble separating the programs from reality.
_____ 10. After she studied French for a year in college, Bonnie had no difficulty understanding the menu of the restaurant in Lyons.

C. *Each of the following sentences contains one or two blanks. If a comma should be inserted in one or both blanks, write "a" on the line in front of the sentence; if no commas should be inserted, write "b."*

_____ 11. Despite the popular myth to the contrary _____ snakes can be found in Ireland.
_____ 12. Although I had heard the joke several times previously _____ I laughed again.

_____ 13. The pianist suddenly stopped playing _____ and swatted a fly buzzing about his head.

_____ 14. The most popular novel _____ written by Ernest Hemingway _____ is probably *The Old Man and the Sea*.

_____ 15. Tamara was brought to this country _____ when she was only an infant.

_____ 16. Vince can jump higher than Stewart can _____ but he can't swim as well.

_____ 17. The Native American _____ who is sometimes called the Indian _____ has been in this country centuries longer than European settlers.

_____ 18. The captain was introduced to the fans _____ as the cheerleaders entered the stadium.

_____ 19. Photographs of Saturn sent from Voyager 2 have added to our knowledge of the universe _____ and to the formation of our own planet system.

_____ 20. The dog growled menacingly _____ but he remained under the porch.

_____ 21. Although Jack has lived in California for several years _____ he still misses the changing of the seasons in the Ozarks of Missouri.

_____ 22. The Hippocratic oath _____ which is administered to physicians _____ reminds them of their obligations to their patients.

_____ 23. When I pull up to a stop sign _____ my car's engine usually dies.

_____ 24. Novels that are popular with the public _____ are sometimes made into successful movies.

_____ 25. Last week the Pulitzer committee announced the recipients of the prizes for outstanding editorial _____ and the outstanding cartoonist.

7-D

CHAPTER TEST

A. *If the italicized group of words in each of the following sentences is an independent clause, write "a" on the line in front of the sentence; if it is a dependent clause, write "b"; if it is not a clause, write "c."*

_____ 1. Do you remember *what you were doing* when you heard the news of John Lennon's death?

_____ 2. *The parents and children argued* over whether they should stop for lunch.

_____ 3. My psychology professor, *who is afraid of cats*, claims that everyone has a phobia.

_____ 4. *Not to be present at the marriage of his daughter* was a disappointment to Mr. Willis.

_____ 5. Ms. Galloway believes *that even newly born babies can be taught to swim.*

B. *Using the appropriate letter, identify the structure of the following sentences.*

a. simple sentence   b. compound sentence   c. complex sentence

_____ 6. Please turn off the lights, and I will lock the doors.

_____ 7. The cattle grazed where the cottage once stood.

_____ 8. Because of the threat of a Chinese veto, the General Assembly reworded the resolution.

_____ 9. At the age of five the English philosopher John Stuart Mill could read Latin.

_____ 10. When the rain stopped, the grounds crew came out and removed the tarpaulin from the infield.

C. *Each of the following sentences contains one or two blanks. If a comma should be inserted in one or both blanks, write "a" on the line in front of the sentence; if no commas should be inserted, write "b."*

_____ 11. After I park my car and climb the seventy steps from the student parking lot _____ I am usually too winded to talk.

_____ 12. The plumber promised he would come back yesterday _____ but he did not return or call us.

_____ 13. Mike is one of those athletes _____ whose enthusiasm and energy make up for any natural talent they may lack.

_____ 14. Although the bus pulled into the station after midnight _____ the band members were greeted by a large welcoming crowd.

_____ 15. Jim Dwyer is the manager of the K-mart store _____ and president of the Rotary Club.

_____ 16. Moses Malone is one of the few professional basketball players _____ who did not attend college.

_____ 17. Richard Pryor _____ the comedian _____ was born in Peoria, Illinois.

_____ 18. Mr. Gordon's oldest daughter _____ who lives in New York _____ works for a television station.

_____ 19. Beverly complained that many of the boys _____ whom she had dated in high school were boring and immature.

_____ 20. Viewer surveys are used to determine the popularity of television programs _____ and to determine advertising rates.

_____ 21. Although the price of gold has dropped in recent months _____ many people still believe that it is a good investment.

_____ 22. Tobacco is a major source of revenue for North Carolina _____ but the state also produces fine furniture.

_____ 23. The workers canceled their plans for a march _____ but voted to remain on strike.

_____ 24. The embezzler was captured after police traced telephone calls _____ and other messages from him to his friends and relatives.

_____ 25. His baby shoes _____ which had been bronzed and given to him by his parents _____ were on the mantelpiece.

8-A

CHAPTER TEST

A. *On the line in front of each number write the letter corresponding to the kind of error each sentence contains. If a sentence is correct, write "d" in front of the sentence.*

a. *sentence fragment*   b. *run-on sentence*   c. *comma-splice*   d. *correct*

_____ 1. Every puppy in the store is adorable, I have no room for a pet in my apartment, however.

_____ 2. I don't understand it you eat only junk food but never gain weight.

_____ 3. Be sure to set your alarm clock so you'll wake in time for the job interview.

_____ 4. Our kitchen is a mess your parents will be here any minute.

_____ 5. Even though he never sends me a Christmas card.

_____ 6. After Alejo gets home from work and before he goes out for the evening.

_____ 7. The leopard has been watching you for several minutes, she hopes you are her next meal.

_____ 8. I have a test in English class, however, your invitation to play softball is tempting.

_____ 9. We searched for Quebec on the map but were unable to locate it.

_____ 10. If you continue to be nasty then I won't share my licorice with you I really mean it.

_____ 11. Spiking the volleyball so high that we couldn't tell whether it would land over the net.

_____ 12. Dr. Erde no longer practices medicine in my city, I still call her for second opinions, though.

_____ 13. Remember to pick up some rice at the supermarket we need tortillas too.

_____ 14. Sometimes it's easier to qualify for college than it is to pay for it.

_____ 15. Winona Ryder's new movie is hilarious, we saw it last night.

_____ 16. New York must be the best city in the world in which to spend New Year's Eve I hope to visit next year.

_____ 17. Until Rita called to tell us that the talent show had been cancelled.

_____ 18. Your eyes are lovely however your punctuation skills are what captured my heart.

_____ 19. Take as many books as you want; I have plenty of others to keep me busy.

_____ 20.   The business meeting was frustrating it began late and ran too long.

_____ 21.   Choosing between Shana's car, a Montero, or Kelly's car, a Volkswagen.

_____ 22.   The thrill of meeting Nelson Mandela, President of South Africa.

_____ 23.   No, I'm not trading my Salt N' Pepa C.D. for your Vanilla Ice C.D.

_____ 24.   The United States has more nuclear reactors than any other nation.

_____ 25.   Physical therapy is only successful if you do the exercises faithfully, otherwise, you will just continue to suffer pain and restricted movement.

8-C

CHAPTER TEST

On the line in front of each number write the letter corresponding to the kind of error each sentence contains. If a sentence is correct, write "d" in front of the sentence.

a. sentence fragment   b. run-on sentence   c. comma-splice   d. correct

_____ 1.   When asked whether I had paid the traffic ticket, which I had received last April.

_____ 2.   Not everyone consumes a big meal on Thanksgiving for example, Trish ate only a salad and some fruit.

_____ 3.   Because Sean is feeling ill, we will play the soccer game without him.

_____ 4.   Jack told me that the chemistry test was difficult, he was right.

_____ 5.   Many Americans are reducing the number of purchases they charge to their credit cards. To help reduce their debts and avoid high interest.

_____ 6.   The word "anecdote" is a Greek word it means "unpublished."

_____ 7.   After the rain stopped, Sheldon finished building the fence. Made of slats and painted white to match the house.

_____ 8.   Realizing that my voice was weak and my dancing was clumsy. I gave up on my plans to be a rock star and I returned to college.

_____ 9.   The tide was too soft, therefore, we couldn't surf as we had hoped to do.

_____ 10. A job that paid well, a beautifully decorated office, and an unlimited expense account were his main career goals.

_____ 11. Just a few of the many friendly and healthy, affectionate animals that are available as pets at the animal shelter.

_____ 12. Few young American couples are able to purchase a home prices are too high for their budgets.

_____ 13. The chocolates look delicious, however, my brother-in-law urged me to eat stringbeans instead.

_____ 14. Keep an eye on the mainsail, meanwhile, we will repair the tiller.

_____ 15. It was a shattering experience. To see with our own eyes the damage caused by the bombs.

_____ 16. Staring out the window, Kent thought of his home in Oregon and the friends he had left behind.

_____ 17. The speech instructor said that anyone can develop confidence when speaking before a group, I signed up for the course immediately.

_____ 18. Encouraging students to remain in school by helping them improve their study habits, according to the counselor.

_____ 19. None of the flowers in James' garden have lived after he planted them he apparently does not have a "green thumb."

_____ 20. Bearing in mind her limited income, and the expensive maintenance involved in owning a large home.

_____ 21. The closing ceremonies of the Olympics were impressive there were music and fireworks everywhere.

_____ 22. To seek a cure for depression and to determine its causes, a group of researchers has been meeting in Sioux Falls all week.

_____ 23. Believing that the threat of flooding had passed, the Miami residents returned to their homes.

_____ 24. Running, talking, and playing with more energy than any other child I have ever met.

_____ 25. Melissa forgot that she had no money or credit cards, she offered to pay for her boy friend's dinner.

8-D

CHAPTER TEST

On the line in front of each number write the letter corresponding to the kind of error each sentence contains. If a sentence is correct, write "d" in front of the sentence.

a. sentence fragment   b. run-on sentence   c. comma-splice   d. correct

_____ 1. The game of chess goes back to ancient times, in fact, its exact origin is unknown.

_____ 2. Proud of her performance on the exam and eager to share the news with her husband, yet aware that more obstacles must be overcome.

_____ 3. Because of the child's crying and hysterical screaming, which gave Veronica a pounding headache.

_____ 4. I cannot believe that James won the marathon he did not train as diligently as the other runners.

_____ 5. A stranger would not be able to tell the difference between the twins it is obvious, however, to their parents.

_____ 6. Bill bought a new suit, rented a sports car, and got a haircut. In order to impress his blind date tonight.

_____ 7. I paid two hundred dollars for tickets to the concert, therefore, I attended the performance despite my painful stomach flu.

_____ 8. Many runners do not eat breakfast until after a race, Lori, however, is convinced that eating a bagel before running brings her good luck.

_____ 9. Claiming that the judges were dishonest and that the outcome of the fight had been decided beforehand, the boxer claimed that he had been cheated of victory.

_____ 10. With an increased concern for health and a decrease in alcohol consumption, except among college students.

_____ 11. "I Feel the Earth Move Under My Feet" is Carole King's best-known song.

_____ 12. Although many students drink coffee while studying for exams, most experts say that it causes nervousness and inability to concentrate.

_____ 13. Growing up in a small home and a poor family in an impoverished farming community. Bard was not able to afford a piano until he had established himself in his career.

_____ 14.   After eating fried chicken, pasta, and salad, followed by generous help-
            ings of ice cream and cookies. Alison still found room for frozen yogurt.

_____ 15.   Containing a fireplace, a balcony, a big kitchen, and an ocean view, Vic's
            apartment is one of Miami's best.

_____ 16.   Because he has five children and two jobs, and because he is a single fa-
            ther. Todd has little free time for hobbies.

_____ 17.   Although they are often not very attractive and can reduce one's periph-
            eral vision, motorcycle helmets frequently save the lives of their wearers.

_____ 18.   I will now sing my favorite song. Despite popular demand.

_____ 19.   The Brazilian jump serve is too difficult for a beginning volleyball player
            to attempt the "floater" serve is recommended, instead.

_____ 20.   Al's dog follows him everywhere, his girl friend objects to its odor.

_____ 21.   Yolanda made the final payment on her car on the same day that it
            stopped running.

_____ 22.   Watching his children playing tag in the backyard, Raynell's memories of
            his own childhood in Alabama.

_____ 23.   The Muslims' holy month of Ramadan, which includes fasting from sun-
            rise to sunset and praying five times a day.

_____ 24.   Telling jokes, dancing with all the ladies, and buying champagne for
            everyone, Pablo was the life of the party.

_____ 25.   You may argue with me until the cows come home I will not change my
            mind.

9-A

CHAPTER TEST

A. *Write the letter of the correct word on the line preceding each sentence.*

_____ 1. Because of the fresh snow, our skis slid (a. smooth   b. smoothly) down the slope.

_____ 2. My brother used to rock me (a. gentle   b. gently) to sleep.

_____ 3. I know her new perfume is popular and expensive, but it smells (a. bad b. badly) and I won't sit by her.

_____ 4. If you want to fly home next week, you'd better reserve a flight (a. quick b. quickly).

_____ 5. Alicio did a (a. good   b. well) job of cooking his first Thanksgiving turkey.

B. *On the line in front of each number write the letter corresponding to the kind of error each sentence contains.*

a. misplaced or dangling modifier   b. illogical/incomplete comparison   c. adjective or adverb used incorrectly   d. faulty parallel structure

_____ 6. Wearing no clothing except a left sock, April laughed loudly at the mannequin in the store window.

_____ 7. My ideal weekend consists of going to a nightclub, restaurant, shopping mall, and to see a good movie.

_____ 8. Held in the Senate chamber, Senator Orozco leads the Finance Committee's annual meetings.

_____ 9. Dad was real disappointed when he realized he'd missed his favorite cooking show.

_____ 10. Sour and curdled, Jack poured the milk down the sink.

_____ 11. Meowing madly and tugging on the Christmas tree until it fell to the floor, Aunt Sylvia was irked by our new cat.

_____ 12. Taking pictures, wearing polka dotted shorts and moaning with wonder, the gorillas watched the zoo visitors intently.

_____ 13. Mary Roberta awoke sudden when she heard her dog bark at a passing cat.

_____ 14. I plan to take a train to Bellows Falls, a bus to Woodstock, and then flying to Montpelier.

_____ 15. To cure the headache, he needs a nap and to take aspirin.

_____ 16. Americans drive to work in cars more often than trucks.

_____ 17. My, you sing beautiful!

_____ 18. Your new car is fast, comfortable, and it is easily driveable.

_____ 19. My girlfriend has brown hair, brown eyes, and an excellent athlete.

_____ 20. Al and Tom enjoy golf more than me.

_____ 21. Massachusetts produces more cranberries than any state.

_____ 22. The United States has more reserves of iron ore than any mineral.

_____ 23. I wish I could learn to bake a pie without getting scorched around the edges.

_____ 24. Westport is closer to Manhattan than Hartford.

_____ 25. Ingrid lost weight by exercising daily and eating good.

9-B

CHAPTER TEST

A. *Write the letter of the correct word on the line preceding each sentence.*

_____ 1. Because the sign painter did not reread his work, he didn't notice that he had spelled several words (a. incorrect   b. incorrectly).

_____ 2. The children looked (a. sad   b. sadly) as their father completed the story.

_____ 3. Because the hamburger had been left on the table overnight, it smelled (a. bad   b. badly) the next morning.

_____ 4. Despite Harriet's inexperience, she did quite (a. good   b. well) in the pool tournament.

_____ 5. We were (a. real   b. really) disappointed to hear that you won't be able to stay with us.

B. *On the line in front of each number write the letter corresponding to the kind of error each sentence contains.*

a. *misplaced or dangling modifier*   b. *illogical or incomplete comparison*
c. *adjective or adverb used incorrectly*   d. *faulty parallel structure*

_____ 6. The governor was tall, slender, and seemed to be middle-aged.

_____ 7. Barking at passing cars and inspecting the shrubbery of the neighborhood, we found the dog that had escaped from its kennel.

_____ 8. Selling shoes during the summer and waiting on tables during the school year, my tuition was paid without the help of my parents.

_____ 9. Ms. Fulkerson claimed that the students of her generation worked harder than the schools today.

_____ 10. Having missed the assignment, my term paper received a low grade.

_____ 11. The supermarket manager felt happily about the sales campaign.

_____ 12. In my opinion, staying up all night to review before an examination is more of a handicap than useful.

_____ 13. The advertisements for the VCR claimed that it was real easy to operate.

_____ 14. Trying to think of a way to begin my speech, a funny story came to mind.

_____ 15.   Life in Las Vegas is not much different from any city its size.

_____ 16.   To her surprise, Roberta made higher grades in chemistry than her brother.

_____ 17.   Prices at a military commissary are usually lower than other retail establishments.

_____ 18.   Many people join health clubs for exercise, for relaxation, and so that they can meet others of the opposite sex.

_____ 19.   Featuring an electric starter and a four-stroke engine, the salesman claimed that the motorcycle was the best on the market.

_____ 20.   Waving and smiling to their friends, the television camera panned slowly across the crowd.

_____ 21.   The firefighters responded very quick when the alarm sounded at the fireworks factory.

_____ 22.   To receive a discount, the advertisement states that we must purchase the lamp before next Monday.

_____ 23.   Despite its small size, the dog barked very ferocious at the mail carrier.

_____ 24.   The natives of the small Pacific island are taller than any of the inhabitants of the area.

_____ 25.   Dorothy has a good sense of humor and can tell a story really good.

_____ 15. The price of the magazine was raised because of an increase in the cost of paper, the cost of printing, and the post office raised the mailing rate.

_____ 16. Clearing his throat and drumming his fingers on the table, the answers of the witness revealed his nervousness.

_____ 17. Working as a volunteer at the hospital gave Steve an opportunity to observe radiology technicians at work and discussing their duties.

_____ 18. Ralph still feels very sorely as a result of the wasp sting.

_____ 19. Although she lettered only in her senior year, Donna received more scholarship offers than anyone in her class.

_____ 20. It takes me more time than Sara to get ready for class in the morning.

_____ 21. Complaining that the new traffic signals were more confusing than the stop sign, they were removed by the city engineers.

_____ 22. The governor recommended a vote for the tax bill both because it was needed and fair.

_____ 23. Mr. Dwyer speaks not only French, but also he is fluent in Italian and German.

_____ 24. Arriving at a decision after discussing the matter with his wife, a raise was demanded by Stan the next morning.

_____ 25. When the villain appeared sudden at the end of the play, the audience booed.

9-D

CHAPTER TEST

A. *Write the letter of the correct word on the line preceding each sentence.*

_____   1.   Our supervisor treats all of us (a. fair   b. fairly).

_____   2.   Please ship the order (a. direct   b. directly) to my office in Sacramento.

_____   3.   It was (a. real   b. really) thoughtful of you to offer me the use of your car last night.

_____   4.   After giving the matter further thought, you may feel (a. different b. differently) in the morning.

_____   5.   The bank returned Ted's check, complaining that he wrote (a. illegible b. illegibly).

B. *On the line in front of each number write the letter corresponding to the kind of error each sentence contains.*

a. *misplaced or dangling modifier*   b. *illogical or incomplete comparison*
c. *adjective or adverb used incorrectly*   d. *faulty parallel structure*

_____   6.   Competition from foreign imports, the price of steel, and also employee absenteeism which stemmed from the flu epidemic contributed to the company's problems.

_____   7.   Carrying antique rifles and wearing replicas of Civil War uniforms, the parade featured hundreds of men and women commemorating the battle.

_____   8.   Genevieve's excuse for not exercising regular was that she was too busy.

_____   9.   Because Jack had not played tennis in several years, I was able to beat him easy in three sets.

_____   10.   The explorers were looking for a new route to the East, lands to conquer, and they were seeking gold and other precious metals.

_____   11.   Joyce felt badly about the incident, but she tried to forget it.

_____   12.   The salads in Greece contain more olive oil than England.

_____   13.   Because I had not been to New York for many years, I could not remember Yankee Stadium very good.

_____   14.   Angry at his partners and unable to pay for the building by himself, the project was finally abandoned.

_____ 15. Alaska is larger than any state in the nation.
_____ 16. The novelist told our class that he had been inspired more by his teachers in college than other writers.
_____ 17. He neglected either to tell his mother or his father of the news.
_____ 18. Afraid that she would forget the words, the announcer spoke rapid and nervously in a quivering voice.
_____ 19. Appointed by the heirs and given the responsibility of managing the estate, the will was read carefully by the youngest son.
_____ 20. The jury believed that the defense attorney's closing statement was more convincing than the prosecutor.
_____ 21. The new word processor in our office is efficient, accurate, and it is easy to operate.
_____ 22. When laughing, tears often roll down Eileen's cheeks.
_____ 23. The new zoning regulation applies not only to commercial buildings but also private residences.
_____ 24. After four years of college, Hank was proud of his ability to dance the cha-cha, deal a straight flush, and also he could make a good martini.
_____ 25. According to the philosopher Zsa Zsa Gabor, it is better to be rich than being poor.

_____ 13. a. My sportscar is enjoyable to drive, moreover, it fits into tiny parking spaces.

b. My sportscar is enjoyable to drive; moreover, it fits into tiny parking spaces.

_____ 14. a. My oldest brother whom you met last week is a talented acupuncturist.

b. My oldest brother, whom you met last week, is a talented acupuncturist.

_____ 15. a. Enclose an essay, transcript, and financial aid form with your application.

b. Enclose: an essay, transcript, and financial aid form with your application.

_____ 16. a. We sang three songs: "Rhiannon," "Shoop," and "Hound Dog."

b. We sang three songs, "Rhiannon," "Shoop," and "Hound Dog."

_____ 17. a. Fu Mingxia a member of China's Olympic team is my favorite platform diver.

b. Fu Mingxia (a member of China's Olympic team) is my favorite platform diver.

_____ 18. a. Phoenix not Tucson is Arizona's capitol.

b. Phoenix—not Tucson—is Arizona's capitol.

_____ 19. a. "Black Slip," by Terry Wolverton, is one of my favorite poems.

b. _Black Slip_, by Terry Wolverton, is one of my favorite poems.

_____ 20. a. I left my ex husband because he overcooked my dinner one night.

b. I left my ex-husband because he overcooked my dinner one night.

_____ 21. a. Although Rose is an expensive attorney, she does some _pro bono_ cases, too.

b. Although Rose is an expensive attorney, she does some pro bono cases, too.

_____ 22. a. I'm moving to Worland, Wyoming so I can practice opera singing, without bothering neighbors.

b. I'm moving to Worland, Wyoming, so I can practice opera singing without bothering neighbors.

_____ 23. a. It's the four boys' responsibility to cook for Sally's birthday.

b. It's the four boy's responsibility to cook for Sallys' birthday.

_____ 24. a. Have you finished wrapping Charles' gift yet?

b. Have you finished wrapping Charle's gift yet?

_____ 25. a. That pizza contains 65 grams of fat and three thousand and five hundred calories.

b. That pizza contains sixty-five grams of fat and 3500 calories.

10-B

CHAPTER TEST

On the line preceding each number write the letter of the sentence that is correctly punctuated.

_____ 1. a. The dress sizes ranged from six to sixteen but I couldn't fit into any of them.
b. The dress sizes ranged from six to sixteen, but I couldn't fit into any of them.

_____ 2. a. Matt's girl friend declined his marriage proposal and enrolled in a convent.
b. Matt's girl friend declined his marriage proposal and enrolled in a convent.

_____ 3. a. Many lawyers, tired of long hours and short vacations, are switching to other careers.
b. Many lawyers, tired of long hours and short vacations are switching to other careers.

_____ 4. a. Nazanin, one of my best friends, plans to study medicine after receiving his undergraduate degree.
b. Nazanin, one of my best friends plans to study medicine, after receiving his undergraduate degree.

_____ 5. a. Leilani looked at her husband and asked "Dave, do you like your new pajamas"?
b. Leilani looked at her husband and asked, "Dave, do you like your new pajamas?"

_____ 6. a. Jonas's sister vacations in Hawaii in winter, and Miami in spring.
b. Jonas's sister vacations in Hawaii in winter and Miami in spring.

_____ 7. a. Although injured, Joani would not sue the motorist who hit her.
b. Although injured Joani would not sue the motorist who hit her.

_____ 8. a. Lindsay wanted an expensive haircut, but her mother would not pay for it.
b. Lindsay wanted an expensive haircut; but her mother would not pay for it.

_____ 9. a. Jean-Yves' copy of *The Martian Chronicles*, a novel by Ray Bradbury, is autographed by the author.

      b. Jean-Yves' copy of "The Martian Chronicles," a novel by Ray Bradbury, is autographed by the author.

_____ 10.   a. The Earl of Sandwich, an English nobleman, gave his name to a well-known food item.

      b. The Earl of Sandwich, an English nobleman gave his name, to a well-known food item.

_____ 11.   a. Although the dog's collar was found on the beach the dog was never located by its owner.

      b. Although the dog's collar was found on the beach, the dog was never located by its owner.

_____ 12.   a. Richard Wright's novel *Black Boy* is about the racism that a young Afro-American must overcome on the way to adulthood.

      b. Richard Wright's novel "Black Boy" is about the racism, that a young Afro-American must overcome on the way to adulthood.

_____ 13.   a. My neighbor last year would often wake me up early in the morning by singing *Home on the Range*.

      b. My neighbor last year would often wake me up early in the morning by singing "Home on the Range."

_____ 14.   a. Shakespeare's birthday, (April 23, 1564), was also the date on which he died, (April 23, 1616).

      b. Shakespeare's birthday (April 23, 1564) was also the date on which he died (April 23, 1616).

_____ 15.   a. Many people who are avoiding alcohol now socialize at coffeehouses instead of bars.

      b. Many people, who are avoiding alcohol, now socialize at coffeehouses instead of bars.

_____ 16.   a. Uncle Don said, "Sylvia's favorite short story, 'The Catbird Seat,' was written by my favorite author: James Thurber."

      b. Uncle Don said "Sylvia's favorite short story *The Catbird Seat* was written by my favorite author; James Thurber."

_____ 17.   a. Buck burst into the room and shouted "Help. I've been bitten by a snake."

      b. Buck burst into the room and shouted, "Help! I've been bitten by a snake."

_____ 18.   a. The examining physician noticed a three-quarter inch scar on Rosa's arm.

      b. The examining physician noticed a three quarter inch scar on Rosa's arm.

_____ 19.   a. Mrs. Jago warned her students "Expect a quiz on tonight's reading when you come to class tomorrow."

      b. Mrs. Jago warned her students, "Expect a quiz on tonight's reading when you come to class tomorrow."

_____ 20. a. Lucia has already bought her school supplies for next semester, pens, paper, a calculator, and aspirin.

b. Lucia has already bought her school supplies for next semester: pens, paper, a calculator, and aspirin.

_____ 21. a. The young handsome Frenchman reminded me to use the phrase _Bonsoir_ only in the evening.

b. The young, handsome Frenchman reminded me to use the phrase _Bonsoir_ only in the evening.

_____ 22. a. Although Chicago is a large and crowded city, it is still possible to find friends and organizations that will give you a sense of belonging.

b. Although Chicago is a large and crowded city it is still possible to find friends and organizations that will give you a sense of belonging.

_____ 23. a. Because Miguel's girl friend is Jewish, he is attending next week's Passover services.

b. Because Miguel's girl friend is Jewish he is attending next weeks' Passover services.

_____ 24. a. "I work for the government, but I am not allowed to discuss my duties," said the man with the dark glasses.

b. "I work for the government but I am not allowed to discuss my duties" said the man with the dark glasses.

_____ 25. a. "Boo!"

b. "Boo"!

10-C

On the line preceding each number write the letter of the sentence that is correctly punctuated.

_____ 1. a. Ramon said that his pulse ranges from fifty to seventy-five depending on how much coffee he has drunk.
        b. Ramon said that his pulse ranges from fifty to seventy-five, depending on how much coffee he has drunk.

_____ 2. a. UCLAs football team is having an unpredictable season, I refuse to predict the outcome of tomorrow's game.
        b. UCLA's football team is having an unpredictable season; I refuse to predict the outcome of tomorrow's game.

_____ 3. a. Mr. Blatz's course which emphasizes in-depth discussions and lengthy research projects is the toughest I have ever taken.
        b. Mr. Blatz's course, which emphasizes in-depth discussions and lengthy research projects, is the toughest I have ever taken.

_____ 4. a. The left headlight, of Nidia's new car, was smashed during the accident.
        b. The left headlight of Nidia's new car was smashed during the accident.

_____ 5. a. The babysitter asked "whether she could play our new stereo."
        b. The babysitter asked whether she could play our new stereo.

_____ 6. a. Uncle Al said "Don't forget to bring me a salad, and a bottle of soda."
        b. Uncle Al said, "Don't forget to bring me a salad and a bottle of soda."

_____ 7. a. Although angry, Victor continued to play as if nothing had happened.
        b. Although angry Victor continued to play as if nothing had happened.

_____ 8. a. Jon wanted to practice on his drums, but his landlord complained about the noise.
        b. Jon wanted to practice on his drums, but his landlord complained, about the noise.

_____ 9. a. I renewed Trish's subscription to "Jet," her favorite magazine.
        b. I renewed Trish's subscription to *Jet*, her favorite magazine.

_____ 10. a. Murphy's, the cafe on Ocean Avenue, is our favorite place for lunch.
        b. Murphy's, the cafe on Ocean Avenue is our favorite place, for lunch.

             b. Marcia said that she divorced her husband because he was a terrible cook.

_____ 11. a. Kathy managed to break four neighbors' windows while practicing golf.

             b. Kathy managed to break four neighbor's windows while practicing golf.

_____ 12. a. My grammar and spelling were ruined for weeks after I read Mark Twain's novel "The Adventures of Huckleberry Finn."

             b. My grammar and spelling were ruined for weeks after I read Mark Twain's novel *The Adventures of Huckleberry Finn*.

_____ 13. a. Matt likes to embarrass me by singing, "Wild Thing," when we're in crowded elevators.

             b. Matt likes to embarrass me by singing "Wild Thing" when we're in crowded elevators.

_____ 14. a. My mother's car (a Mercedes convertible) is almost as sporty as mine (an old Nissan).

             b. My mother's car, (a Mercedes convertible) is almost as sporty as mine, (an old Nissan).

_____ 15. a. Champagne glasses that are made by Baccarat are of the highest quality.

             b. Champagne glasses, made by Baccarat, are of the highest quality.

_____ 16. a. My encyclopedia states, "Washington Irving's short story 'The Legend of Sleepy Hollow' introduced one of his most famous characters: Ichabod Crane."

             b. My encyclopedia states "Washington Irving's short story *The Legend of Sleepy Hollow* introduced one of his most famous characters: Ichabod Crane."

_____ 17. a. Randy exclaimed "That's Julia Roberts sitting at that bus stop"!

             b. Randy exclaimed, "That's Julia Roberts sitting at that bus stop!"

_____ 18. a. Much of the world's oil comes from Saudi Arabia.

             b. Much of the worlds' oil comes from Saudi Arabia.

_____ 19. a. Brent laughed and said "This isn't the first time I've accidentally put my clothes on backwards."

             b. Brent laughed and said, "This isn't the first time I've accidentally put my clothes on backwards".

_____ 20. a. Laura has three annoying habits: smoking, snapping her gum, and borrowing my clothes.

             b. Laura has three annoying habits, smoking, snapping her gum, and borrowing my clothes.

_____ 21. a. The German phrase *Tchüss* is used by Austrians to say goodbye.

             b. The German phrase, *"Tchüss,"* is used by Austrians to say goodbye.

_____ 22. a. Although "Happy Birthday" is a copyrighted song few people pay royalties to its author after singing it to their friends or family.
           b. Although "Happy Birthday" is a copyrighted song, few people pay royalties to its author after singing it to their friends or family.

_____ 23. a. Because she wants to converse with her new classmate from Brazil Shewonda is learning Portuguese.
           b. Because she wants to converse with her new classmate from Brazil, Shewonda is learning Portuguese.

_____ 24. a. "Why didn't you warn me that you sing old show tunes in your sleep?" demanded Hector's new bride.
           b. "Why didn't you warn me that you sing old show tunes in your sleep" demanded Hector's new bride?

_____ 25. a. To help control his blood pressure Charles runs two or three miles daily.
           b. To help control his blood pressure, Charles runs two or three miles daily.

11-B

CHAPTER TEST

Put an "X" next to the number of any word that should be capitalized.

1. Although Susan earned a (1) bachelor's degree in anthropology, she teaches (2) english and enjoys reading (3) philosophy.

    (1)_____   (2)_____   (3)_____

2. The (4) governor of the state has decided not to attend the (5) labor union's rally in Kansas (6) city next (7) labor Day.

    (4)_____   (5)_____   (6)_____   (7)_____

3. Adriana started to read F. Scott (8) fitzgerald's novel (9) *the Great Gatsby* last (10) summer, but did not finish reading it.

    (8)_____   (9)_____   (10)_____

4. We saw the name of Kim Spire's (11) father on the (12) vietnam (13) war (14) memorial during our visit to Washington, (15) d.c.; he had been a (16) pilot in the air force.

    (11)_____   (12)_____   (13)_____   (14)_____   (15)_____   (16)_____

5. Martin Luther was a (17) catholic priest who challenged some of the teachings of his (18) church. He later became one of the leaders of the Protestant (19) reformation and a key figure in the (20) lutheran church.

    (17)_____   (18)_____   (19)_____   (20)_____

6. Chris and I had the same (21) professor for American (22) literature during our (23) junior year at (24) northwestern University, and we each graduated at the end of the (25) spring semester the following year.

    (21)_____   (22)_____   (23)_____   (24)_____   (25)_____

11-C

CHAPTER TEST

Put an "X" next to the number of any word that should be capitalized.

1. Newport (1) beach is a great place to visit in the (2) spring, but it is too chilly in (3) february.

   (1)_____   (2)_____   (3)_____

2. A *Critique of (4) pure Reason*, by the German (5) philosopher Immanuel Kant, was written when he taught at Konigsberg (6) university in the late (7) eighteenth (8) century.

   (4)_____   (5)_____   (6)_____   (7)_____   (7)_____   (8)_____

3. I informed (9) aunt Bridget not to expect my (10) husband and me for (11) thanksgiving dinner because (12) doctor Fishman said that our (13) flu is contagious. Bridget said that our (14) uncle would be disappointed.

   (9)_____   (10)_____   (11)_____   (12)_____   (13)_____   (14)_____

4. The Lincoln (15) memorial in Washington, (16) d.c., was the site of Martin Luther King, (17) jr.'s famous "I have a dream" (18) speech.

   (15)_____   (16)_____   (17)_____   (18)_____

5. My (19) brother Bobby speaks the Russian (20) language fluently with a Moscow (21) accent, although he has never visited the former Soviet (22) union or taken formal classes in (23) college.

   (19)_____   (20)_____   (21)_____   (22)_____   (23)_____

6. Margaret grew up in the (24) city of Baltimore, but now she lives in (25) southern Maine.

   (24)_____   (25)_____

11-D

CHAPTER TEST

Put an "X" next to the number of any word that should be capitalized.

1. If you fall asleep before nine o'clock (1) p.m., you'll miss (2) *cheers*, my favorite television program, and I'll eat your share of the (3) pizza.

   (1)_____ (2)_____ (3)_____

2. Let's ask our (4) rabbi when (5) chanukah services will be held before we make plans for dinner Friday (6) night.

   (4)_____ (5)_____ (6)_____

3. Jay caught more than a dozen (7) trout while fishing in the (8) sierras last (9) summer, but he still prefers to eat (10) catfish from the (11) midwest.

   (7)_____ (8)_____ (9)_____ (10)_____ (11)_____

4. *The Adventures of Huckleberry Finn* is a (12) novel that many (13) americans read in their (14) sophomore year of (15) high school and fondly remember well into adulthood.

   (12)_____ (13)_____ (14)_____ (15)_____

5. Do you remember meeting (16) professor Barbolla at our (17) barbecue last (18) fourth of July?

   (16)_____ (17)_____ (18)_____

6. Joan plays the (19) bass guitar in a (20) band and also stars as a (21) nurse on a popular (22) television show.

   (19)_____ (20)_____ (21)_____ (22)_____

7. If you let my (23) cousin Don drink any more (24) coffee, he will stay awake until next (25) spring.

   (23)_____ (24)_____ (25)_____

_____	20.	carere	carear	career
_____	21.	eliminate	elimanate	eleminate
_____	22.	desease	diseese	disease
_____	23.	critacism	critisism	criticism
_____	24.	elegible	eligible	eligable
_____	25.	deceive	diceive	decieve

12-B

CHAPTER TEST

A. *Identify the correct word by using the appropriate letter.*

_____ 1. Frankly, Sheila is (a. to   b. too) angry to talk to you now.

_____ 2. Although we bought our concert tickets at the same time, we were not able to sit (a. all together   b. altogether).

_____ 3. Why would you (a. by   b. buy) an expensive deli sandwich that you could prepare at home for half the price?

_____ 4. José is much admired for the campus improvements he initiated while serving on the student (a. council   b. counsel).

_____ 5. San Juan is the beautiful (a. capitol   b. capital) of Puerto Rico.

_____ 6. Yun-Kim blushes when anyone gives her a (a. complement   b. compliment).

_____ 7. Gerald has just had his (a. fourth   b. forth) cup of coffee, and it's not even noon yet.

_____ 8. It is unlikely that our generation will see complete world (a. piece   b. peace).

_____ 9. Sam's dog has nearly chewed through (a. it's   b. its) new leash.

_____ 10. Luisa had (a. already   b. all ready) completed the quiz as the professor finished giving the instructions.

B. *Identify the correctly spelled word by using the appropriate letter.*

	a.	b.	c.
11.	acuracy	accuracy	acuraccy
12.	competent	compitent	competant
13.	license	lisense	lisence
14.	legitamate	legitemate	legitimate
15.	unnecessary	unneccessary	unecessary
16.	restaraunt	resturant	restaurant
17.	medecine	medicine	medicene
18.	recomend	recommend	reccomend
19.	prejudice	prejadice	prejudace

_____	20. wheather	whether	wether
_____	21. anonimous	ananymous	anonymous
_____	22. committee	comittee	commitee
_____	23. accommodate	acomodate	accommadate
_____	24. begining	beginning	beggining
_____	25. existance	existince	existence

12-C

CHAPTER TEST

A. *Identify the correct word by using the appropriate letter.*

_____ 1. To Jolene's surprise, she (a. knew   b. new) none of the guests at the wedding.

_____ 2. Although my dog Charley (a. bares   b. bears) her teeth frequently, she is actually very gentle and friendly.

_____ 3. Sean enjoyed his math (a. course   b. coarse) more than he had expected when he registered for it.

_____ 4. The picnic was canceled because the invasion of the ants made it (a. altogether   b. all together) impossible to eat on the lawn.

_____ 5. Sometimes it's difficult to accept the (a. principals   b. principles) of our parents when making our own decisions.

_____ 6. When his wife was not looking, Ken sampled a (a. peace   b. piece) of the pie she had just removed from the oven.

_____ 7. Each secretary was given a supply of company (a. stationary   b. stationery) for writing letters to customers.

_____ 8. Vince's family has not yet decided (a. weather   b. whether) to give him a surprise party.

_____ 9. Jason and his sister will visit (a. their   b. there) cousins in Florissant next month.

_____ 10. Jamie auditioned for a (a. role   b. roll) in a music video.

B. *Identify the correctly spelled word by using the appropriate letter.*

	a.	b.	c.
_____ 11.	sophmore	sophamore	sophomore
_____ 12.	absence	absense	abcense
_____ 13.	maintenance	maintanance	maintenence
_____ 14.	tendensy	tendency	tendancy
_____ 15.	beautiful	beatiful	buetiful
_____ 16.	cematary	cemitary	cemetery

_____ 17. goverment	govermint	government
_____ 18. embarass	embarrass	emberress
_____ 19. litarature	literiture	literature
_____ 20. desperate	desparate	despirate
_____ 21. knowlidge	knowledge	knoledge
_____ 22. hypocrysy	hypocrisy	hipocrycy
_____ 23. mischeveous	mischievious	mischievous
_____ 24. Wensday	Wednesday	Wendsday
_____ 25. personnel	personnal	personell

12-D

CHAPTER TEST

A. *Identify the correct word by using the appropriate letter.*

_____ 1. Most people would agree that honesty is a (a. principal b. principle) that should be followed.

_____ 2. I have never (a. scene b. seen) traffic as confusing as that in Mexico City.

_____ 3. Because the medicine has (a. affected b. effected) her appetite, Helen eats only one regular meal daily.

_____ 4. Mitchell finally accepted the fact that his winning the state lottery was an (a. allusion b. illusion).

_____ 5. Before beginning a strenuous exercise program, you should seek the (a. advice b. advise) of a doctor.

_____ 6. Clarence's unkind treatment of his employees is finally bothering his (a. conscience b. conscious).

_____ 7. Toni sat (a. among b. between) Isley and me during the movie.

_____ 8. The car engine hummed (a. continually b. continuously).

_____ 9. Lupe could not (a. bare b. bear) to look at the grades on the final exam that were posted on her instructor's window.

_____ 10. Are you (a. all ready b. already) for tomorrow's soccer game?

B. *Identify the correctly spelled word by using the appropriate letter.*

	a.	b.	c.
_____ 11.	innocense	innocence	inocence
_____ 12.	desirable	desireable	desirible
_____ 13.	criticism	criticesm	criticm
_____ 14.	sargent	sargeant	sergeant
_____ 15.	preceding	preceeding	preceading
_____ 16.	canidate	candedate	candidate
_____ 17.	Febuary	Febrary	February
_____ 18.	paralel	parallel	paralell
_____ 19.	succede	sucede	succeed

_____	20. garantee	guarantee	gaurantee
_____	21. abundance	abundence	abundense
_____	22. marriage	marrage	mariage
_____	23. adiquate	adequate	adiquette
_____	24. akward	awkard	awkward
_____	25. awesome	awsome	awssome

Final Examinations
(Forms A, B, C, and D)

Part Four: *Using the appropriate letter, identify the correctly punctuated sentence.*

_____ 41. a. Most recipes for pie dough include: flour, water, salt, and shortening.
           b. Most recipes for pie dough include flour, water, salt, and shortening.

_____ 42. a. Although the audience pleaded I continued to sing my favorite Madonna songs.
           b. Although the audience pleaded, I continued to sing my favorite Madonna songs.

_____ 43. a. I was treated by Stacia Berlin, M.D., at the clinic.
           b. I was treated by Stacia Berlin M.D. at the clinic.

_____ 44. a. Sheldon found three articles (*Corn, Sugar Products,* and *Uses of Bran*) to include in his report on nutrition.
           b. Sheldon found three articles ("Corn," "Sugar Products," and "Uses of Bran") to include in his report on nutrition.

_____ 45. a. "Stop it!" cried the frustrated mother.
           b. "Stop it"! cried the frustrated mother.

_____ 46. a. Mr. Dabirian subscribes to two magazines: "Progressive Architecture" and "American Scholar."
           b. Mr. Dabirian subscribes to two magazines: *Progressive Architecture* and *American Scholar.*

_____ 47. a. My ex-girlfriend used to bake cookies with all-purpose flour.
           b. My ex-girlfriend used to bake cookies with allpurpose flour.

_____ 48. a. I like the sweaters you made for the Rosenfields' dog; can you make one in my husband's size?
           b. I like the sweaters you made for the Rosenfield's dog; can you make one in my husbands' size?

_____ 49. a. It's my favorite team, the San Diego Chargers.
           b. Its my favorite team, the San Diego Chargers.

_____ 50. a. You can have either four thousand and one hundred pennies or 41 dollar bills.
           b. You can have either 4100 pennies or forty-one dollar bills.

C

FINAL EXAM

Part One: *On the line in front of each number write the letter corresponding to the kind of error each sentence contains. If a sentence is correct, write "d" in front of the sentence.*

a. sentence fragment   b. run-on sentence   c. comma-splice   d. correct

_____ 1. Some of the salesmen who had met their quotas and who had received large bonuses for their performances.

_____ 2. Moistening his lips, glancing at first base, and trying to ignore the taunts from the fans behind first base.

_____ 3. Dodger Stadium in Los Angeles, which seats over 60,000 fans, is privately owned.

_____ 4. Taking a walk in the park at night used to be a safe activity, in many large cities, however, it would be risky.

_____ 5. Most medical schools in this country are experiencing a decline in applications a few, however, report an increase.

_____ 6. Hundreds of alleged cures for hiccoughs have been claimed, few, if any, seem to have any value.

_____ 7. Paula made twelve consecutive free throws, but finally she missed one in the fourth quarter.

_____ 8. A feature story on a grandmother who climbs mountains, published in last Sunday's newspaper.

_____ 9. Encountering hordes of wasps and afraid that they would attack him, he jumped into his car.

_____ 10. He was known for his hot temper and unpredictable behavior he decided, on the advice of his manager, to change his actions on stage.

Part Two: *On the line in front of each number write the letter corresponding to the appropriate word in each sentence.*

_____ 11. (a. Are   b. Is) there any news from your parents concerning the accident?

_____ 12. Neither a belt nor suspenders (a. was   b. were) needed to hold up his pants.

_____ 13. Everything about his appearance, including his clothes and his speech mannerisms, (a. suggest   b. suggests) that he is from France.

_____ 14. Were you as surprised as (a. I   b. me) by her remark?

_____ 15. As a young man, Einstein reportedly taught (a. himself   b. hisself) mathematics.

_____ 16. Mandy is one of those students who (a. studies   b. study) at the last minute but still seem to do well.

_____ 17. The benefits offered by the company (a. are   b. is) superior to those of other companies.

_____ 18. Forty-five dollars (a. are   b. is) not an unusual amount to pay for a science textbook.

_____ 19. As a result of campaigns against drinking, the number of arrests for drunken driving (a. has   b. have) declined noticeably.

_____ 20. The aging movie star admitted that he had never (a. rode   b. ridden) a horse in his life.

_____ 21 When the bell (a. rang   b. rung), the boxers ran to the middle of the ring.

_____ 22. Several divers explored the ruins of the old ship that (a. sank   b. sunk) in the harbor last year.

_____ 23. As soon as the last tourist had (a. gone   b. went), the hotel closed for the summer.

_____ 24. Helen's lungs almost (a. burst   b. bursted) because of the underwater pressure.

_____ 25. I could tell immediately which painter had (a. did   b. done) the etching.

_____ 26. Last month some of the delegates (a. began   b. begun) to regret their votes.

_____ 27. Mr. Gomez will take only two students to the meeting with him: Sean and (a. I   b. me).

_____ 28. Vern's brother complained about (a. him   b. his) keeping a pet python in their room.

_____ 29. The custodian accused (a. us   b. we) evening-shift workers of leaving the door to the factory unlocked.

_____ 30. Was it Mr. Montgomery or (a. her   b. she) who called you last week?

Part Three: _Using the appropriate letter, identify the error in each of the following sentences._

a. adjective or adverb used incorrectly   _b. misplaced or dangling modifier_
c. unclear pronoun reference   _d. illogical or incomplete comparison_

_____ 31. Parker's contribution to the team was more than Bell.

_____ 32. New York has more inhabitants than any city in the United States.

_____ 33. Rene speaks French perfect as a result of his growing up in Toulouse.

_____ 34. When preparing for a marathon, plenty of rest and the right diet are important.

_____ 35. Because the microphone would not function, the speaker had to yell real loud.

_____ 36. I remember hearing that President Kennedy had been shot during the afternoon newscast.

_____ 37. Reaching for my hat, the wind suddenly gusted.

_____ 38. Chris has never had a lesson on the guitar, which surprises me.

_____ 39. The performance of every swimmer improved great as a result of the training schedule introduced by the new coach.

_____ 40. Fay dropped out of nursing school shortly before graduation and married a much younger man, which disappointed her parents.

Part Four: *Using the correct letter, identify the correctly punctuated sentence.*

_____ 41. a. The dean said that, living in a dormitory is an excellent way to make friends quickly.
　　　　 b. The dean said that living in a dormitory is an excellent way to make friends quickly.

_____ 42. a. "I am sorry to report," the sales manager announced. "That sales for the last quarter are down almost twenty percent."
　　　　 b. "I am sorry to report," the sales manager announced, "that sales for the last quarter are down almost twenty percent."

_____ 43. a. Margie watches the ten o'clock news, and then goes to bed.
　　　　 b. Margie watches the ten o'clock news and then goes to bed.

_____ 44. a. Four hockey teams from the South were selected to play in the tournament.
　　　　 b. Four hockey teams from the south were selected to play in the tournament.

_____ 45. a. The country faced several problems: the devaluation of its currency, political turmoil, a shortage of food, and drought.
　　　　 b. The country faced several problems; the devaluation of its currency, political turmoil, a shortage of food, and drought.

_____ 46. a. The comedian, Rich Little, is known for his impersonations.
　　　　 b. The comedian Rich Little is known for his impersonations.

_____ 47. a. His father who came from Italy was a tenor in the San Carlo Opera Company.
　　　　 b. His father, who came from Italy, was a tenor in the San Carlo Opera Company.

_____ 48. a. Many readers of Conrad's novel *Lord Jim* do not know that it is partially based on his own experiences at sea.

D

FINAL EXAM

Part One: *On the line in front of each number write the letter corresponding to the kind of error each sentence contains. If a sentence is correct, write "d" in front of the sentence.*

a. *sentence fragment*   b. *run-on sentence*   c. *comma-splice*   d. *correct*

_____ 1. Devotion to his country and the determination to survive capture, the major cause of his ability to endure the rigors of torture.

_____ 2. Asked what was their favorite fast food, over half of the respondents named pizza.

_____ 3. Child abuse and wife-beating are not isolated or rare events, many police departments report that these crimes are increasing.

_____ 4. Norman and Lois drove for miles without seeing a sign of human habitation, much of their trip was through the Sahara desert.

_____ 5. Earl has an old radio that he bought in 1950 he is able to receive short-wave broadcasts from Europe and South America.

_____ 6. Insulation had been removed from the wires leading to the telephone, investigators concluded that the telephone had been tapped.

_____ 7. Smoking among adults has declined in recent years some studies report, however, that teen-agers are still smoking in equal numbers.

_____ 8. Mrs. Caruso gave a lecture on Italian art and architecture, a subject she teaches at the university.

_____ 9. The changing borders of the countries of the Middle East, which makes mapmaking very difficult.

_____ 10. Mr. Dawkins continues to keep his records by hand, he refuses to buy a computer.

Part Two: *On the line in front of each number write the letter corresponding to the appropriate word in each sentence.*

_____ 11. (a. Were   b. Was) there any people who did not claim their tickets?

_____ 12. Neither Greece nor Morocco (a. plan   b. plans) to attend the conference.

_____ 13. Everything in the classroom, including the desks, books, and computers, (a. was   b. were) vandalized over the weekend.

_____ 14. Mrs. Willis is just as enraged as (a. he b. him) about the decision.

_____ 15. Greg claimed that he did not eat the entire cake by (a. himself b. hisself).

_____ 16. There (a. appear b. appears) to be more than two winners in the fifty-yard dash, incredible as it seems.

_____ 17. A check-out procedure based on scanners and bar graphs (a. has b. have) replaced the old technology.

_____ 18. (a. Has b. Have) either of the candidates conceded the election yet?

_____ 19. The manager of the team, together with his captain and the owner of the franchise, (a. was b. were) presented a commendation for having won the championship.

_____ 20. Because the buttons on his suit had been (a. shined b. shone), he realized that he should polish his shoes.

_____ 21. The cat (a. sitting b. setting) on my doorstep is waiting for me to bring it some milk.

_____ 22. The cat has (a. sat b. set) there for over an hour.

_____ 23. The newspaper boy claims that he (a. laid b. lay) the paper on the porch safely out of the rain.

_____ 24. I had scarcely (a. laid b. lain) my head on the pillow and begun to doze when the telephone rang.

_____ 25. The decision of the company to lay off forty employees was a disappointment to Linda and (a. I b. me).

_____ 26. Everyone except George and (a. I b. me) appeared confident as the date of the wedding approached.

_____ 27. Three miles (a. are b. is) a relatively short distance for an experienced runner.

_____ 28. When the telephone (a. rang b. rung), Clyde jumped up to answer it before his sister could reach it.

_____ 29. A number of interesting books on Russian politics (a. has b. have) been written within the last year.

_____ 30. Howard and Lisa (a. has b. have) gone to Montreal for two weeks to visit her mother.

Part Three: _Using the appropriate letter, identify the error in each of the following sentences._

a. adjective or adverb used incorrectly   _b. misplaced or dangling modifier_
c. unclear pronoun reference   _d. illogical or incomplete comparison_

_____ 31. While shopping for groceries last night, a wheel on my shopping cart fell off while I was pushing it down an aisle.

_____ 32. The population of Los Angeles is now larger than Chicago.

_____ 33. Containing too much water and not enough cement, I could not make the mortar stick on the wall.

_____ 34. The memories of his youth in Europe weighed heavy on his subconsciousness as he read the newspaper account of the revolution.

_____ 35. Because the air conditioning system rattled and hummed loud, we had to talk in loud voices.

_____ 36. Pablo loved the flamenco music of Seville, and he decided that he would become one.

_____ 37. Laura laughed very excited when she heard the news.

_____ 38. Having been accepted as a new member of the United Nations, the vote for the small African nation was overwhelming.

_____ 39. Stan painted his motorcycle bright yellow, which confused his wife.

_____ 40. You should plan very careful the route you will drive, making sure that gasoline and food can be purchased along the way.

Part Four: _Using the appropriate letter, identify the correctly punctuated sentence._

_____ 41. a. The rock star's bodyguard, who stayed by his side, pushed back the fans seeking autographs.
  b. The rock star's bodyguard who stayed by his side pushed back the fans seeking autographs.

_____ 42. a. Moviegoers of all ages like the movie "Fantasia."
  b. Moviegoers of all ages like the movie _Fantasia_.

_____ 43. a. Although Loretta was eligible to retire she decided to work for another year.
  b. Although Loretta was eligible to retire, she decided to work for another year.

_____ 44. a. Scientists claim that, the disappearance of the ozone layer over North America is affecting the temperature and rainfall.
  b. Scientists claim that the disappearance of the ozone layer over North America is affecting the temperature and rainfall.

_____ 45. a. "I'm happy to announce," stated the President's press secretary, "that the President has been awarded first prize in the baking contest."
  b. "Im happy to announce," stated the president's press secretary, that, the president has been awarded first prize in the baking contest."

_____ 46. a. The prospective buyer of a computer faces several decisions, what brand to purchase, what type of printer to use, and what kinds of hardware to purchase.
  b. The prospective buyer of a computer faces several decisions: what brand to purchase, what type of printer to use, and what kinds of hardware to purchase.

_____ 47. a. Mitzi has a staff meeting every morning at nine o'clock, and then consults with her personal secretary.

b. Mitzi has a staff meeting every morning at nine o'clock and then consults with her personal secretary.

_____ 48. a. Because she was accustomed to swimming in the Pacific, Muriel had developed a powerful backstroke.

b. Because she was accustomed to swimming in the Pacific Muriel had developed a powerful backstroke.

_____ 49. a. Lincoln Center in Manhattan, is the home of the Metropolitan Opera.

b. Lincoln Center in Manhattan is the home of the Metropolitan Opera.

_____ 50. a. Hugh could not decide between: the purchase of a compact disc player, or a new typewriter.

b. Hugh could not decide between the purchase of a compact disc player or a new typewriter.

Form C

1. a   2. b   3. a   4. b   5. a   6. b   7. a   8. a   9. b   10. a   11. a
12. a   13. b   14. a   15. b   16. a   17. a   18. b   19. a   20. b   21. a
22. b   23. a   24. b   25. b

Form D

1. b   2. a   3. b   4. b   5. b   6. b   7. b   8. b   9. b   10. a   11. a
12. a   13. b   14. a   15. b   16. a   17. a   18. b   19. b   20. b   21. a
22. b   23. b   24. a   25. a

Chapter Four

Form A

1. c   2. a   3. a   4. b   5. c   6. c   7. b   8. a   9. a   10. c   11. b   12. a
13. b   14. b   15. a   16. a   17. a   18. a   19. a   20. b   21. b   22. b   23. b
24. b   25. b

Form B

1. a   2. c   3. b   4. a   5. b   6. a   7. b   8. a   9. c   10. a   11. b
12. a   13. a   14. a   15. a   16. b   17. a   18. a   19. b   20. a   21. a
22. a   23. b   24. a   25. a

Form C

1. b   2. c   3. a   4. a   5. c   6. b   7. a   8. b   9. a   10. b   11. b
12. a   13. b   14. a   15. a   16. b   17. a   18. a   19. b   20. a   21. b
22. b   23. a   24. c   25. a

Form D

1. c   2. a   3. b   4. b   5. a   6. a   7. a   8. c   9. a   10. b   11. b
12. a   13. b   14. b   15. b   16. a   17. a   18. a   19. b   20. b   21. a
22. b   23. a   24. b   25. a

Chapter Five

Form A

1. d 2. b 3. c 4. c 5. a 6. a 7. b 8. d 9. c 10. c 11. b 12. d
13. a 14. b 15. b 16. a 17. b 18. b 19. a 20. b 21. b 22. b 23. a
24. b 25. b

Form B

1. a 2. c 3. b 4. c 5. b 6. b 7. d 8. d 9. b 10. b 11. a
12. b 13. b 14. a 15. a 16. a 17. b 18. a 19. b 20. a 21. a
22. a 23. b 24. a 25. a

Form C

1. a 2. c 3. d 4. a 5. b 6. a 7. b 8. b 9. c 10. b 11. c
12. a 13. b 14. d 15. a 16. b 17. a 18. b 19. a 20. a 21. a
22. a 23. a 24. b 25. a

Form D

1. a 2. c 3. d 4. a 5. b 6. a 7. b 8. b 9. c 10. b 11. c
12. a 13. d 14. b 15. a 16. b 17. a 18. b 19. b 20. a 21. a
22. a 23. a 24. a 25. a

Chapter Six

Form A

1. d 2. a 3. b 4. b 5. c 6. a 7. c 8. b 9. d 10. a 11. a 12. a
13. b 14. a 15. b 16. b 17. b 18. a 19. a 20. b 21. a 22. a 23. a
24. a 25. b

Form B

1. b 2. a 3. d 4. b 5. c 6. a 7. b 8. a 9. b 10. d 11. b
12. b 13. a 14. a 15. b 16. a 17. b 18. b 19. b 20. a 21. a
22. a 23. a 24. a 25. b

Form C

1. a 2. d 3. b 4. c 5. a 6. c 7. b 8. d 9. d 10. a 11. a
12. a 13. b 14. b 15. a 16. b 17. b 18. b 19. b 20. b
21. b 22. a 23. b 24. b 25. a

Form D

1. d 2. b 3. a 4. c 5. c 6. a 7. b 8. d 9. b 10. a 11. b
12. b 13. b 14. a 15. b 16. a 17. b 18. a 19. a 20. a 21. a
22. b 23. a 24. a 25. b

Chapter Seven

Form A

1. c 2. a 3. a 4. b 5. c 6. a 7. c 8. c 9. c 10. c 11. a 12. b
13. a 14. b 15. b 16. a 17. b 18. b 19. a 20. a 21. b 22. b 23. b
24. a 25. a

Form B

1. c 2. a 3. b 4. b 5. c 6. b 7. c 8. a 9. c 10. a 11. b
12. b 13. b 14. a 15. a 16. b 17. a 18. a 19. b 20. b 21. a
22. b 23. a 24. b 25. a

Form C

1. a 2. a 3. a 4. c 5. b 6. a 7. a 8. c 9. b 10. c 11. a
12. a 13. b 14. b 15. b 16. a 17. a 18. b 19. b 20. a 21. a
22. a 23. a 24. b 25. b

Form D

1. b 2. a 3. b 4. c 5. b 6. b 7. c 8. a 9. a 10. c 11. a
12. a 13. b 14. a 15. b 16. b 17. a 18. a 19. b 20. b 21. a
22. a 23. b 24. b 25. a

Chapter Eight

Form A

1. c   2. b   3. d   4. b   5. a   6. a   7. c   8. c   9. d   10. b   11. a   12. c
13. b   14. d   15. c   16. b   17. a   18. b   19. d   20. b   21. a   22. a   23. d
24. d   25. c

Form B

1. a   2. d   3. b   4. c   5. b   6. d   7. a   8. a   9. c   10. d   11. b
12. a   13. b   14. a   15. a   16. b   17. c   18. a   19. d   20. c   21. d
22. b   23. c   24. d   25. a

Form C

1. a   2. b   3. d   4. c   5. a   6. b   7. a   8. a   9. c   10. d   11. a
12. b   13. c   14. c   15. a   16. d   17. c   18. a   19. b   20. a   21. b
22. d   23. d   24. a   25. c

Form D

1. c   2. a   3. a   4. b   5. b   6. a   7. c   8. c   9. d   10. a   11. d
12. d   13. a   14. a   15. d   16. a   17. d   18. a   19. b   20. c   21. d
22. a   23. a   24. d   25. b

Chapter Nine

Form A

1. b   2. b   3. a   4. b   5. a   6. a   7. d   8. a   9. c   10. a   11. a   12. a
13. c   14. d   15. d   16. b   17. c   18. d   19. d   20. b   21. b   22. b   23. a
24. b   25. c

Form B

1. b   2. a   3. a   4. b   5. b   6. d   7. a   8. a   9. b   10. a   11. c
12. d   13. c   14. a   15. b   16. b   17. b   18. d   19. a   20. a   21. c
22. a   23. c   24. b   25. c

Form C

1. b   2. a   3. b   4. a   5. b   6. b   7. a   8. b   9. d   10. b   11. d
12. a   13. c   14. c   15. d   16. a   17. d   18. c   19. b   20. b   21. a
22. d   23. d   24. a   25. c

Form D

1. b   2. b   3. b   4. a   5. b   6. d   7. a   8. c   9. c   10. d   11. c
12. b   13. c   14. a   15. b   16. b   17. d   18. c   19. a   20. b   21. d
22. a   23. d   24. d   25. d

Chapter Ten

Form A

1. a   2. b   3. b   4. a   5. b   6. b   7. b   8. b   9. a   10. a   11. a   12. a
13. b   14. b   15. a   16. a   17. b   18. b   19. a   20. b   21. a   22. b   23. a
24. a   25. b

Form B

1. b   2. b   3. a   4. a   5. b   6. b   7. a   8. a   9. a   10. a   11. b
12. a   13. b   14. b   15. a   16. a   17. b   18. a   19. b   20. b   21. b
22. a   23. a   24. a   25. a

Form C

1. b   2. b   3. b   4. b   5. b   6. b   7. a   8. a   9. b   10. a   11. a
12. a   13. b   14. a   15. b   16. a   17. b   18. a   19. a   20. a   21. a
22. a   23. b   24. a   25. a

Form D

1. b   2. b   3. b   4. b   5. a   6. b   7. a   8. a   9. a   10. b   11. a
12. b   13. b   14. a   15. a   16. a   17. b   18. a   19. b   20. a   21. a
22. b   23. b   24. a   25. b

Chapter Eleven

Form A

1. X   2. X   3. X   5. X   6. X   7. X   8. X   9. X   11. X   12. X   13. X
14. X   15. X   23. X   24. X

Form B

2. X   6. X   7. X   8. X   9. X   12. X   13. X   14. X   15. X   17. X
19. X   20. X   24. X

Form C

1. X   3. X   4. X   6. X   9. X   11. X   12. X   15. X   16. X   17. X
22. X

Form D

2. X   5. X   8. X   11. X   13. X   16. X   18. X

Chapter Twelve

Form A

1. b   2. a   3. a   4. b   5. a   6. b   7. b   8. b   9. a   10. b   11. a   12. c
13. c   14. a   15. b   16. a   17. c   18. b   19. b   20. c   21. a   22. c   23. c
24. b   25. a

Form B

1. b   2. a   3. b   4. a   5. b   6. b   7. a   8. b   9. b   10. a   11. b
12. a   13. a   14. c   15. a   16. c   17. b   18. b   19. a   20. b   21. c
22. a   23. a   24. b   25. c

Form C

1. a   2. a   3. a   4. a   5. b   6. b   7. b   8. b   9. a   10. a   11. c
12. a   13. a   14. b   15. a   16. c   17. c   18. b   19. c   20. a   21. b
22. b   23. c   24. b   25. a

Form D

1. b 2. b 3. a 4. b 5. a 6. a 7. b 8. b 9. b 10. a 11. b
12. a 13. a 14. c 15. a 16. c 17. c 18. b 19. c 20. b 21. a
22. a 23. b 24. c 25. a

Final Examination

Form A

1. b 2. c 3. d 4. a 5. c 6. d 7. a 8. a 9. c 10. d 11. a 12. b
13. a 14. b 15. a 16. b 17. b 18. a 19. a 20. b 21. b 22. a 23. a
24. a 25. b 26. a 27. a 28. b 29. a 30. a 31. d 32. b 33. a 34. a
35. d 36. c 37. b 38. c 39. c 40. a 41. b 42. b 43. a 44. b 45. a
46. b 47. a 48. a 49. a 50. b

Form B

1. a 2. a 3. d 4. c 5. b 6. c 7. c 8. d 9. a 10. a 11. b
12. a 13. a 14. a 15. a 16. a 17. a 18. a 19. b 20. b 21. b
22. b 23. a 24. a 25. b 26. a 27. a 28. a 29. a 30. a 31. b
32. b 33. d 34. c 35. c 36. a 37. d 38. b 39. a 40. a 41. b
42. b 43. a 44. a 45. b 46. b 47. a 48. b 49. b 50. b

Form C

1. a 2. a 3. d 4. c 5. b 6. c 7. d 8. a 9. d 10. b 11. b
12. b 13. b 14. a 15. a 16. b 17. a 18. b 19. a 20. b 21. a
22. a 23. a 24. a 25. b 26. a 27. b 28. b 29. a 30. b 31. d
32. d 33. a 34. b 35. a 36. b 37. b 38. c 39. a 40. c 41. b
42. b 43. b 44. a 45. a 46. b 47. b 48. a 49. a 50. b

Form D

1. a 2. d 3. c 4. c 5. b 6. c 7. b 8. d 9. a 10. c 11. a
12. b 13. a 14. a 15. a 16. a 17. a 18. a 19. a 20. a 21. a
22. a 23. a 24. a 25. b 26. b 27. b 28. a 29. b 30. b 31. b
32. d 33. b 34. a 35. a 36. c 37. a 38. b 39. c 40. a 41. a
42. b 43. b 44. b 45. a 46. b 47. b 48. a 49. b 50. b